FACE

Penetrating through Hong Kong's glamorous urban skyline and into its labyrinthine interior, one finds that the power of this city's spatial matrix lies in an urban architecture shaped and textured by daily use—a three-dimensional city fabric composed of diverse, urban vernacular expressions with their multi-levelled infrastructural provisions. Be it shop-houses or tenement structures, podium-towers or new-town-style housing, industrial blocks or shopping malls, urban escalators or sky bridges, these typical physical patterns compose a mosaic of urban experiences and define how one dwells or works, rests or entertains, walks or drives. The ability to make and remake the fabric of the city in a way that cultivates the diversity of everyday life in Hong Kong is a key challenge for those concerned with its future.

Hong Kong can in some ways be considered a model city. It combines lively streets with lush parks, beautiful waterfronts, and a perfectly arranged public transportation system. Its density is ecologically highly efficient. And it has an intense housing program that creates a socially attractive model.

This deserves attention, though. The housing towers are based on the simple extrusion of a relatively uniform floor plan; all packed closely together, creating a truly monotonous 'sea of needles.'

The approach not only produces unattractive and low quality housing stock, but it reduces economical variety and hampers social diversity. This model of development fails to make use of the enormous potential inherent to such a dense metropolitan city, and in many ways, it impedes Hong Kong's competitiveness with surrounding cities.

Towers of Choices is an invitation to designers, planners and politicians to envision and realize a more varied Hong Kong cityscape through a focused investigation of Hong Kong's housing typologies and towers. The publication stems from a series of studios hosted at Hong Kong University that examined Hong Kong's existing housing stock and its relation to building regulations. New means have been proposed with which a more harmonious balance between population density and quality of life has been explored. This book synthesizes this body of research and proposes various new concepts for housing towers — concepts that go beyond simple extrusion. *Towers of Choices*.

Towers of Choices by The Why Factory: Winy Maas and Tihamér Salij with Martine Vledder, Arend van Waart, Sander Mulders, Claudia Mainardi, Anna Dolcetta and Sylwia Franczak

Editors: Winy Maas and Tihamér Salij

Guest contributions by: Weijen Wang, Tris Kee and Wah Sang Wong

Table of Contents

PRE

Rethinking Hong Kong Housing Typologies

Text by Weijen Wang

Hong Kong's Vertical Fabric and Urban Spaces

Standing on the Peak and looking down on Victoria Harbor, one can see a wave of vertical housing towers rising from the sloping terrain and extending down to the water's edge. This tightly woven, vertical fabric continues to the harbour front, ribboning through Wan Chai and undulating along the coastline toward Chai Wan. The verticality is only punctuated by the horizontality of a few elevated freeways and momentarily interrupted by multi-level junctions: highways, subways, and skywalks that overlap or intersect with the vertical towers. With today's podium towers rising alongside yesterday's tenement blocks, portending to rapidly subsume them, the current urban topography of Hong Kong is characterized by its complex totality, which is rapidly being remade through acts of dismantling what came before with little hesitation and in the name of progress.

In the past two decades, the dynamic complexity of Hong Kong's urbanism, manifested through an aesthetic of labyrinthine density and constant regeneration, has been gradually threatened by the dominating typology of the podium tower. Not only are newly built podium towers overwhelmingly replacing other housing forms, but newly developed mega-structures consisting of residential towers with shopping podiums below are also aggressively occupying the landscape in the reclaimed lands along the urban fringe. Driving from Central and Kowloon along the Metro line towards the New Territories, one sees repetitive configurations of towers. New towns like Tseung Kwan O, organized by four Metro stations and hundreds of identical residential towers that sit on interconnected mega-shopping podiums and provide homes for half a million people, best illustrate Hong Kong's new generation of urban development.

The City of Towers

After the 1980s, the formulation of new building regulations allowed private developers to work with high plot ratios to develop podiums supporting several pencil-like towers and cover 100 percent of their sites. This facilitated the mass replication of the efficient radiant-unit layout, and the extrusion of these efficient floor plans to heights of around 40 stories. One tower designed this way can easily furnish 320 units (8 units per floor multiplied by 40 stories), and one mega-podium development of eight towers can accommodate 2,500 households, instantly creating a community of roughly 10,000 people. If one Metro station can serve 120,000 people living in 12 mega-podium street blocks, four Metro stations would make a new town with a population of nearly half a million, equivalent to the scale of a typical European city. The city's Buildings Ordinance, which has filtered general concerns over health and safety into overly prescriptive regulations on building, and planning codes that are geared toward maximum efficiency, have created a fast-growing city with little room for architectural design in housing.

Hong Kong, a city that has long taken pride in its active public housing policy, is now facing multiple challenges: a shortage of land, a deficiency in affordable flats, and a lack of design innovation in architecture. Despite the mass construction of efficiency-driven, large-scale developments, with the continuous speculation over high-profit real-estate, demand still always surpasses supply in Hong Kong, and housing remains an issue of quantity more than quality. Both private developers and public housing authorities follow the same formulas for producing uniformly efficient apartment layouts that maximize interior space with views, reinforce standardized domestic programmes such as TV-centred living rooms with bay windows, and give off the appearance of a luxurious clubhouse, with marble-tile-finished bathrooms and granite-floored lobbies. Little room is left for elements that prioritize design sensitivity over predictable formulas for domestic comfort, such as patio gardens, balcony lounges, rooms with cross-ventilation, kitchen-centred dining spaces, and bathtubs with views or adjacent playground for children.

Hong Kong can be considered one of the few cities that put a progressive housing proposal in the spirit of early-twentieth-century European modernism into action. However, it is now facing challenges for having implemented efficient high-rise housing solutions with little variation in design. The overly successful model of high-density housing is now filling the city with cookie-cutter architecture based on simple plan extrusions, and the need for diversity and innovation in housing design is becoming apparent. How can we design beyond plan extrusion while also satisfying pressing needs for quantity and efficiency? How can we design vertical towers that allow for horizontal variation? How can we design compact living spaces that are porous enough to make room for different communities? How can we support smaller changes in how spaces are used, so as to build from the bottom up, from the grassroots, even in the case of mega-scale housing?

From urban and planning perspectives, how can we provide variety in housing design within the framework of the mega-structure and its system of operation? How do we regenerate Hong Kong's high-density housing by allowing alternative mechanisms rather than perpetuating a homogeneous mode of planning? If the nature and scale of urban planning leaves little allowance for the facilitation of small adjustments and the regular re-making of the urban fabric, how can we adjust the planning mechanism to promote smaller developments that allow for greater diversity? How can we build smaller granules of dwellings in the city while sustaining the habitation of the metropolis? How can we learn from other cities and open up the design process for public housing?

Strategies for Developing a New Housing Typology

The Master of Architecture studio led by Winy Maas at the University of Hong Kong set out to explore alternative designs for high-density tower housing. After reviewing the history, the market, and the current building codes and housing typologies in Hong Kong, the studio challenged basic assumptions underlying the podium-tower design that has been heedlessly adopted by developers and the city's building authorities.

By focusing on the spatial aspects of one particular daily activity—such as reading, cooking, eating, sleeping or bathing—students developed ideal images of domestic life and proposed unit designs based on their particular perspectives. Each of the resulting unit plans can be plugged into a standard lobby core, clustered into typical floor layouts, and stacked up into a housing tower. When over twenty models of housing towers were arranged on the floor of the studio room, the sheer variety among them demonstrated how we could design housing differently by re-imagining how we would like to live. This is not only an effective method to prove our capacity for breaking away from the overly prescriptive norms of housing design, but it also challenges the current model of extrusion and repetition from a very pragmatic user's view and stimulates our imagination of what is possible for Hong Kong. Other studio design exercises explored the potential for change by considering how the configuration of housing towers could reshape community spaces and city life, how working and leisure spaces within the towers could be reimagined, how variety and porosity could be created with outdoor balconies and patios, and also how light, water, and energy consumption could be better moderated in towers.

Cities are living organisms that constantly evolve. Their vitality depends on the dynamic relationships in which parts and fragments regenerate and join into an everchanging whole. They require a continuous process of transformation, wherein new parts are generated into multiple assemblages from within, forming layers of permeable, heterogeneous spaces. How can we foster the essential complexity that emerges only from the mixing of the new with the old? How can we link the city's past with its present and its future? If the city reaches a limit for expansion, can we find ways to re-organize housing? We hope that through processes of fabrication and re-fabrication, strategies can be developed, allowing cities and housing to be sustained, transformed, generated and regenerated. And it is through such processes that architecture and cities move into the future.

Hong Kong can in some ways be considered a model city. It combines lively streets with lush parks, beautiful waterfronts, and a perfectly arranged public transportation system. Its density is both ecologically efficient and socially attractive.

Despite the integration of idyllic features, however, the profusion of housing and office towers, packed closely together, creates a truly monotonous 'sea of needles'. Hong Kong's towers — its housing towers in particular — exude an overwhelming uniformity and heighten the sense of anonymity.

Make your Tower!

Text by Winy Maas

The monotony of Hong Kong's housing stock can be attributed to overly prescriptive building regulations and the exorbitant demand for affordable housing. Small spaces and strained construction budgets have led to the overproduction of a limited repertoire of typologies that fail to reflect the diverse needs and desires of Hong Kong's expanding and differentiating population.

While monotonous extrusions of small and efficient floor plans can relieve some of the pressures of having to house a dense and still-growing population, this kind of urban development has had a fundamentally negative impact on quality of life. It not only produces unattractive and low-quality housing stock, but it also hampers social diversity. Rather than making use of the enormous potential inherent to such a dense metropolitan city, such development constrains Hong Kong's vital heterogeneity and, as a result, impedes its economic competitiveness with surrounding cities.

How can Hong Kong's housing express the diversity of the communities it serves rather than perpetuate and impose uniformity? How might architects and developers bypass strict planning and building regulations? How might they experiment with the parameters of current regulations and realize more innovative and attractive housing—housing that could radically help Hong Kong? What value can be added through creative design? How might these designs help illustrate how to adapt or reform existing rules, to make room for more possibilities?

In a series of studios hosted at Hong Kong University, we analyzed and reviewed Hong Kong's current housing stock and its relation to building regulations.

We identified what aspects of life were severely compromised in contemporary Hong Kong, what needs and desires were routinely sacrificed, neglected, or untapped. From there, we proposed architectural and urban means to reinvigorate these aspects and propose new concepts for housing towers—concepts that go beyond the current model of simple extrusion.

We started at the scale of the apartment unit. How could we imagine apartments based on considerations other than those of mere efficiency? Could the same minimum amount of space produce homes with more expressive and distinctive characteristics, with features that facilitate new uses of space? What would happen if we softened the emphasis on certain functions and let other potential uses of architecture and urban space prevail? How could the use of bunkbeds open up space and diversify the uses of the bedroom? Or could we imagine domestic spaces designed primarily around cooking and eating? Homes dominated by food production? Or homes formally planned like villages? Homes designed like theatrical stages? Could we live in homes that speak to our dreams of truly sleeping under the stars? Or homes in which we could swim from room to room?

We thus set out to imagine a catalogue of apartment typologies in which room configurations would be organized based on a specific hierarchy of functions. For instance, cooking, dining, storing, studying, bathing or relaxing could be emphasized or deemphasized through design. How could these new types of apartments enhance quality of life, even within the model of mechanical replication and extrusion? How can they inspire incremental change? As a second step,

we imagined creating precise combinations of apartment typologies, experimenting with combinations that were rich with specificity and therefore had the potential to catalyze distinct urban interactions. Finally, we asked how we could free ourselves from conceiving of vertical space in terms of conventionally stacked floors. We imagined homes that could be arranged vertically so that every floor had a different configuration.
We envisioned shared staircases that transformed towers into Escher-like compositions, central gardens leading to waterfalls and forming vertical parks, and private chimneys festooning towers that, in turn, enliven the cityscape with intriguing palaces of pipes. We could go on and on with these fantasies.

By generating these new models, we intend to inspire innovative approaches to architecture and urban planning that will allow for greater diversity and more open space…

Pick your choice! *Make Your Tower!*

OBSERV

ATIONS

More than seven million people currently live on the 1,110 square kilometers of land that comprises Hong Kong. According to statistics from the Hong Kong Planning Department, only 24.1 percent of this area is developed, of which only 6.9 percent is residential. [1] With such a high population density, the city stands out for its efficient management of space and its comprehensive infrastructure system, but it is also the site of the highest real estate prices in the world. It seems that high land prices, combined with strict building and planning regulations, have squeezed many Hong Kong residents into ever-smaller, uniformly designed homes.

State of Housing in Hong Kong

Text by Tihamér Salij

Over the past decades, Hong Kong has produced an enormous amount of overpriced but monotonous housing towers, which represent and reinforce a highly mediocre quality of life. The reasons are manifold, but a few stand out: government authorities have heavily influenced the city's housing development by setting exacting regulations and guidelines, while property developers have responded with predictable and minimally varying design schemes. As a result, most contemporary housing developments in Hong Kong express little beyond simple compliance with the many building regulations and the maximization of short-term profit for developers. They fail to provide desirable living conditions and to express the architectural excitement that can come from designing in response to the complex needs of a community.

Undesirable Quality of Life

Hong Kong is one of the world's most economically powerful cities, next to London, Tokyo, Paris, and New York. By some measures, it can be considered one of the wealthiest cities in the world. Hong Kong citizens have the highest life expectancy rate in the world, with an average life span of 81.24 years for men and 87.32 years for women. [2] But wealth and high life expectancy do not equate to a good quality of life. Hong Kong ranks 70th on the 2016 Quality of Living Index, and the city scored very high on the 2016 Worldwide Cost of Living Index, ranking as the third most expensive place to live, just behind Zurich and Singapore. [3,4] For the majority of people living in Hong Kong, life is extremely difficult, and the increasing demands and costs of everyday life are putting residents under greater and greater amounts of stress.

The city of Hong Kong has the world's least affordable housing market. Homes in Hong Kong have an average price of US$1,501.88 per square foot, making them the most expensive in the world. [5] The property value in Singapore, which ranks in second place, is 40 percent lower (about US$920 per square foot). A research report by UBS, a Swiss global financial services company, ranks Hong Kong second in the Global Real Estate Bubble Index with a score of 1.67 after London, which has a score of 1.88. In Hong Kong, as in London, housing prices are mainly driven by global investment demand rather than local household earnings, saddling residents with a record-high price-to-income ratio of 21 and a price-to-rent ratio of 33 points. As stated by the UBS Global Real Estate Bubble Index, 'this has made Hong Kong one of the world's most expensive cities for private housing. The average yearly income of a highly skilled worker can buy only around 3m^2 of living space in the private transactional market. For low income workers, social housing programs mitigate the high prices, though housing conditions remain strained.' [6] While the city has been successful in attracting international businesses and global investment, urban life in Hong Kong is, critically, losing its appeal.

In general, quality-of-life aspects in Hong Kong are deteriorating: Hong Kong suffers from extremely high property prices, shrinking living spaces, a surfeit of uninteresting public spaces, underdeveloped and non-pedestrianized shopping streets, the disappearance of traditional shops and multigenerational businesses, increasing numbers of large shopping malls, and worsening pollution. While the government holds on to strict building regulations, and most property developers hold on to their tested, profit-maximizing development strategies, Hong Kong continues to be dominated by a mediocre urban fabric ruled by rigid and unimaginative ideas of how to keep the city compact and functional.

According to the Hong Kong Housing Authority, the average living space in Hong Kong is 13.1 square meters per person, which is among the smallest in the world. [7] There is intense competition for any affordable housing in Hong Kong. About half of Hong Kong's population lives in some form of subsidized housing, though the demand is significantly higher. Affordable housing units are currently distributed through oversaturated lottery systems, or awarded to residents who have been on a waiting list for years. Younger generation Hong Kong residents are often forced to live with their parents, or they live in homes that are too small to start families in. It is not uncommon for a family of six individuals, representing three generations, to share an apartment smaller than 40 square meters. The majority of Hong Kong residents are forced to sacrifice the quality and size of their homes and to adjust their social and family lives accordingly.

Not only are most Hong Kong residents being priced out of the city, but the profusion of high-end apartment towers, luxury hotels, giant shopping malls, and a car-based infrastructure in Hong Kong have also increasingly displaced the city's precious public space, urban greenery, independent shops, street markets, and other small-scale facilities. The mix of stringent building regulations and shortsighted, profit-maximizing approaches to development have led to the adoption of generic building typologies designed to minimize costs and rely heavily on standardized design and construction processes. The lack of urban diversity and the increase of extremely small housing units at high prices have significantly contributed to the low quality-of-life standards and the reduced well-being of Hong Kong residents.

Standardized Housing Production

Hong Kong has a rich history of building tall, which has resulted in an astoundingly vertical urban topography with more than 1,294 towers of over 150 meters high. [8] While the island served as the site of relatively distinctive skyscraper designs starting in the 1950s, since the 1970s, Hong Kong's housing tower typologies have diminished to a narrow spectrum of so-called 'podium towers'. Despite its great history in building tall, Hong Kong has not been able to fully explore and experiment with its tallness and its desire for density. Instead, the urban fabric of Hong Kong has evolved into a vertical sprawl of extremely homogeneous residential towers on top of (over)commercialized podiums, reflecting shortsighted responses to land scarcity and market forces.

Hong Kong seems to have evolved into a grotesque realization of the utopian Ville Contemporaine city plan proposed by the French-Swiss architect Le Corbusier in 1922. Importantly, the original plan was meant as a hypothetical experiment to explore the possibility of an efficient, high-density city for three million inhabitants, centered on a cluster of gigantic cruciform-shaped towers. Le Corbusier's plan identified cruciform-shaped towers as the perfect standard, reproducible forms for sustaining high efficiency and high density. In Hong Kong, where city dwellers have to contend with a shortage of developable land, most residential towers are characterized by predictable, standard designs, with floor plans dictated by the city's building regulations and extruded upwards with minimal variation. The result is an aesthetic of sameness.

It is important to note that the plan of the Ville Contemporaine was not meant to function as a blueprint for actual construction. There is also another crucial difference between Le Corbusier's Ville Contemporaine plan and its seeming manifestation in Hong Kong. The efficiency-driven planning of Hong Kong does not take into account the vast, open, green spaces and low-rise buildings that surround the central cluster of cruciform towers in Le Corbusier's vision, separating the towers from other grouped high-rises to ensure an abundance of clean air, light, and great views in the city. Rather than realizing the concept of large towers on a vast green space, Hong Kong has implemented the concept of large towers on vast shopping spaces and infrastructural nodes.

Many claim that Hong Kong has no space to extend – that new developments would threaten its natural sites and waterfronts. In fact, the opposite is true. Hong Kong has plenty of space to build. Over 60 percent of Hong Kong is unbuilt land, and the city has plenty of vacant industrial buildings as well.

Sites in areas such as Kwun Tong, Wong Chuk Hang and Aberdeen have the potential to be converted into residential buildings. The Hong Kong government could loosen the current restrictions to support and facilitate the redevelopment of vacant industrial buildings in these areas and convert them into affordable residential buildings. Theoretically, Hong Kong should have enough developable land to house all inhabitants in an acceptable housing unit size with relative comfort and without harming the environment.

Over the past few decades, the cruciform-shaped tower has been perfected and fine-tuned, emerging as the dominant housing typology in Hong Kong. Many of these towers exemplify architectural design that cleaves precisely to the minimum amounts of light, air, sanitation, and accessible outdoor space for dwellings as prescribed in Hong Kong's Buildings Ordinances and its Building (Planning) Regulations. While the trident- and cross-shaped tower typologies are often developed for the high-end housing market for higher-income residents, the cruciform-shaped tower typology seems to be the most popular housing tower typology for the mid- and lower-income housing market in Hong Kong.

A few developers and architects have made efforts to promote the use of different tower typologies, but for the most part, Hong Kong developers have not adopted these new typologies. Instead, they seem resistant to such creativity, preferring to stick closely to the cruciform model while camouflaging this conservatism with innovative marketing. Without doubt, the cruciform model will continue to exist for some time. It has been stamped so many times onto the Hong Kong cityscape that it dominates the collective memory of the people and the housing market.

The typical residential high-rise in Hong Kong has a central core, which becomes the pivot for basic design maneuvers such as flipping and mirroring standardized apartment units with identical layouts. These simply designed floor plans are then extruded vertically along the core without any variation between floors, which keeps production cost and construction time at a minimum. Hong Kong's housing designs have thus become extremely repetitive, often generating apartment units that lack variation in size and form and fail to provide sufficient outdoor space or adequate spatial accommodations for daily activities such as dining, cooking, bathing, or studying. Typical apartments also lack adequate storage and other important elements such as daylight, natural ventilation, or unblocked views. People are forced to choose from a selection of the same, low-quality options.

Endless repetition

Sameness

Podiums kill street life

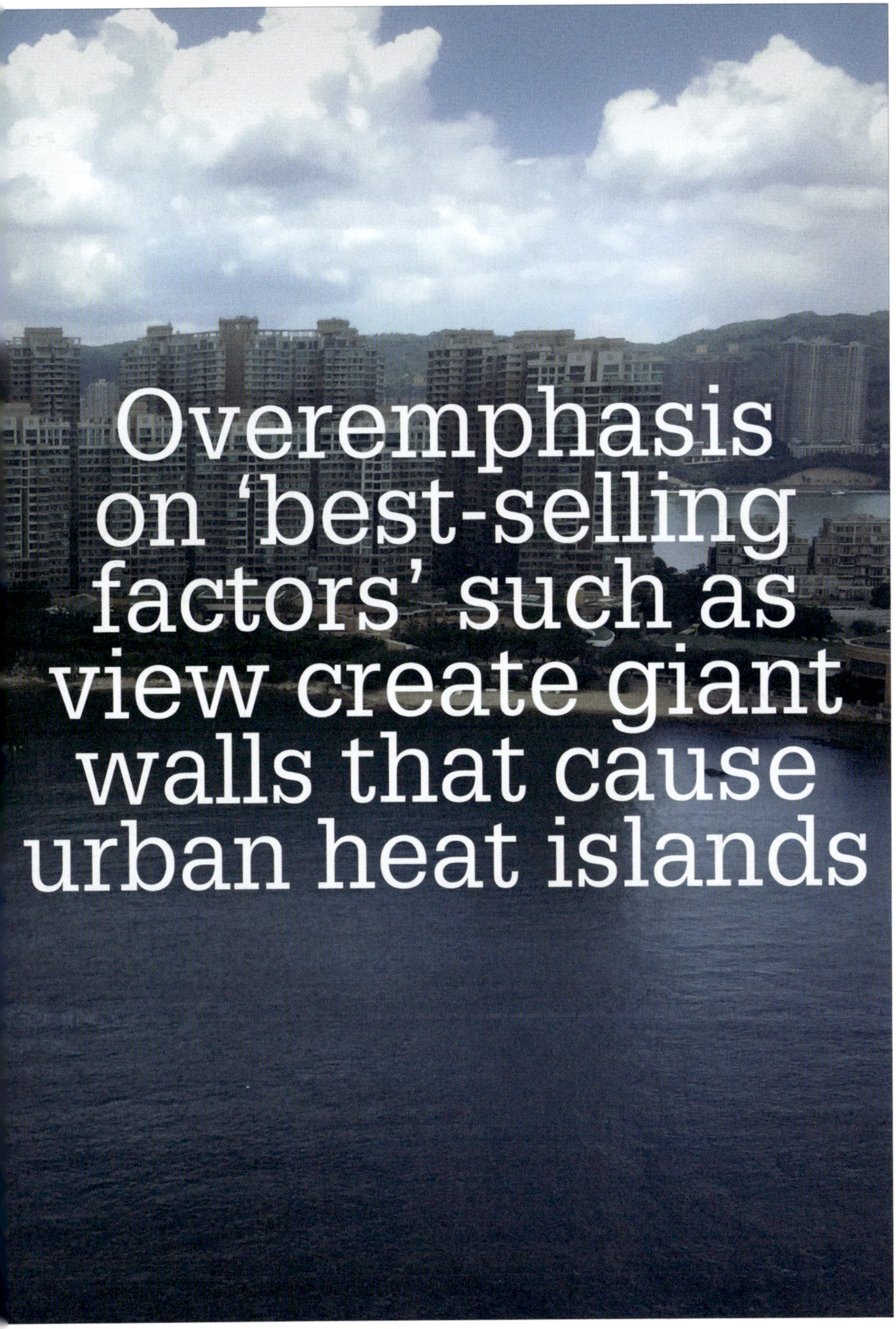
Overemphasis on ‘best-selling factors’ such as view create giant walls that cause urban heat islands

"MPH, PHRMPH"

Sky-high housing prices force people to live in cramped spaces

Cage-homes
have become
the norm

Disappearing low-rise housing typologies

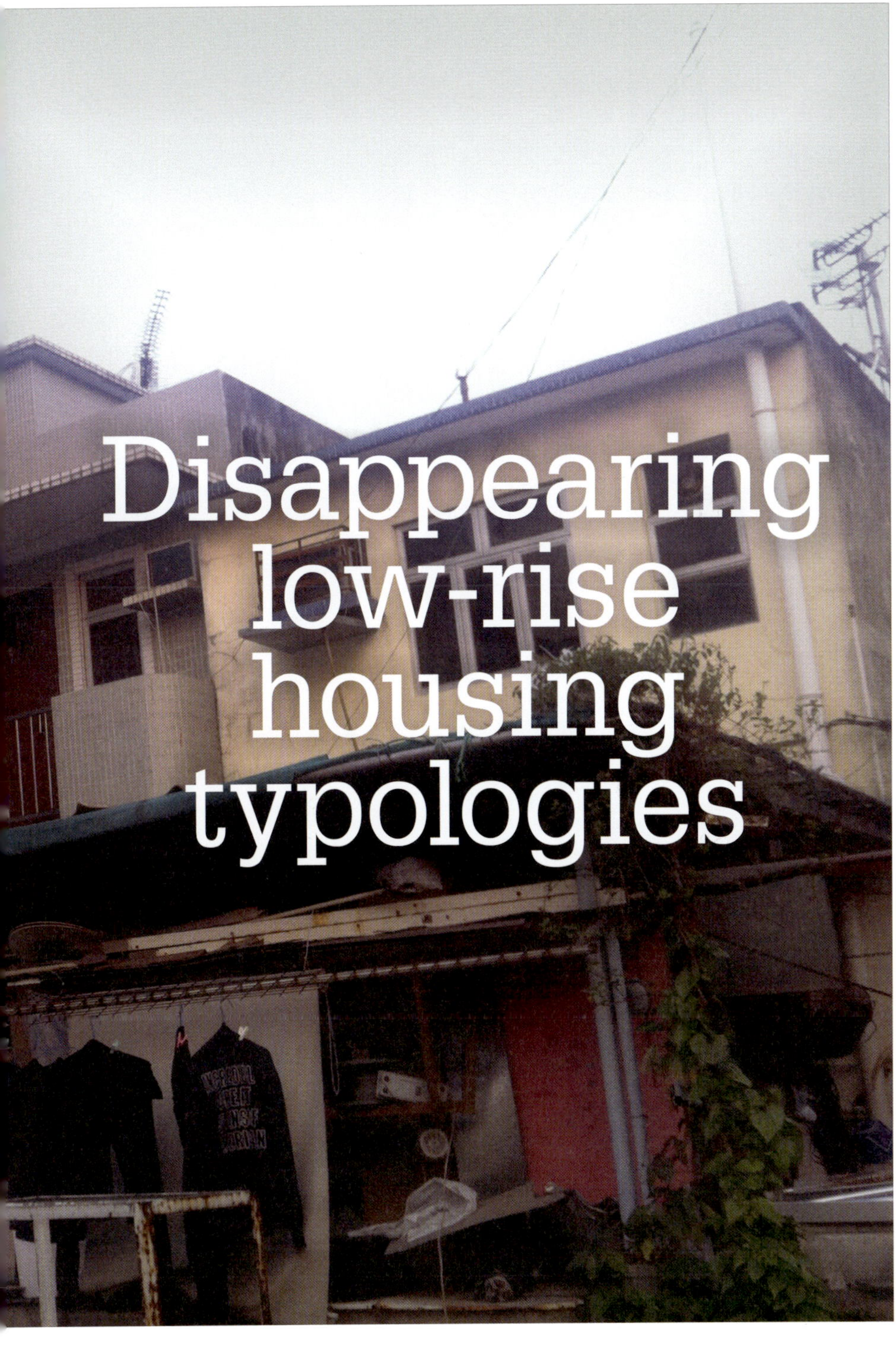

Stringent building regulations destroy diversity and reduce quality of life

Large-scale new town developments suffer from social isolation

Apartments
without
sufficient light
and natural
ventilation

Useless balconies

No regulations for the maid's room

Since the 1950s, Hong Kong's housing problem — including the lack of public housing, the unaffordability of private housing units, and the apparent scarcity of land to develop — has been a frequent topic for public discussion. Significant social unrest could be attributed to Hong Kong's housing-related deficits. Despite all the debate, housing development in Hong Kong has remained fundamentally unchanged. In the past few decades, the government has launched campaigns to supply more housing, but there has been little progress towards establishing viable long-term solutions. The following collection of newspaper headlines will illustrate how the lack of affordable housing, the poor general conditions of the city's housing, and continuously rising real estate prices have dominated public debate over the past 60 years — and continue unabated to this day.

What Do the Media Say?

Text by Tihamér Salij

This text is adopted and modified from a conceptual text by the students.

Collection of newspaper articles compiled by the students of The Why Factory's "Hong Kong Tower Revolution" studio at the Department of Architecture (Architecture and Urban Design III, ARCH 5001) at the Hong Kong University, during Fall 2013,
and students of The Why Factory's "Towers Beyond Extrusion" studio at the Department of Architecture at the Hong Kong University, during Fall 2014.

Hong Kong Tower Revolution, Architecture and Urban Design III (ARCH 5001), Hong Kong University.
Studio Tutors: Prof. Winy Maas and Tihamér Salij with Sander Mulders and Arend van Waart
Students: Au Wing Yi, Chak Tsz Kin, Chan Chung Man, Chan Ian Yin Yan, Chan Pui Yin, Chau Shek Lun, Cheng Ching, Ip Kai Hong, Liu Kemeng, Mok Wang Chee, Tang Ho Yin, Kong Ho Ching, Kwok Ka Ching, Lau Xin Yee, Lee Kin Wai, Li Mei Yu, Lung Man Ching, Ma Ching Yi, Suen Wing Yin, Sze Ivy, Sze Ying Ying, Yeung Cho Yui, Yeung Ho Man

Towers Beyond Extrusion, Architecture and Urban Design III (ARCH 5001), Hong Kong University
Studio Tutors: Prof. Winy Maas, Tihamér Salij, Martine Vledder with Donn Holohan
Students: Au Yeung Chun Yu JOEY, Chan Fong Tong FRED S, Cheng Pok Him BOB, Ching Ka Ho FRED, Henao Granda Jan Esteban, Ho Sheung Hay TERENCE, Hu Xiangdong HOCK, Ko Pak Kan ZETH, Li Zhixin ALLISON, Liu Chuen Yung VINCENT, Ma Yue, Qin Liting TING, Tang Tak Shing KELVIN, Wen Fan, Wu Yucong, Xie Junni, Ffion Zhang, Ho Yin SUNNY CHA, Sai Bond, Man Hei KENNIF, Han PAT

Housing Shortages and Poor Conditions

Housing has long been subject to enormous pressures in Hong Kong. Providing proper and affordable living spaces for citizens is arguably the city's biggest obstacle to growth. Too many Hong Kong residents are living in tiny homes, such as two- to three-square-meter 'coffin cubicles', formed by the illegal subdivision of flats, or rooftop squats with deteriorating walls, ceilings, and staircases, leaking roofs, insanitary toilet facilities, and no running water, cooking facilities, or windows. The prevalence of such poor-quality housing is the result of rapid population growth and a lack of long-term planning, which has kept the city from working toward sustainable and affordable housing development.

According to the media, even residents with relatively high incomes have difficulty making down payments on housing. The huge difference in the average cost of rent between public and private housing is forcing a large majority of residents with middle to relatively high incomes to pay two-thirds or even more of their income on rent. In 2016, the average rental price for permanent private housing in Hong Kong Island, according to the Rating and Valuation Department, was HK\$377/m^2. In districts such as Kowloon, the average rental price for permanent private housing reached an average of HK\$298/m^2, and HK\$227/m^2 in the New Territories. The rental prices for public housing in the same districts are dramatically less expensive, averaging HK\$55/m^2 for Hong Kong Island, HK\$61/m^2 for Kowloon and HK\$49/m^2 for the New Territories. But housing affordability and resource management remain critical issues, and as many news outlets have reported, the city's efforts to increase public housing development has been far from sufficient. The waiting list for public housing remains extremely long.

1950s and '60s: Crisis and Response

Since the 1950s and '60s, Hong Kong's housing policy has undergone drastic changes. In the 1950s, Hong Kong's economy was still underdeveloped, and its deficiencies were compounded by the large influx of refugees from Mainland China. This exacerbated the demand for housing and ramped up the construction of illegal squats all over Hong Kong. On Christmas Eve 1953, a fire in Shek Kip Mei destroyed the homes of more than 50,000 residents. This event, which brought new attention to the ongoing housing shortage, prompted the Hong Kong government to formulate a public housing policy in the early 1960s. This government initiative led to the construction of housing with improved standards of quality for more than 500,000 inhabitants. During that same period, the government implemented a low-cost housing programme to provide higher quality rental accommodations.

1970s: Population Rise and Urban Expansion

Later, during the 1970s, the media began covering stories that highlighted the unremitting population rise and widespread dissatisfaction with the quality of Hong Kong's public housing estates. The government reacted by building new housing estates and initiating the construction of whole new towns in the New Territories of Hong Kong. More experimental housing typologies were developed to provide living spaces with more natural light, better ventilation, larger unit sizes, and improved communal spaces with better facilities. Yet the supply of housing could not meet the growing demand, and the continued shortage of housing and land prompted private landowners to speculate for profit maximization of their properties.

1980s and '90s: Financial Crisis, Unrest, and Recovery

During the 1980s and '90s, Hong Kong suffered a financial crisis, spurred by political unrest in China and other global events. Asset values of the stock market, property and land values, as well as the foreign exchange market fell to record lows. In 1997, sovereignty over Hong Kong was returned from the United Kingdom to China. Despite these major political and financial events, which spurred a dramatic plunge of the Hung Seng index, Hong Kong's economy recovered quickly as if nothing had happened, setting conditions for real estate speculation.

2000s to the Present: Speculation on the Real Estate Market

In the last twenty years, speculation on the property market has increased, becoming one of the most hotly debated topics in the media. Landowners, developers, and people with higher incomes from Hong Kong as well as Mainland China continue to speculate on housing for short-term profits, leaving many apartments vacant in a city continuously struggling to house its residents. According to a survey of 360 cities by the U.S.-based consultancy bureau Demographia, in the past few years, Hong Kong has topped the list as the most unaffordable city due to its soaring property prices and the inability for most salary incomes to catch up. Unaffordable housing and a lack of quality housing stock will likely remain pressing topics of debate in Hong Kong.

"Shek Kip Mei - Area to Prese

1953

Shek Kip Mei – From Former Squatter Area to Present Diverse Community

"From Former Squatter Diverse Community"

Source: Wordpress, http://cedarbarefootwalk.wordpress.com/2011/10/13/shekkipmei/

In the 1950s, many refugees from Mainland China moved to Hong Kong. Since the then Hong Kong government had no housing policy for the grassroots people at that time, refugees squatted in wooden huts built along the hillside, many of them in Shek Kip Mei. These primitive huts had very limited facilities and poor hygiene; the high-density nature of these settlements are susceptible to constant outbreaks of fire. In order to resettle the victims of one of these disastrous fires, the government built resettlement blocks which were subsequently redeveloped into Shek Kip Mei Estate, Pak Tin Estate, Nam Shan Estate and Tai Hang Tung Estate in the 70s.

"Mei Ho Estate – Resettlement Estate for the homeless victimes of the great fire."

1954

Source: http://www.inmediahk.net/node/1003895

"Sai Wan Estate - The Public Housing on Slope"

Source: Blog, http://memory-of-child-year.blogspot.hk/2014/08/1-1.html

1959

Source: http://www.inmediahk.net/node/1003895

1960

"Li Cheng Uk Estate - Resettlement Area"

"Living in the Cage"

1960

Source: http://www.welovehkhist.com/activity/Activity_09_01_images/07.jpg

"The Rapid Development of Public Housing in Chai Wan"

1961

Source: British Pathe, https://www.youtube.com/watch?v=qY5wLZKglpM

"More than 10,000 starving illegal immigrant from China"

1962

Source: Newspaper Ming Pao

"China's Refugees: Something can be done now."

1962

Source: Life, http://books.google.com.hk/books?id=3U4EAAAAMBAJ&printsec=frontcover#v=onepage&q&f=false

It was in their faces for all the world to read—the hunger for enough food and a little joy. Both were just out of reach. Over the border into British territory flooded thousands after thousands of refugees from Red China. They straggled in crowds by day down hot, bare mountainsides, and by night lost their families and friends in the confusion of the dark. They cowered bewildered in the underbrush, listening to Chinese from Hong Kong hopefully calling out the names of relatives who might be in hiding.

A 14-year-old boy from Chungking traveled about 1,000 miles to the border by train and foot, was caught twice by Red border guards, talked his way free and finally smuggled himself into Hong Kong in a freight car full of cabbages. Two brothers and a sister who had journeyed 125 miles crossed the border unmolested by the Red guards, expecting to be welcomed. But, like most of the fleeing Chinese, they were tragically disappointed.

Hong Kong is so saturated with refugees—a million and a half in the past 12 years—that it cannot absorb any more. Formosa has too little room for them. And the U.S. will take only skilled workers with sponsors in America. So British troops and police at Hong Kong, helpless to do otherwise, rounded up the refugees and returned them to the Communists.

Perhaps 15,000 made it to the s
Hong Kong. At least 55,000 wer
return to their homeland. Then, su
pathetic inundation ceased. Either
gime clamped down on those tryin
or word got back into China that
were closing the border. But the
the great flight remained. "All we
commune was work," one man w
into Hong Kong told LIFE Cor
Charles Elliott. "We went to wor
sun rose and when the sun set w
home to bed so we could work th
But the hunger was the worst thing
lage one out of every 10 has died

"Wanchai Reclamation"

Source: Wah Kiu Yat Po Daily

1964

"Mei Foo Sun Cheun - Role Model For Residential Housing"

1962

Source: http://www.inmediahk.net/node/1003895

“Walled City builders flouting regulations”

Source: South China Morning Post

1972

South China Morning Post. Dec. 21, 1972.

Walled City builders flouting regulations

Multi-storey buildings are being constructed inside the Kowloon Walled City on sketches and plans that have not been approved by the Public Works Department, according to some residents in the area yesterday.

Reliable sources told the S.C.M. Post last night the Public Works Department does not normally extend its jurisdiction into the Walled City.

In normal circumstances, unlike Hongkong Island or the rest of the Colony, buildings within the Walled City need not secure any approval for construction.

But, the sources believed, the PWD would not sit back and watch potentially dangerous structures being built.

S.C.M. Post reporters who toured the area yesterday saw feverish building activities there.

There are buildings of 12 or more storeys built during the past few years while several more are being constructed on the fringes of the Walled City.

Some of the buildings, the residents claimed, had been constructed without piling. Holes were dug into the ground about 10 feet deep, into which reinforced concrete pillars were placed to bear the weight of the whole structure.

However, th[…] these buildings w[…]

Occasionally, […] were told, one […] floors were adde[…] completed an[…]

[…] averaging a little over $1 a square foot.

A ground floor shop with an area of between 250 and 300 square feet fetches about $[…] a month in rent.

The new buildings are ri[…] on the fringes of the Wa[…] City. Its centre remains unchanged with many old structures.

In a court case more than 10 years ago, the Supreme Court ruled that the Walled City was […]

Source: South China Morning Post

“No authoritative ruling on Walled City’s legal status”

1973

No authoritative ruling on Walled City’s legal status

[…] have frequently asserted and reasserted their claims since 1899.

As a matter of Hongkong’s municipal law, however, there is no doubt: the Walled City is legitimately “part and parcel of Her Majesty’s Colony of Hongkong” until the expiry in 1997 of the New Territories lease.

The Public Works Department, therefore, has equal justification with the police and other Government agencies to carry on its functions inside the city. But it has never done so. In consequence there are dozens of large, multi-storey buildings erected over the last 20 years in defiance of building regulations and town-planning principles; the six and a half acres of the Walled City are a jumble of tiny lanes and tall blocks of flats built without benefit of proper foundations or Government supervision.

The reasons for the curious restraint of PWD officers are primarily political. China has not been prepared to relinquish her claim to title over the Walled City and has protested whenever the Hongkong […]

[…] before the war and still available is detailed enough to admit an accurate description of where the wall’s foundations were, and the few remains are of little help. The Japanese demolition teams did a thorough job, taking every possible piece of stone for the work then being carried out on Kai Tak improvements.

The conventional assumption is that the Walled City is bounded by Tung Tau Tsuen Road, Sai Shing Road, Lung Chun Road and Lung Shing Road. The second and third of these, however, do not appear from modern plans to follow exactly the line of the old wall. It is not surprising that Mr Wong Yat-kwan, owner of the nearly-completed block of flats on Lung Shing Road now being demolished by Government, had hoped to take advantage of the uncertainty to lessen building costs by avoiding PWD regulations.

His claim, however, is not a good one, for the address of his condemned building places it on the wrong side of the street. The contractor maintains that it was the site of a small river in the Walled City; yet old maps […]

[…] action against a developer on Lung Shing Road.

The illustrations published with this article are republished by kind permission of the Law Journal.

[…] feet in width and in total length about 2,200 feet, a considerable area of territory is involved.

Such niceties do not, of course, concern the PWD, which seems to be interested only in checking the clearly untenable assertions of immunity based on location within the Walled City.

But the exaggerated caution of its general policy may be unwarranted. Building regulations are designed to protect residents, and presumably the erection of large buildings, by unlicensed constructors able to ignore technical requirements relating to piling and standard of concrete, endangers those who use them. China does not object to police activities inside the city, and could allow PWD supervision there without weakening her ideological and legal claim to the whole area.

In fact it is now rather late for the Hongkong Government to intervene, for nearly all available space for illegal construction has been taken up: the “unsafe” buildings are already there, providing accommodation at reasonable rental for many thousands of people and profits for landlords who have been led to expect continuance of such income. And the Walled City could not be razed without expensive resettlement, bitter resentment and damaging political controversy.

THE WALLED CITY, 1902

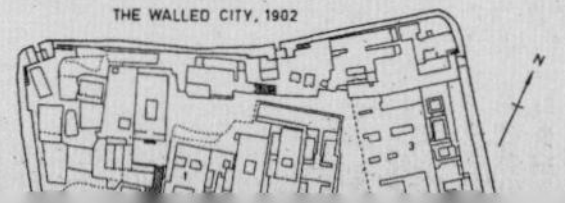

1974

"Shek Kip Mei Estate reconstruction work slow, living condition is worse"

Source: Wah Kiu Yat Po Daily

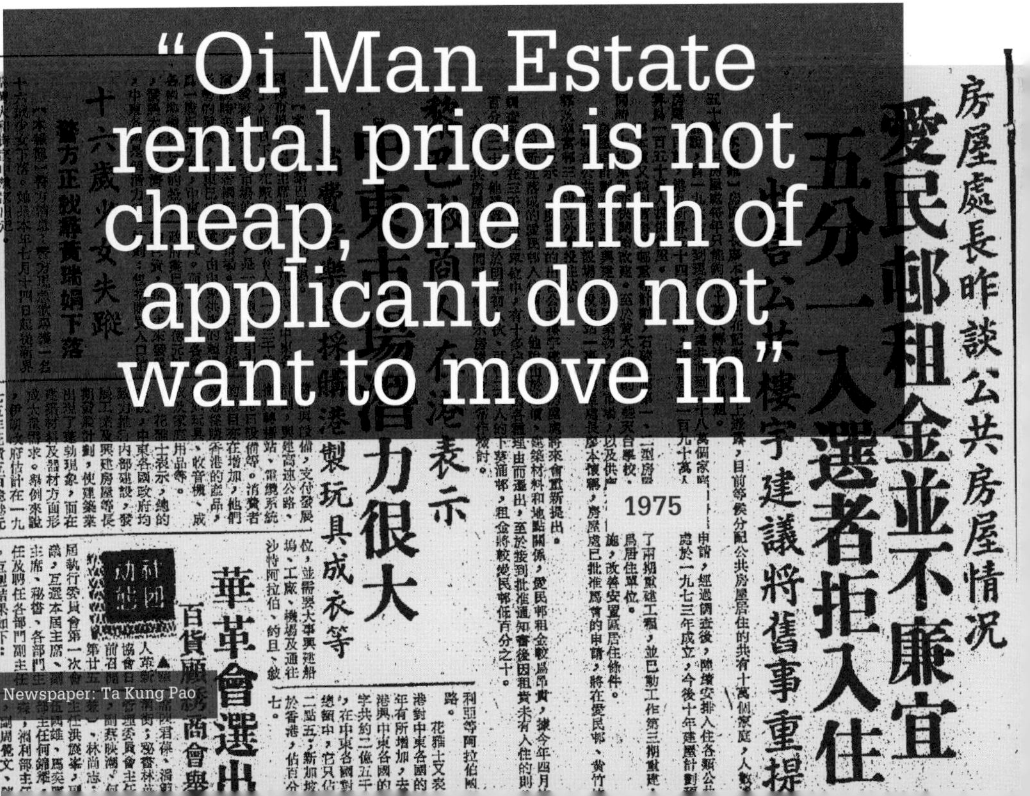

"Oi Man Estate rental price is not cheap, one fifth of applicant do not want to move in"

1975

Newspaper: Ta Kung Pao

1976

Project aims at better homes for 350,000 in NT

"Project aims at better homes for 350,000"

A development programme will soon start to give better homes and facilities to about 350,000 people in the rural areas outside the new towns at Shatin, Tsun Wan and Tuen Mun.

Blueprints have been completed and work on the first site formation is to begin after Christmas.

The programme will provide public housing estates in 12 rural areas in the New Territories and outlying islands – Taipo, Shek Wu Hui, Fanling, Yuen Long, Sai Kung (Tui Min Hoi), Mui Wor, Cheung Chau, Tai O, Peng Chau, Lau Fau Shan, Tan Kwai Tsuen and Sham Tseng.

Feasibility studies for these areas were submitted recently by Public Works Department consultant engineers. Detailed design work for much of the engineering and building is either in hand or underway.

The Government Engineer (New Territories), Mr Kenneth Kwok, said yesterday the development of the new market towns is similar in concept to the new towns, but on a smaller scale.

The aim, he said, is to provide balanced development with all basic facilities and essential services for residents. These will include schools, clinics, community halls, shopping centres and recreational areas.

In addition, sites will also be made available to private developers for commercial and industrial use, he said.

He said about $371 million has been earmarked in the public works programme for various engineering projects in the rural development areas.

Development will first concentrate on Taipo, Shek Wu Hui, Fanling, Yuen Long, Sai Kung, Mui Wor, Cheung Chau and Tai O.

"The first contract in the programme, involving the reclamation of about 27 hectares in Tolo Harbour, Taipo, will be signed in a few days' time and work will start immediately afterwards," he said.

The reclaimed land will be used to build a public housing estate for about 10,000 people with ... facilities.

The reclamation will take about 26 months to complete with piling work for the housing estate to start by July. The first tenants will be moving in by the latter part of 1979.

Meanwhile, tenders are about to be invited for the formation, reclamation, ... and drainage works in the ... Kung (Tui Min Hoi) area, work to start early next year.

The completed site formation will provide land for a p... ... and a ho... scheme for fishermen disp... by the High Island W... Scheme – a total of about ... people.

At Shek Wu Hui, tender... expected to be called in ... latter half of next year fo... formation of 21 hectare... land for various uses, incl... a public housing estate ... 5,000.

Also included in the ... stages of the Shek Wu ... development is the wideni... Jockey Club Road and ... Road from the Wo Hop ... railway crossing to the ex... Shek Wu Hui town.

Mr Kwok said the form... of 14 hectares of lan... Fanling has also been pla... and work there is expect... begin soon. Initial develop... will include an estate for 1... together with associ... community facilities.

At Yuen Long, plans a... land for a smaller estat... 5,000 people.

At Mui Wor, in... development will consis... forming about 10 hectares ... the ferry concourse fo... estate to house 800 an... building of a new ferry pier.

Tenders will also be c... soon for site formation wo... Tai O on Lantao where an... housing estate will be bui... 3,000 people. Building w... expected to start in July.

At Cheung Chau, Mr K... said about nine hectares w... formed for early developm...

Source: South China Morning Post

"$140 million housing boost"

$140 million housing boost

THREE contracts worth more than $140 million were signed yesterday for the construction of the second phases of two housing estates to accommodate a further 26,000 people.

The larger of the contracts, valued at $70 million, was for building the second phase of Stage II of Shunleetsuen Estate.

Four 18-storey blocks will provide 2,400 flats for up to 12,000 people, as well as 130,000 square feet ... complex, two estate carparks and three cooked-food pavillions.

Work starts at the end of next month and will be completed by March 1979.

The contract was awarded to the Shun Shing Building Construction Company.

The second contract worth $69 million was awarded to the Kwan Lee Construction Company for building Phase IIB of Ngauchiwan Estate.

In this stage, 2,039 flats for more than 14,000 people will be built in two standard twin "H" shaped blocks, a single "H" block and a slab block.

COMPLEX

The work also includes a three-storey commercial complex, a multi-story, three cooked-food pavillions, a kindergarten annex and a nursery.

Construction starts at the end of this month and be completed by October 1979.

Both contracts were signed by the Acting Director of Housing, Mr Bernard Williams.

The third contract, valued at $3.1 million and awarded to Franki Piling and Engineering (Hongkong) Limited, is for piling work for three secondary schools at the recently completed Woohe estate. It was signed by the Housing Architect, Mr Cheung Sing-hoi.

The awarding of these contracts brings to $339.7 million the value of building and piling contracts awarded since April 1 this year.

Last year, the value of eight building contracts awarded by the Housing Department totalled $265 million.

Source: South China Morning Post

1977

at better homes for
n New Town"

1977

"Before 1981, 380,000 people move into housing estate; Sha Tin, Tsuen Wan, Tai Po build more public housing"

沙田屯門荃灣大埔再建公屋

八一年前卅八萬人入住屋邨

工程合約未來八月批出

新鎮增建屋邨加速發展

九八零年七月至一九八一年五月，將有二萬八千個居住單位落成。

這二萬多個單位，公佈於五座新建屋邨內。該四屋邨爲荃灣石圍角邨，屯門安定邨及友愛邨，沙田的沙角邨，及大埔第十六區一尚未命名的屋邨。

石圍角邨在荃灣新市鎮內興建，工程共分四期進行，在八座大廈內約有六千個居住單位。第一期建築合約於八月份批出，包括興建兩座住宅大廈及一間小學，建築費約爲三千七百六十萬元。整個屋邨將於一九八〇年十二月落成，費用超過一億三千六百萬元。

沙角邨位於沙田新市鎮，分三期興建，共有八座大廈，內有四千八百間房舍，第一期打樁工程合約於八月內招標，價値爲八百六十萬元。整個屋邨的建築工程預料於一九八一年一月完竣，全部建築費用高達一億三千萬元。

在屯門新市鎮亦將興建另外兩個新屋邨，名爲安定邨及友愛邨。全部工程分五期進行，共有十八座大廈，內有一萬四千間房屋，於本月批出之第一期打樁合約價値爲二千七百萬元，這項浩大工程應可於一九八一年一月完成，全部建築費爲四億零五百萬元。新界大埔第一個公共屋邨將分兩期興建，在十座大廈內共有五千四百個居住單位，第一期打樁工程合約於本月批出，價値約爲一千三百萬元。這屋邨可望於一九八〇年七月落成，總建築費爲一億四千六百萬元。

政府大建屋計劃，使房屋委員會向其工作目標邁前一步。爲促使這些計劃如期完成，該委員會將於本（八）月份，開始批出此等屋邨的建築工程合約。并外，建築工程方法及樓宇設計，採用特別適合機械建築技術，以縮短工程時間。上述五個屋邨將會有學校，市場，購物中心及其他的社區設施。這四項建築工程可爲十五萬人提供居住單位，聯同現時已在施工十一個公共屋邨建築工作在內，估計在一九八一年時，可有足夠單位容納三十八萬人。新建屋邨單位增加，除可爲現時居於私人樓宇而收入較低市民，提供一些租金較廉的獨立單位外，更有助於減輕舊屋邨住客的擠逼程度。房屋委員會公共屋邨計劃表面上爲收入較低家庭提供住於市值而具有合理設備的單位外，實際

Source: Wah Kiu Yat Po Daily

"Rent increases are undemocratic"

1979

Source: South China Morning Post

'Rent increases are undemocratic' — housing watchdog

By ANGELA LAU

The Housing Department was yesterday attacked for deciding "undemocratically" on a "large-scale" rent increase in 14 public housing estates and several converted estates from September.

"The council is highly dissatisfied with the one-sided decision of the Government," said the chairman of the Hongkong People's Council on Public Housing Policy, Mr Lau Wai-yin, at a press conference yesterday.

"We will conduct an opinion survey this month among estate residents affected," he added.

"We have already heard of opposition to the increase," he said.

The two-year-old council, which concentrates on public housing policies, consists of social work agencies and professionals.

"Results of the survey will be submitted to the Government," said Mr Lau.

The council was referring to the recently announced 10 to 15 per cent rent increase for 14 public housing and two converted estates built between 1973 and 1977.

The increase will take effect from September 1, and will affect about 40,000 people.

The estates include Lai King and Lai Yiu in Tsun Wan, Lek Yuen in Shatin and Oi Man and Shek Kip Mei (converted) in Kowloon.

Mr Lau said that the increase is "a way of making profit out of residents who have no other choice but to accept it."

"This increase is unnecessary because the Housing Authority has been reaping a $400 million surplus every year for the past few years," said Mr Lau.

Referring to the Housing Authority's budget for 1973-74 and 1978-79, Mr Lau pointed out that while rents provide for 97 per cent of the authority's income from the estates, only a "meagre 16 per cent of this income is spent on the residents."

"About 29 per cent of this income goes to the Government in the form of rates and interests," he said.

He added that another 16 per cent of this income goes to the Housing Authority in the form of surplus and reserve.

"Besides, maintenance services within the estates have not improved over the past five years," he continued.

Mr Lau explained that in 1973-74 the HA spent 15 per cent of its income on maintenance services for the estates.

"The expenditure on maintenance services remained at 17 per cent in 1978-79."

Mr Lau further added that the residents cannot shoulder this financial burden.

"According to the Labour Department's annual report last year, the average salary increase last year for workers was only five to eight per cent, and yet the prospective rise in rents amounts to 15 per cent, which is double their pay rise," he said.

"Obviously, the Housing Authority has forgotten the difficulties of the labourer."

Besides, Mr Lau pointed out, "the residents have never been really satisfied with the management of the estates."

"We have received numerous complaints about bad management — no salt water for the toilets for months,

"HK can absorb 12mill people"

1980

Jones talks of long-term scenario:

HK can absorb 12m people

By WAT KIT-BING

Hongkong can absorb a total population of up to 12 million people in the long term, the Secretary for the Environment, Mr Derek Jones, said yesterday.

And he outlined three ways in which this could be done — urban development of Hongkong Island's rugged interior, the filling in of reservoirs and further reclamation around Victoria Harbour.

Mr Jones told a lunch meeting of the Zonta Club that the inner harbour scenario will involve a series of measures.

These would include the maximum redevelopment of the existing urban area, the development of Kai Tak and further reclamations around the harbour, possibly around Stonecutters Island.

"It could also entail the removal of the small reservoirs on Hongkong Island and development of the large water catchment area in its centre, together with the provision of large quantities of fill for further reclamation around the harbour.

"This would be urban core development with a vengeance, but the possibilities should be investigated," he said.

Another proposal is the belt of territory just beyond the inner harbour stretching from Lantao, through Tsun Wan, across to Shatin and Ma On Shan and extending round to Junk Bay.

The third scenario is the outer belt, much closer to the border, stretching from Tuen Mun and Pillar Point in the west through the northwest New Territories, Yuen Long and across to Fanling, Sheung Shui and the north-east.

Each of these pockets can accommodate an extra two million people, Mr Jones said.

He said Hongkong should do what it can to utilise the urban area because it is the centre of activity.

Mr Jones emphasised that none of the three scenarios will necessarily happen and Hongkong may end up with bits of each.

He said that both the Government and the community have to ponder this issue in coming years and have to make choices, "whether consciously or by default."

Mr Jones also said that Hongkong is now moving so fast in various directions that "we are faced with a serious problem of choice in how to apply the considerable, but limited, resources we have for public sector capital expenditure to a whole galaxy of development options."

He said until recently there had been no great problem in financing the public works programme, but now the rate of expenditure has increased sharply.

"This year, it is estimated to be $7,080 million, a 290 per cent increase in five years."

He said the two major factors in this increase have been the new towns and public housing programmes and

HK 'can absorb 12m people'

(Cont'd from Page 1)

new towns of Shatin, Tuen Mun, Taipo, Fanling-Sheung Shui and Yuen Long will have a combined population of almost 2½ million, compared with less than a million now.

But, Mr Jones said, "the spreading out of the population to the new towns demands also adequate communications linking the new towns with each other and with the inner urban areas around the harbour."

He said the expenditure on this area is overstraining the economy and particularly the construction industry and is producing serious overheating.

Mr Jones cited another set of problems which he said are longer term and concern the future direction of Hongkong's development and the future distribution of the population.

"Their inter-relationships are now being examined by the new Strategic Planning Unit in the Environment Branch."

Source: South China Morning Post

decision has to be made on building a bridge linking Lantao with the mainland via Ma Wan and Tsing Yi, plus a first class road and possibly a rail link to the new airport, said Mr Jones.

A decision on the building of a new airport will be made in 1982.

Mr Jones said that by 1990, after the removal of the airport, the redevelopment of Kai Tak, with appropriate reclamations, would provide a very large area of land in a central location for urban development.

Also some of the building height restrictions in Kowloon could be removed.

"The location of another container port will be an important added factor in decisions on future population distribution and transport links."

Possible locations suggested by Mr Jones include Tuen Mun, Lantao, an extension of the existing Kwai Chung

"Air-con rooms in flats 'not saleable area"

Surveyors' institute says many developers abuse system and confuse buyers

Flat buyers were warned yesterday that a flat's saleable area should not include the area of the air-conditioning plant room, an increasingly popular facility designed for luxury residential developments.

The warning came as the Hong Kong Institute of Surveyors issued its latest clarification of the definition of a flat's saleable area.

Under the current regulations, no land premium is required for building an air-conditioning plant room, which used to be designed for detached houses to store a centralised air-conditioner. But some flat owners have in fact paid for the room, as some developers include it as part of the saleable area.

The new definition announced by the institute yesterday includes the 'utility platform' - a balcony-like platform - but not the air-conditioning plant room as saleable area.

'The air-conditioning plant room is commonly found in multi-storey residential developments in recent years,' the institute's vice-president, Stephen Yip Moon-wah, said. 'It should not be counted as saleable area because people living in the flat do not practically use it.'

A number of surveyors said that some developers were abusing the right to build an air-conditioning plant room. They were building the rooms larger and describing them as storerooms.

Air-conditioning plant rooms are commonly found in floor maps of newly built developments. In the floor map of one luxury apartment in Kowloon Tong, the air-conditioning plant room is roughly the size of the kitchen or small bedroom.

The size of a plant room can vary from 10 sq ft to over 30 sq ft, said Charles Chan Chiu-kwok, managing director of valuation and professional services at property consultant Savills.

Source: South China Morning Post

... for the plant room under current building regulations, 'but its size has to be justifiable and approved by the Buildings Department', he added.

'Some developers include the room's area as saleable area because, they

"Board urges war on those 'city warts'"

By MATTHEW LEUNG

The proliferation of "city warts" — illegal extensions to buildings — is a source of worry to many Kowloon City District Board members.

And they have blamed the Government for not monitoring the situation closely enough.

Members yesterday called on the Government to detail officers immediately to conduct investigations to prevent the spread of these illegal extensions and demolish existing ones.

However, the Government said it did not have sufficient manpower to do the job

... Kowloon City, Mr D.U. Ramanayake, told members at the board meeting.

But he added that if residents complained officials would inspect the sites and if illegal structures were found to be in dangerous positions they would be demolished.

The District Lands Officer (Kowloon West) of the Lands Department, Mr D.G. Dear, suggested that a specialist team be set up under the Building Ordinance Office to handle the problem.

He said the team should have all means to remove and demolish cages and illegal structures.

Mr Dear said the ultimate

... could not find a word other than "hell" to describe the ...

... Shamshuipo were the two areas most seriously affected by the problem.

Another board member, Mr Luk Wai-kong, said the Government should consider the effect of aircraft noise on students.

He said aircraft noise affected people living in Kowloon City, Sai Tau, Kowloon Tong, Matauwai and To Kwa Wan.

The problem became a controversial issue recently with the decision not to proceed with plans for an alternative airport.

He said the hardest hit were students, particularly those in Kowloon Tong and

Source: South China Morning Post

1983

"Big drive to clear illegal extensions"

Source: South China Morning Post

1984

Big drive to clear illegal extensions

By JULINA CHAN

The Government is about to launch its biggest clearance operation against a multi-storey building in San Po Kong with nearly 650 illegal extensions.

Orders will be issued today by the Building Ordinance Office requiring owners of the units to remove all the illegal extensions within three months.

The building involved is the 17-year-old, 20-storey San Po Kong Mansion, at the junction of Choi Hung Road and Yin Hing Street.

If the owners do not comply with the removal order, the Government will hire contractors to clear the illegal units and the costs involved will be charged to the owners.

The contractors could begin work in October and have the job completed by April, a Government spokesman said.

The move has drawn mixed reaction from tenants, with most claiming yesterday they had never been informed of the problem.

This is despite the fact that a spokesman for the Buildings Ordinance Office said owners were ordered almost three years ago to remove defective reinforced concrete features on th side walls as they wer sidered liable to becom gerous.

The unauthorised tures included 19 fla structures at the first level, 445 cages and structures and 190 ca and racks.

"No action has ye taken in response to th ernment order," the man said.

This, together wi complaints about building activities, pro further detailed surve said.

The spokesman sai of the structures were tially dangerous.

They also obstructe ing and ventilation and a health hazard.

The Government the building as one worst in the area in te breaching building laws

One flat owner, Mr lung, who moved in ju months ago, appealed Government to exte deadline for the clearan

Mr Lo said he had more than $46,000 b an extention to his house a kitchen and room.

Mr Lo said he wo have built it if he had it was illegal.

"Nobody told me that," he said.

"To be fair, the G ment should remove illegal structures in all premises — why sho pinpoint us only?" he a

Mr Lo will conside ing compensation fro Government if his ext is demolished against h

"The Government at least give us more he said.

A ninth floor ten Mrs Chow, said she follow the majority o on whether to compl the Government order go against it.

She personally h strong objections to the ance, although the ext to her flat had been more than 10 years ago.

1985

"Relaxed housing rules benefit 2,000 families"

Relaxed housing rules benefit 2,000 families

TWO thousand more families will become eligible for public rental housing under the new income and space eligibility limits, the Housing Authority announced yesterday.

Over-income applicants who have been dropped from the waiting list may be reviewed and reinstated as the limits have been relaxed with retrospective effect to September 1.

The new standards are about 10 to 15 per cent higher than the limits announced last December.

The new household income eligibility limits are $3,700 per month for a three-person unit; $3,900 per month for a four-person unit; $4,100 for a five-person unit; $4,400 for a six-person unit; $4,700 for a seven-person unit; $5,000 for an eight-person unit; $5,300 for a nine-person unit and $5,600 for a unit of 10 or more people.

These limits will be further increased by 20 per cent for the Elderly Persons Priority Housing Scheme.

The new levels for the elderly are $4,400 per month for a three-person unit; $4,700 for a four-person unit and $5,000 for a five-person unit.

The revised space eligibility limit has now been set at four square metres per person.

For applicants living in accommodation of durable material but without one or more basic living facilities, or in accommodation shared with one or more other households, or for those whose rent-income ratio exceeds 20 per cent, the new space limit is 4.5 square metres per person.

INVITED

Meanwhile, the Housing Authority has also invited piling tenders for the second phase of a new Home Ownership estate in Tuenmun new town.

Work will comprise piling for three 37-storey tower blocks with 1,680 flats, a commercial centre and a five-storey car park plus associated walkways.

Work is expected to start next February and to be completed in about six months.

To be built in two phases near Wuking estate, the new HOS estate will be fully completed by 1985 providing 2,800 flats for about 12,000 people plus a wide range of commercial and educational facilities.

Piling work for two blocks under the first phase will start next month.

Source: South China Morning Post

“Building law ‘ridiculous’”

Source: South China Morning Post

1985

Building law ‘ridiculous’

([illegible] from [illegible]age 1)

The first impl[illegible] while the latter w[illegible] an im[illegible]ative.

Counsel said [illegible] was ambiguous and absurd.

There were so many various considerations the Building Authority [illegible]d to take into account before issu[illegible] notice, he said.

Mr Bernacchi al[illegible] said it was unfair of the tr[illegible]unal to dismiss the appea[illegible] hearing as there may have been a good excuse.

His client had initially corresponded with the Lands Department on this matter which was under the auspices of the Director of Public Works.

But the notice was sent by the Building Authority, which was a separate entity and some confusion may have resulted, counsel said.

Furthermore, if the notice was a compulsory order, it would affect an innocent third party whose building adjoined the structure concerned.

In reply, Crown Solicitor Mr Neil Strawbridge said the object of the ordinance was to protect the public from unsafe buildings and to ensure that they were properly built in accordance with the law.

He said the appeals tribunal was only empowered to hear cases that involved a decision that the Building Authority made in exercising its discretion.

“May” in this context [illegible] mandatory [illegible] appeal [illegible], Mr Strawbridge said.

[illegible] sed the whole ordinance, this was not one of the powers the Building Authority had discretion [illegible] there was no discretion involved, there could be no appeal.

However, in sections where the words “in his opinion” preceded the word [illegible] appealed, said Mr Strawbridge.

But those words did not appear in this section.

In his judgment, Mr Justice Jackson-Lipkin said that the construction of this word was often a practitioner's delight and a Crown counsel's nightmare.

“The draftsman could not have been in control of himself by using it in section 24 or he would not have got the law into such a state,” he said.

The judge noted that the definition of “may” in the Oxford dictionary took up a full nine columns.

But as far as the ordinance was concerned, there were four constructions.

The first was to confer and enable power; the second a directory; the third discretion of a limited nature and the fourth, unlimited discretion.

The judge said frequently it was easy to decide which [illegible] But, [illegible] this ordinance it had been scattered [illegible], he said.

[illegible] said his job was to try [illegible] discover which colour of confetti the draftsman was writing [illegible].

Normally, he would have no hesitation in saying that “may” never meant “must” and the section meant complete discretion.

But in this instance, it was [illegible] law drafting has been broken in this ordinance,” the judge said.

“Unhappily, I have to try to make sense out of it.

“Two things are perfectly clear: one is that ‘shall’ means ‘shall’ and there is no discretion whatsoever, and the other “in the opinion of the Building Authority may” means there is an unfettered discretion.”

The judge said half way between the two was what he had to determine — if “may” is directory as opposed to “shall be” mandatory.

The judge said he had to look at the half way mark and see if “may” in section 24 fell on the “shall” side or “in the opinion of” side.

If it was minutely “in the opinion of” side, the appeal tribunal must have been wrong as it did not matter what type of discretion was involved.

Mr Justice Jackson-Lipkin noted that in [illegible] preceding [illegible] — section 2[illegible] — [illegible] “in the opinion [illegible] appeared.

[illegible] deals with the situation [illegible] the Building Authority may make an order requiring the works to cease until the order is withdrawn,” he said.

“It [illegible] can consider what is being [illegible] is in contravention of the ordinance.”

However, to make sense of section 24, the judge said he found it of limited use to look through the ordinance as a whole.

What he did find useful was to look at sections 23, 24, 24a together and possibly section 26.

The draftsman put the words “in the opinion of” to indicate complete and unfettered discretion and that in such cases the appeal must go to the appeals tribunal.

Where the draftsman used “may” in a directory sense, the parties aggrieved may come to the court for a judicial review.

And where he used “shall” in a consequential situation it was mandatory.

The judge said that only in this way could he avoid repugnance or absurdity.

“I have reached this conclusion with the greatest of hesitation and personal repugnance,” he said.

“I, for the life of me, cannot see why the legislation should give the Building Authority complete discretion in section 23 which allows for a [illegible] simple and [illegible] yet uses the same [illegible] in relation to [illegible] situation in section 24 . . . which subjects the citizen to an expensive and difficult [illegible] for judicial [illegible] cannot allo[illegible] sonal feelings to [illegible] but I say them [illegible] that Mr Strawbridge will return to his chambers and say to someone ‘it's about time we went through this ordinance and put it into shape’.”

The judge suggested that some definition clauses be inserted at the beginning of the ordinance so that “everyone knows what everything means.”

“Alternatively, someone could be put into a small room for three weeks to decide which of these sections should involve an appeal to the tribunal and which should not,” he said.

“It may be necessary by way of an amendment to ensure that this is done.”

The judge said it was with regret that he had to dismiss the motion and awarded costs to the Crown.

Mr Bernacchi stated his intention to take the matter further.

The stay on the execution of the notice will therefore continue.

Mr Kenneth Chan appeared with Mr Bernacchi on the instructions of T. M. Chow and Co.

"Development density stays"

Source: South China Morning Post

1989

Development density stays

By Johnson Sze

HONGKONG'S dense cityscape won't be allowed to become more crowded, despite proposed legislative amendments allowing the use of modern construction materials.

Architects would enjoy greater flexibility if the proposed amendments allowing new building materials were approved, according to Principal Building Surveyor, Mr Anthony Samson.

"But there should be no inference that the plot ratio or development density will alter. There is no intention of changing development density," he said.

"Developers will only be able to build skyscrapers within existing planning controls."

Hongkong land is classified into three categories of development density. Developers are required to adhere to a plot ratio — the size of the site to total floor area of the proposed building.

Density allowed is determined by community facilities available in the area and the types of development the Government wants carried out there.

Property developers are not optimistic that a relaxation in the choice of building materials will enable them to create more floor area.

"New buildings may be allowed to go higher but they will also be more slender if plot ratios do not change accordingly," said a property developer who declined to be named.

"The proposed amendment will, to some extent, give architects more leeway in designing the shape of their buildings," he said.

Development control in Hongkong is enforced by the Building Ordinance Office (BOO). It is responsible for vetting all development plans for new buildings and clearing illegal structures from existing buildings.

Mr Samson said the Finance Branch had finally agreed to boost staffing levels. An extra 60 posts had been created for this year, representing about half the quota for recruitment earmarked for the Buildings and Lands Department.

The department comprises four offices responsible for land administration, town planning, building control and land surveying.

More than half the new staff would be deployed to seek out dangerous buildings in Hongkong, said Mr Samson.

> "There should be no inference the plot ratio or development density will alter. There is no intention of changing development density. Developers will only be able to build skyscrapers within existing planning controls.
>
> Mr Anthony Samson,
> Principal Building Surveyor

The BOO drainage unit would also be boosted to support the battle against pollution, he said. The unit's staffing level would eventually be doubled and it would be responsible for monitoring industrial drainage systems to ensure effluents were not discharged into stormwater drains.

Another major task of the office is ensuring existing buildings are free from illegal structures. About two-thirds of the BOO's 480 staff are responsible for this.

Mr Samson said unauthorised structures were rife on Hongkong's buildings and the Control and Enforcement Division would continue its action against infringements.

The BOO would continue to publicise its crackdown on illegal structures and let the public know what infringed the law, he said.

"Stopping flatowners doing their illegal work in the first place must be a much better way to tackle the problem than issuing orders bureacratically."

"Controls on height of buildings to continue"

Source: South China Morning Post

1991

Controls on height of buildings to continue

By KENNETH KO

THE Government is likely to further extend control over the height and density of buildings in Kowloon if the airport project is shelved, according to property analysts.

The relocation of Kai Tak airport has lead to rumours that the severe height restrictions imposed on the Kowloon peninsula because of the flight path may be relaxed.

But in view of the deadlock in the airport issue, property analysts are sceptical of a relaxation.

It is also believed that the town planning blueprint, Metroplan, will have to be refined accordingly if the new airport plans are scrapped.

Mr Kenneth Chan, director of Jones Lang Wootton, said the relaxation in height restriction would increase the redevelopment potential in some areas of Kowloon.

However, if the airport projects were scrapped, the height restriction would probably remain even after 1993, he said. The Government has extended the Temporary Control of Density of Building Development (Kowloon and New Kowloon) Ordinance 1989 until the end of 1993.

In order to assure the safety of the flight path, Mr Chan said, the Government might even introduce new regulations to control the height of buildings in Kowloon.

Another consideration was the capability of local infrastructure support to cope with the scale of possible redevelopment arising from any relaxation in building height and density, he said.

Mr Koh Keng-shing, of First Pacific Davies, agreed that the Government would uphold the restrictions on the height of buildings in Kowloon as long as it continued to use Kai Tak airport.

But he said any relaxation in height restrictions would be a long-term process, and it was difficult to assess and project the possible consequences.

● Legislative Councillor, Mrs Peggy Lam Pei Yu-dja, said yesterday she was confident the new airport could be built and hoped the two governments would consider the well-being of Hongkong people.

But she did not believe Hongkong would suffer any immediate setback even if the new airport plan was shelved.

Other airports which would open in neighbouring areas would help divert some of the China-bound flights, Mrs Lam said.

She rejected suggestions that yesterday's drop in stock prices was caused by the unfavourable news about the airport project, saying the downturn was only a market adjustment as prices had been at too high a level.

1991

"Building regulations tightend"

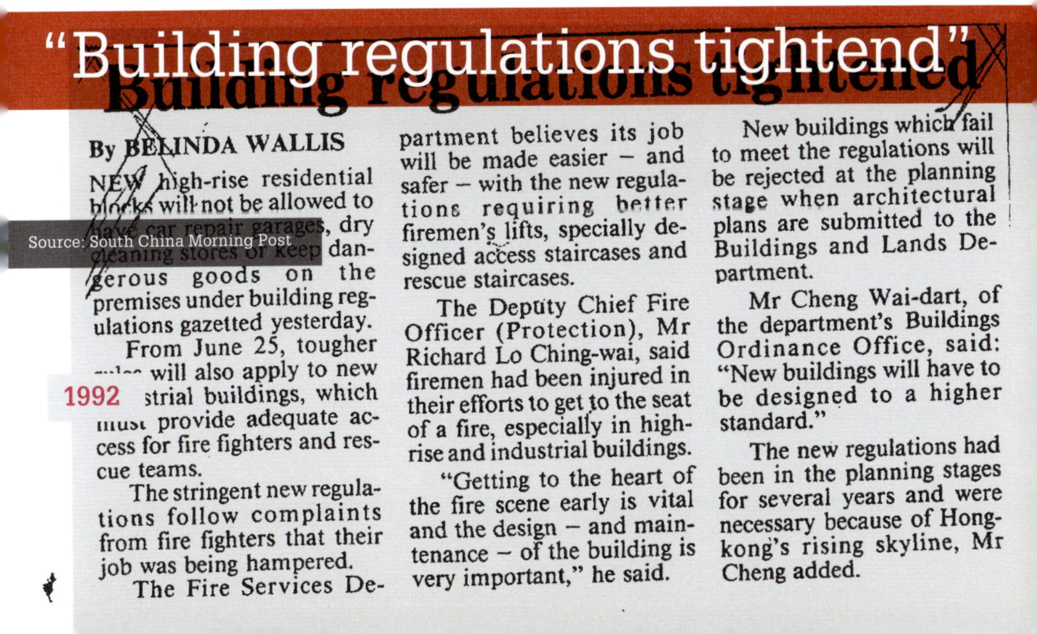

Source: South China Morning Post

1992

Building regulations tightened

By BELINDA WALLIS

NEW high-rise residential blocks will not be allowed to have car repair garages, dry cleaning stores or keep dangerous goods on the premises under building regulations gazetted yesterday.

From June 25, tougher rules will also apply to new industrial buildings, which must provide adequate access for fire fighters and rescue teams.

The stringent new regulations follow complaints from fire fighters that their job was being hampered.

The Fire Services Department believes its job will be made easier – and safer – with the new regulations requiring better firemen's lifts, specially designed access staircases and rescue staircases.

The Deputy Chief Fire Officer (Protection), Mr Richard Lo Ching-wai, said firemen had been injured in their efforts to get to the seat of a fire, especially in high-rise and industrial buildings.

"Getting to the heart of the fire scene early is vital and the design – and maintenance – of the building is very important," he said.

New buildings which fail to meet the regulations will be rejected at the planning stage when architectural plans are submitted to the Buildings and Lands Department.

Mr Cheng Wai-dart, of the department's Buildings Ordinance Office, said: "New buildings will have to be designed to a higher standard."

The new regulations had been in the planning stages for several years and were necessary because of Hong-kong's rising skyline, Mr Cheng added.

Cheung Kong makes breakthrough in selling from balcony under new rules

South China Morning Post | 2001-08-… Newspaper | … Business-HongKong | | By RICHARD WOO

“Cheung Kong makes breakthrough in selling from balcony under new rules”

Source: South China Morning Post

2001

2001 Cheung Kong (Holdings) has secured sales consent for the first residential project incorporatingexempted spaces of balconies under the Government's new building facility incentives. Caribbean Coast phase one at Tung Chung Station had its building plan and deed of mutual covenantrevised for including balconies in units on the upper floors of its five residential blocks. Sales manager William Kwok said the consent was received last week. He said balconies would beincorporated into units above the 33rd floors of the buildings. Units of about 600 square feet wouldhave balconies of about 19 sq ft each while 1,000 sq ft units would have 27 sq ft balconies. Mr Kwok said about 700 of the 1,500 units at the phase one development would have balconies. In February, the Buildings Department introduced new incentives to encourage developers to erectgreen or environmentally friendly buildings, with balconies being one of the main features. A balcony is considered a green facility because it can act

New rules encourage ‘greener’ buildings

2001

“New rules encourage ‘greener’ buildings”

South China Morning Post | 2001-02-2… Newspaper | HongKong | | By ANTOINE SO

2001 Balconies and open spaces in new homes will be exempted from land premium charges in an attemptto promote more environmentally friendly buildings, the Director of Buildings, Leung Chin-man, saidyesterday. The latest government move to exempt the "green" features of buildings from the grossfloor area was spelt out in a joint code drawn up between lands, buildings and planning departments. The exemptions include open balconies, public corridors, lift lobbies, podium gardens and sky gardens. Apart from balconies, the listed features shared by residents cannot be sold by developers. Under the new rules, all exemptions from the gross floor area must be stated in sales brochuresfor consumer reference. A team within the Buildings Department will be set up to monitor whetherdevelopers are following the rules. Mr Leung said developers found to be squeezing exempted areas into saleable areas would besubject to prosecution. The department will also be able to withdraw occupation permits to a siteviolating the code. Mr Leung also said prices for the "green" flats would be subject to market forces anddevelopers would not be able to raise prices against the market trend. "At the end of the day, it's supply and demand which determines the price. In the long run,when those green features become part of all housing, no one will be able to have higherprices," he said. "So there should be no question of exploitation." Exemptions to the gross floor area would, for now, not be applicable to sites with land leasesrestricting total gross floor areas. Land premiums for balconies, for example, would have to be paidin these buildings. To prevent buildings from becoming too "bulky", Mr Leung said the green facilities tobe exempted would not exceed eight per cent of the total gross floor area. The president of the Hong Kong Institute of Architects, Professor Lau Sau-shing, praised themove, saying more open spaces would give residents a sense of relief and identity as they did in the1970s and 1980s, when balconies were excluded from the gross floor area. "Hong Kong is unique in having many tall buildings. With a balcony, one could have contactwith the outside and decorate a balcony with plants," Professor Lau said. The secretary-general of the Real Estate Developers' Association of Hong Kong, Louis Loong Hon-biu, urged the Government to consider being more flexible over land premium charges for greenfacilities on projects covered by previous restrictive land leases.

Source: South China Morning Post

"New rules good first step but open to abuse"

2001

Source: South China Morning Post

New rules good first step but open to abuse

outh China Morning Post | 2001-03-14Newspaper | Property | PANG SHIU-...

2001 The Joint Practice Note on Green and Innovative Buildings issued by the Buildings Department, Lands Department and Planning Department is the first step by the Government to honour its pledge toencourage the property industry to incorporate green features in new residential developme... try will be exempted from gross floor area (GFA) and site coverage calculation for greenfeatures, subject to conditions. The cumulative GFA exemption for all green features, excluding sky and podium gardens, should notexceed 8 per cent of the total permitted GFA for the development. The advantages of this jointpractice are: <ul><li>The architect will have more freedom in designing green features. The building will lookmuch better when the following features are incorporated. <li>The occupier will have a higher efficiency-ratio flat when a balcony is incorporated. Theincrease in efficiency ratio in "pencil" developments (which generally have lowerefficiency ratios) is more than mass residential buildings. <li>The micro-climate of the development will be enhanced when green features areincluded.</ul></li> While there are advantages to designers and occupiers, developers will pay more to implementgreen features. In Hong Kong, about 95 per cent of flats are built for sale. Most developers will compare the additional cost incurred with the marginal profit from the sale,although some may take a longer view, seeing green features as a good tool to enhance corporateimage. Balconies are drawing the most attention. The cost of construction, the premium payable to apply for a lease modification (if the leasestipulates the balcony area is part of the permissible GFA of the development) and the interestincurred pending the outcome of lease modification applications are the main concerns of developers. The construction cost for a two- square-metre balcony is estimated to be about HK$60,000 toHK$70,000 and the shared extra premium could be in the range of HK$15,000 to HK$20,000 per balcony. Disregarding the extra interest incurred (in the lease modification application), the totalprovision cost for one balcony could be as high as HK$90,000. Any profit mark-up will mean buyers need to pay an ... w-end flats. Flats in this category usually ...

South China Morning Post 南華早報

"Cage-home dwellers' income dwindle"

Cage-home dwellers' incomes dwind...

Audrey Parwani

People forced to live in ... economy, a survey shows

People who live in cage homes and partitioned rooms have not benefited from Hong Kong's improving economy and average incomes have dropped, a survey has found.

Source: South China Morning Post, https://www.scmp.com/article/577210/cage-home-dwellers-incomes-dwindle

2007

The Society for Community Organisation conducted the survey from July to September. It interviewed 202 households from 25 registered and 32 unregistered cage homes, and 266 partitioned rooms in properties with more than five rooms each. It found the unemployment rate had improved for cage-home dwellers, down to 30.9 per cent from 36.1 per cent in 2004. It also improved for lodgers of partitioned rooms, to 16.4 per cent last year from 30 per cent in 2004.

But over the same period, the median monthly income dropped. The median income for those living in cage homes and some partitioned rooms was HK$3,400 and HK$3,250. This reflected a drop of 15 per cent and 30 per cent, respectively, from HK$4,000 for cage-home dwellers and HK$5,000 for people living in partitioned rooms. In 2004, 10.2 per cent of room lodgers earned less than HK$3,999 a month. This rose to 21.2 per cent last year. Although 57.1 per cent of people living in partitioned rooms earned HK$4,000 to HK$5,999 a month in 2004, this has now dropped to 34.8 per cent.

The society's chairman, Ho Hei-wah, urged the government to set a minimum wage for workers to protect this group from a further decline in their living standards.

'Their living environments are critical. [Cage-home dwellers] get an average of 18 square feet per person. This has shrunk from an average of 30 square feet two years ago.'

Yu Mei-wan arrived from the mainland five years ago. She is not entitled to public housing until she has lived in the city for seven years. Her son and daughter, 20 and 18, arrived from the mainland in August.

Source: http://hk9707.blogspot.hk/2009/09/blog-post_8978.html

2009

第一章　山雨欲來風滿樓
外篇七　經濟大蕭條

董建華連任前夕，北京力挺他繼續當特首，可是人們對他怨聲載道，親共人士只好以諸多藉口來為他未能帶領香港經濟復甦而開脫

"10 years history of SAR - the economic depression"

港的失業率不過是每十二個人之中有一人，美國卻是四個人已有一個失業（失業率高達25%），甚至有鄉郊農民
死。

經濟大蕭條發生的時候，正值總統胡佛（Herbert Hoover）在位。此君在經濟頂峰時上任，半年後泡沫就爆破。他在就職時說的「美國史上最接近消滅貧窮的一天（We in America today are nearer to the final triumph over poverty than ever before）」，和董建
台前喊的「中國好，香港更好」，同樣令人苦笑。而胡佛預言經濟快將復甦（Prosperity is just around the corner），跟董建華和
深信香港將是「金融風暴裡最快復甦的地區」，一樣是空頭支票。經濟困難時期，無奈的群眾分別對兩位領袖極盡挖苦之能事，董
喊作「老懵董」，美國都市裡的貧民窟則被諷為胡佛鎮（Hooverville）。

面對困局，兩人皆不願向窮人開倉派米，直接把錢塞到貧民手中，只肯減稅、增加臨時工或推動一些建設項目。可是經濟早已出現
環－－消費下跌，導致公司倒閉或裁員減薪，破產數目增加，消費再萎縮。除此以外，董建華的「八萬五」被香港人指為摧殘樓市
則冒昧地下令大幅增加關稅以求自保，換來外國報復，全球貿易大減，讓大蕭條擴散至全球各地，成為二次大戰的遠因。當兩人的
期完結時，經濟非但沒有好轉，反而比幾年前更糟，失業情況更形惡劣。只是香港人眼白白看著董建華被北京欽點，讓「經驗豐富
在毫無對手挑戰下，「當仁不讓」地順利連任，再幹五年，美國國民則有幸可以運用手上的選票，擡走共和黨的胡佛，在一九三二
舉中高票把民主黨的小羅斯福（Franklin Roosevelt）送進白宮。

早在當選以前，羅斯福已組織了一班智囊（Brain Trust）密謀對策，並在上任後的頭一百天簽署多項法令，推行名垂千古的「新政
（New Deal），先把金融機構整頓，然後派錢救濟數以千萬名失業者和補貼農民，讓工會擁有集體談判權，推行大規模基建計劃
水霸、種樹等等，以解決失業問題。雖然羅斯福的做法被後人指其貫徹了經濟學家凱恩斯（John Maynard Keynes）的「大政府」
過度干預經濟，而當時工會也嫌聯邦政府太過保守，對貧困者的幫助不夠，但畢竟羅斯福能扭轉繼續下墮的形勢，哪怕經濟尚未完

"With speculation from mainlanders, the price moved far beyond that of 1997"

[神州股票資訊]內地客炒熱香港樓市 房價遠超1997年 @ 2011-05-21 18:22:50

成为好友中第一个点赞的人吧!

2011

Source: http://www.21cbh.com/HTML/2011-5-19/0NIMDAwMDlzOTE0NA.html

http://www.21cbh.com/HTML/2011-5-19/0NMDAwMDlzOTE0NA.html

受中國房地產熱影響，香港的房產價格創下歷史新高，成為全世界房價最高的城市之一。近日，香港淺水灣赫蘭道11號的一幢豪宅以6.6億港元（約合5.5億人民幣）的價格售出。

80後少婦3.4億在香港購買豪宅，只是內地客搶購香港豪宅的縮影。年初至今，香港樓市在內地限購、通脹等因素助推下，吸引大批內地資金，價格逐步上漲，目前香港樓市均價已遠超1997年高位，這也引發了香港本地對於樓市泡沫的擔憂。

大多數香港本地地產從業者認為，本輪樓市行情及價格、市場環境與1997年很不相同，買家很多為一次性付款，目前香港私宅空置率約為5%，屬合理水平。

但從民間的反應來看，有機構及學者認為，港府有必要進一步採取措施控制樓市升溫，並增加供應來穩定預期。

特色豪宅受內地客追捧

5月初，「香港九龍最貴住宅九龍站凱旋門頂層名花有主，來自惠州的80後少婦黎嘉敏以3.45億港元買下」的消息，將內地客搶購香港豪宅這一事件推向了高潮。

按照香港中原地產研究的分類，總價在1200萬港元以上的住宅可歸入豪宅。香港中原地產市場部數據顯示，2007年上半年，內地買家在香港購買豪宅的整體金額佔比不過9.7%，此時中小戶型的購買比例為4.3%；但2010年下半

"High demand creates record prices in Hong Kong"

2011

High Demand Creates Record Prices In Hong Kong

July 28, 2011 - Hong Kong

Like Send 8 people like this. 0

Luxury residential prices in Hong Kong continue to climb, edging up 3.8 per cent QoQ to HK$19,520 (US$2,505) per sq ft, according to the latest research from Colliers International.

This new figure is a record high, and with demand continuing to grow prices may continue to rise in the future.

Total residential sales in Hong Kong slowed down in the second quarter of the year, but the high-end market remained active, with sales of properties exceeding HK$20 million (US$2.56 million) increasing by 11 per cent QoQ.

Simon Lo, Executive Director of Research and Advisory Services for Colliers International said a good portion of the increases in luxury purchases came from mainland Chinese buyers, unhindered by mortgage insurance issues that are slowing down locals.

In addition to sales, the rental market is performing strongly. As rents continue to rise, some tenants have found themselves moving towards smaller units or less prestigious neighborhoods.

Average rent in the luxury districts currently stands at HK$47.30 (U$S6.07) per sq ft per month, an increase of 4.1 per cent QoQ and a record high.

In the longer term, interest rate hikes and tightening measures from local banks could cause some consolidation in the near future, but a dramatic

"Young cage home residents 'isolated from family"

South China Morning Post 南華早報

NEWS HONG KONG HOUSING

Young cage home residents 'isolated f

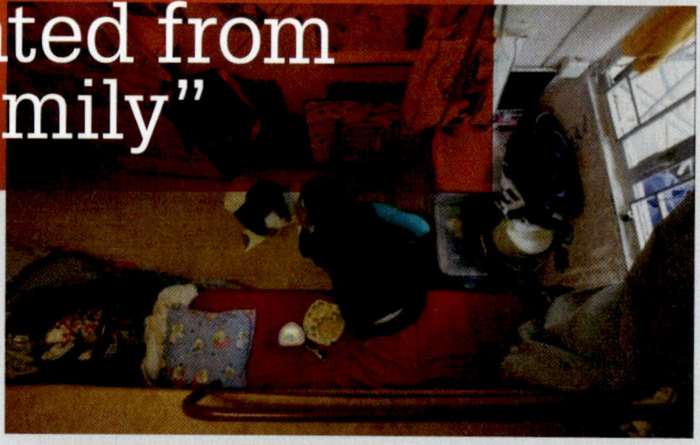

A single mother plays with her daughter in the bedroom of an 80 square-foot sub-divided flat. Photo: Reuters

Amid the public housing crunch, single people earning a low wage are taking up residence in subdivided flats and cage homes, but the cheaper rent comes with a steep emotional price: isolation from loved ones.

More than 70 per cent of people living in such cramped places ... visited them ... has found.

The number of non-elderly, single people who are on Hong Kong's public housing waiting list

"Normal things like meeting with family members has become a rare thing for many of them," said Angela Lui Yi-shan, a community organiser with the Society for Community Organisation, which conducted the survey. "People may have the impression that they are a flexible group, but 90 per cent of them have no savings. Housing is a ... obstacle to their personal development."

She announced the survey ... she said was unreasonable ... of the economic ladder.

2013

Source: South China Morning Post, https://www.scmp.com/news/hong-kong/article/1262379/young-cage-home-residents-isolated-family

"Overdrawn by speculation, a city with no future"

呢個，亦係香港人作爲一個整體，自私自利嘅共業。

受惠物業升值而身家暴增嘅人，只係間接剝削緊下一代嘅年青人，
上一代人憑着運氣，輕鬆步入中產，遺下居高嘅樓價
新一代年輕人就忍受高樓價，用微薄嘅薪水日捱夜捱

呢個零和遊戲入便當然有好多人接火棒，結果就係負資產燒炭。
當中當然有人係為炒賣暴富而盲目入市，但亦有營營役役為求有安樂窩嘅人。
佢哋會大力鞭笞政府冇防止樓價下瀉。但，其實係炒賣之下，點都會有人死。
分別在你依家班負資產死，或者將來樓價繼續高企下置業人士死。
常言道沙士掏空香港中產，但我不禁反問，呢班中產係點樣嚟？

樓宇，作爲會折舊嘅物品，唯一非炒賣升值潛力在於社區環境改善，實質需求增加。
但香港作爲一個已發展地區，仲有幾多空間去引入移民提高需求？
正常而言，樓宇係會隨折舊而貶值，加上維修等支出，根本就唔應該祈望有升值潛力。

Source: South China Morning Post, https://www.scmp.com/comment/insight-opinion/article/1311149/subdivided-flats-hong-kongs-housing-conundrum

2013

"Subdivided flats: Hong Kong's housing conundrum"

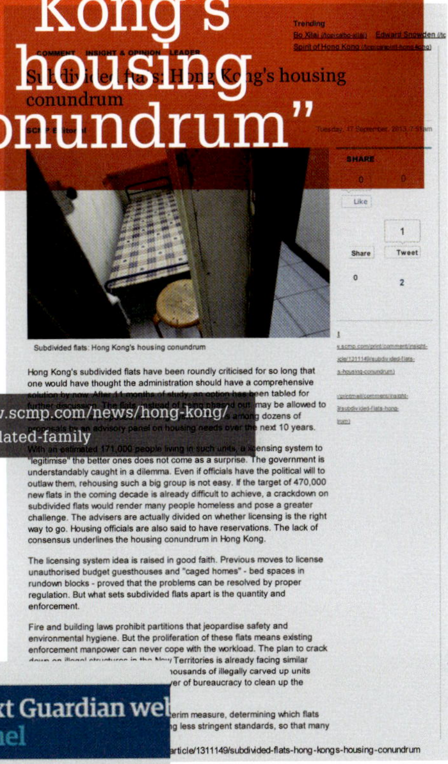

Source: South China Morning Post, https://www.scmp.com/news/hong-kong/article/1262379/young-cage-home-residents-isolated-family

"Housing bubble 2.0 can only end badly"

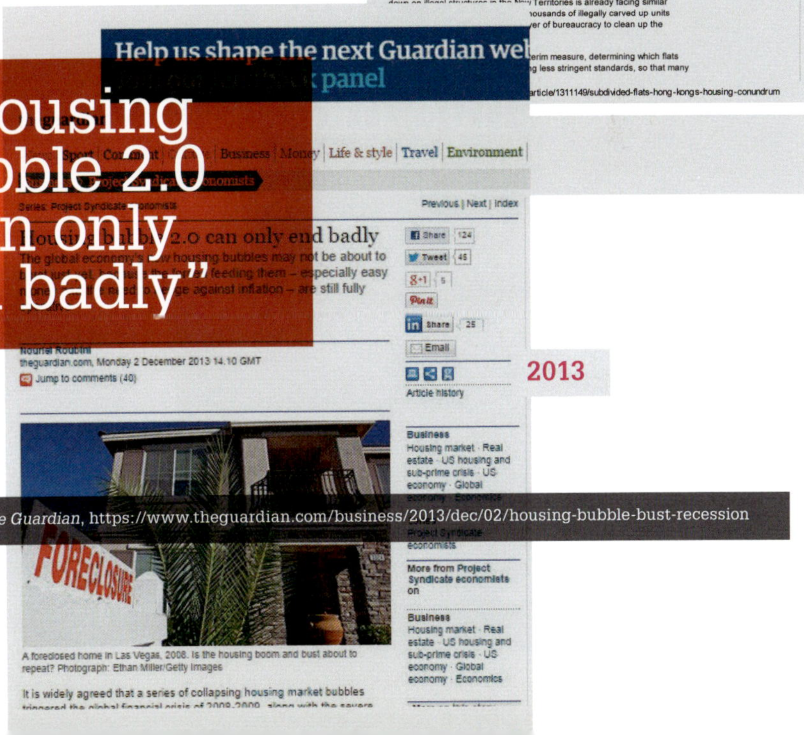

2013

Source: *The Guardian*, https://www.theguardian.com/business/2013/dec/02/housing-bubble-bust-recession

2013

"License subdivided flats and build 470,000 new flats over decade, says housing report"

NEWS HONG KONG

License subdivided flats and build 470,000 new flats over decade, says housing report

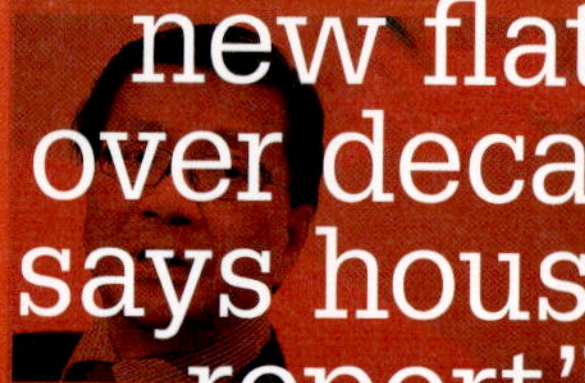

Secretary for Transport and Housing Anthony Cheung Bing-leung. Photo: K.Y. Cheng

A committee studying Hong Kong's long-term housing plans on Tuesday recommended introducing a licensing system for subdivided flats, dropping a proposal to impose rent controls, and setting a modest target for building more flats.

The committee proposed a building target of 470,000 flats over the next 10 years. Sixty per cent of these flats should be for public housing and the rest private. It also suggested speeding up construction of public housing flats and reforming a point system to make it easier for single young people to ...

... other measures would do little help to shorten the waiting time for public housing applicants.

The recommendations came as the Hong Kong government launched a three-month public consultation on the commitee's proposals to deal with the the city's long-term housing needs and the increasing number of people from low income groups that are forced by rising rents to live in subdivided flats.

A University of Hong Kong study commissioned by the government in May estimated that more than 170,000 people are forced to live these flats.

The licensing system proposed by the committee would only apply to units in residential buildings, those in industrial buildings should be banned, the Long Term Housing Strategy Steering Committee suggested in a consultation document.

Source: South China Morning Post, https://www.scmp.com/news/hong-kong/article/1302643/license-subdivided-flats-and-build-470000-new-flats-over-decade-says

"Hong Kong's cubicle apartments: could you live like this?"

Hong Kong's cubicle apartments: could you live like this?

City living can feel cramped – but can you imagine anywhere more cramped than these homes in Hong Kong? According to the human rights group, Society for Community Organization, which commissioned this series of photographs, taken from above, more than 100,000 people are cooped up in such places in the city, often with whole families living together in these tiny spaces

2013

Source: *The Guardian*, https://www.theguardian.com/world/gallery/2013/feb/22/hong-kong-flats-tiny-cubicles

"Poverty rooted in housing shortage"

2013

Friday, August [illegible], 2013, 15:20

Michael Tien: Poverty rooted in housing shortage

By Joseph Li

The shortage of affordable housing lies at the root of the city's poverty problem, says poverty commission member Michael Tien. He notes the plight of low-income people, who are forced to pay unconscionable rents and left with too little for life's other necessities. Joseph Li writes.

Source: Focus Hong Kong, http://epaper.chinadailyasia.com/focus-hk/article-447.html

Snapshot

Michael Tien Puk-sun, 63, is the founder/owner of a large fashion retail chain. He is a lawmaker, district councillor and vice-chairman of New People's Party. He is a member of the Commission on Poverty and is in the second term as a deputy to the National People's Congress. He had previously held many posts in public service, including chairman of the Employees Retraining Board, chairman of the Standing Committee on Language Education and Research and also board chairman of Kowloon-Canton Railway Corporation.

"The big question for Generation Y: How can we buy a home?"

The big question for Generation Y: How can we buy a home?

A third of young Hongkongers say their dream is to own a home, but that will be far from easy

Yvonne Liu

Tuesday, 16 July, 2013, 5:16am

SHARE

9 Like 6

2 Share 7 Tweet

0 4

The big question for Generation Y: How can we buy a home?

ıp.com/print/property/hong-
ɔle/1283473/big-question-
ɔw-can-we-buy-home)

ntmail/property/hong-
'3/big-question-
-buy-home)

Buying a home seems to be the biggest dream of young Hongkongers.

A recent survey conducted by the University of Hong Kong at the behest of financial services company MassMutual interviewed 500 young people born in the 1980s and 1990s - known colloquially as Generation Y.

A third said their biggest ambition was to own their own home, while just less than one in five said they dreamed of owning a business or landing a dream job and one in eight said their main wish was to have more money. Only one in nine young people said their dream was to travel around the world.

The home ownership ambition will be a difficult one for young people to achieve, however. My friend lives with her parents in a public housing estate. Buying a flat in a private housing estate has been a dream of hers for many years.

2013

Source: https://www.scmp.com/property/hong-kong-china/article/1283473/big-question-generation-y-how-can-we-buy-home

Finding alternative accommodation could also become a matter of necessity. "Only my parents are eligible to live in this public housing flat," she said. "If they pass away, I can't live in the flat any more."

My friend studied hard and went to university, but she did not earn very much in the first few years after she graduated.

However, having gained more experience, she now earns nearly HK$30,000 a month, enough to be classified as middle class, based on the definition used by Chinese University's sociology department.

Even so, her salary is not enough for her to buy a flat. "I have to give HK$9,000 a month to my parents, as they have retired," she said. "My personal spending is about HK$8,000 a month. I have about HK$10,000 left.

"A second-hand Home Ownership Scheme flat costs more than HK$3 million. If I use the 'green form' to buy the flat, I have to prepare a down payment of more than HK$900,000."

People who live in public housing are eligible to buy an HOS flat without paying the land premium levy, by filing a "green form" application. But it would take my friend more than six years to save the down-payment. And she would be unable to save money for her retirement while doing so.

"Even if I got the down-payment, it is difficult for me to afford the monthly mortgage expenditure," she said. "If I rent a flat, I can't save money after

"Shanghai investors wary of Hong Kong market"

2014

Source: South China Morning Post,
http://scmp.com/business/money/markets-investing/article/1590347/shanghai-investors-wary-Hong-kong-market

South China Morning Post
MONEY
SAT Sep 27, 2014 Updated: 9:5_ pm

BUSINESS • MONEY • MARKETS & INVESTING • STOCKS

Shanghai investors wary of Hong Kong market

Through train fails to impress some mainlanders, who say they are unfamiliar with local regulations and are put off by higher share prices

Bloomberg in Shanghai

PUBLISHED : Friday, 12 September, 2014, 6:19am
UPDATED : Friday, 12 September, 2014, 6:19am

Investors look at stock prices in Shanghai but whether they will peer as closely into Hong Kong markets is another question. Photo: AFP

SHARE

Jiang Siqiang has a whole list of reasons he is not interested in shifting any of his money from the mainland's equity markets into Hong Kong.

As the 67-year-old retiree sips tea and watches stock prices flicker across the screen at a brokerage in Shanghai, he ticks them off one by one. Shanghai shares tend to trade at cheaper valuations than those listed 1,224km to the south in the former British colony. Hong Kong's market rules are unfamiliar, and he is also turned off by the poor track record of many mainland money managers who have bought foreign shares through the qualified domestic institutional investor programme (QDII).

"Even QDII funds are losing money overseas, and they are managed by experts," Jiang said at a Changjiang Securities outlet in Shanghai's Pudong district. "I wouldn't buy Hong Kong stocks" any time soon.

Jiang's misgivings provide a look into why 77 per cent of mainland investors surveyed by CLSA last month said they would not take part in a planned exchange link between Shanghai and Hong Kong. Their lack of interest contrasts with Hong Kong traders' growing appetite for mainland stocks, which are luring record inflows through exchange-traded funds. That suggests Hong Kong shares are poised to underperform their Shanghai counterparts, according to Aviate Global, an institutional equity brokerage.

China, the biggest emerging economy, is counting on a successful exchange link to help liberalise its financial system, increase the role of the yuan and give its citizens more investment channels amid a slumping property market

Most Popular (/most-popular)

VIEWED
SHARED
COMMENTED

1 Shanghai stock market link-up with Hong Kong's 'ready for launch' (http://scmp.com/business/money/markets-investing/article/1601378/shanghai-stock-market-link-hong-kongs-ready-launch)

2 Kerry Logistics seeks quality over quantity (http://scmp.com/business/companies/article/1601281/kerry-logistics-seeks-quality-over-quantity)

3 ... set minds rolling (http://scmp.com/business/article/1582406/rumbling-pla-carriers-hong-kong-set-minds-rolling)

4 China steel demand drops for first time in 14 years due to slowing economy (http://scmp.com/business/commodities/article/1600767/mainland-steel-demand-drops-first-time-14-years-due-slowing)

5 Established rivals may keep Shanghai trade zone's gold exchange in check (http://scmp.com/business/commodities/article/1597536/established-rivals-may-keep-shanghai-trade-zones-gold-exchange)

We recommend

NEWS
Chinese woman wrongfully jailed for theft given apology and payout 25...
05 Sep 2014

(http://www.scmp.com/news/china/article/1585998/chinese-woman-wrongfully-jailed-theft-given-apology-and-payout-25-years)

NEWS

A Brief History of the Buildings Ordinance and Tower Typologies in Hong Kong

Text by Tris Kee

Drawings by Jan Henao and Claudia Mainardi

Housing has always been a critical social issue in Hong Kong, in terms of both quality and affordability. Developers, government officials, architects, and other stakeholders responsible for shaping Hong Kong's built environment are constantly negotiating a delicate balance between financial gain and concerns for quality of life as they struggle to allocate land and cope with a growing urban population.

Building regulations have historically played a significant role in the shaping of Hong Kong, often by defining the city's planning requirements and setting volumetric constraints that influence the design of buildings. Today, what is known as the Buildings Ordinance and a series of other statutory building regulations and Practice Notes have set requirements that affect the development of all private buildings in Hong Kong, including residential buildings. Even slight amendments to regulations have triggered major changes in built forms.

Through clues such as building height, layout disposition, façade length, the arrangement of balconies, and fenestration design, it is possible to identify which generation of building regulations was likely in place when a given housing block or tower was constructed.

This section gives an abridged account of the events and phenomena that influenced the development of Hong Kong's building regulations and the various formal expressions and typologies that have emerged in response to social, economic, and legislative changes. The current Hong Kong cityscape can be seen as a historical cross-section, reflecting several generations of housing development, including some increasingly dominant contemporary typologies that are characterized by repetition and uniformity.

1856 – The First Generation of Regulations

Some of the earliest building regulations in Hong Kong were created by the colonial government to regulate the construction of British occupied buildings. The first official Buildings and Nuisances Ordinance in Hong Kong was established in 1856 under Sir John Bowring. It included a total of 19 clauses that defined major building elements and listed requirements for foundation depth, as well as the construction materials for certain buildings and the dimensions of the various materials. Distinctions were made between residential and non-residential buildings, and the number of storeys allowed in certain buildings was defined. With the implementation of this ordinance, houses affected by the law had to be constructed with stone or brick walls, and they were required to have safe working places and sufficient water closets and privies.

Buildings considered to be in ruinous or dangerous conditions were to be labelled as 'nuisances'. For instance, if buildings were constructed with flammable material or if they had any design projections that 'negatively affected' passers-by, they would be considered nuisances. A Surveyor General was appointed to carry out the surveillance and inspection of buildings to satisfy the Ordinance.

Since the Buildings and Nuisances Ordinance only applied to British occupied buildings, it left the majority of buildings in Hong Kong—typically three-storey Chinese tenements built in timber and without private kitchens or bathrooms—completely unregulated. It was poorly received by the public, and it was jointly protested by both European and Chinese residents.

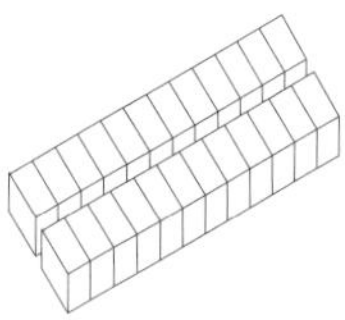

1887 - The Public Health Ordinance

The Public Health Ordinance of 1887 completely revised the previously enacted Buildings and Nuisances Ordinance. With a broader scope than its predecessor, the 1887 Ordinance aimed to improve the overall sanitary conditions of Hong Kong by addressing the dire need for water supply, drainage, and waste collection infrastructure in the city. It defined several key ideas, including overcrowded living conditions, and it established requirements for backyards in construction in an effort to improve levels of natural light and ventilation. A magistrate was designated with the power to control nuisances stated in the ordinance, and a statutory approval procedure from the Sanitary Board was created to more closely monitor compliance with these new requirements.

The new ordinance notably revised regulations on the construction and maintenance of water closets. It was no longer acceptable to connect water closets to underground sewers, and waste was to be collected through separate channels and disposed of discretely. Privies had to be provided in factories and other industrial buildings for sanitation purposes. One obvious improvement resulting from the ordinance was the emergence of private bathrooms in newly constructed public housing. However, these requirements were only applied to new buildings, leaving older buildings with poorer levels of sanitation unchanged. As a result, the overall sanitation levels in Hong Kong underwent little improvement.

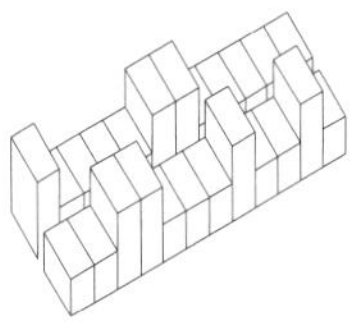

1894 - Outbreak of Bubonic Plague

In 1894, Hong Kong experienced an outbreak of the bubonic plague, which killed more than 2,500 people. In response to this catastrophic event, the colonial government established various new regulations, such as the Closed Houses and Insanitary Dwelling Ordinance, to mandate the inclusion of window openings to the outside, control window sizes, and manage living density and building height.

1903 - Overcrowded Living Conditions and Building Height Restrictions

Escalating concerns about overcrowding and unhygienic living conditions in the city prompted Hong Kong's colonial government to consolidate its existing laws relating to public health and city planning into a new piece of legislation known as the Public Health and Buildings Ordinance. Enacted in February 1903, this integrated ordinance, which regulated matters pertaining to public health and building design and construction, consisted of 271 sections.

Part of the 1903 ordinance builds upon an existing piece of legislation known as the English Public Health Act of 1875, which served to restrict building heights to ensure that sufficient sunlight reached the streets. Under the 1875 Act, buildings had to observe a maximum 45-degree light angle, defined as the diagonal angle between the ground-level building line on one side of a street and the skyline formed by edge of the roof on the other side. The legacy of this height restriction is still evident in Hong Kong's older districts, where one can measure diagonal light angles of roughly 45 to 54.5 degree in older buildings that typically reach 25 to 35 feet in height.

Under the 1903 Ordinance, all developments on land leased from the British Crown were to be regulated at a light angle of 63.5 degrees, which effectively capped building heights at a 1:1 ratio to the width of the street. In other words, the height of new buildings was not to exceed the width of the street it faced (s.188). The depth of buildings was also controlled for the first time.

The 1903 Public Health and Buildings Ordinance also established regulations specifically for residential buildings, including how rooms were sub-divided and how floors, mezzanines, cubicles, storerooms, and cocklofts were defined. Its definitions reflect a time when the long, narrow interiors of tenement houses were frequently subdivided into so-called 'cubicles', and commercial operations were frequently situated in spaces behind residential suites. Overcrowding was also redefined under the 1903 Ordinance.

Before 1903, kitchens were typically constructed without specific lighting or ventilation requirements and shared among residents on all floors of the building. After the enactment of the ordinance, kitchens were required on every floor, significantly influencing the design of residential buildings. Staircases were also precisely regulated for the first time, so that they had to observe a minimum tread of eight inches and a maximum rise of eight and a half inches per step (s.121). A new section on fire escapes was added (s.149), and window provisions were clearly spelled out (s.150).

Notably, this Ordinance generally did not apply to buildings or structures belonging to the Crown or to the colonial government, or to any land vested in any person on behalf of the royal naval or military departments of his Majesty's service. It also proved ineffective shortly after Hong Kong received an influx of refugees from China, which exacerbated its already overcrowded conditions and incited another epidemic of plague. Under such trying circumstances, the Buildings Ordinance revealed real practical deficiencies and became widely criticized, prompting the introduction of another iteration of the Buildings Ordinance.

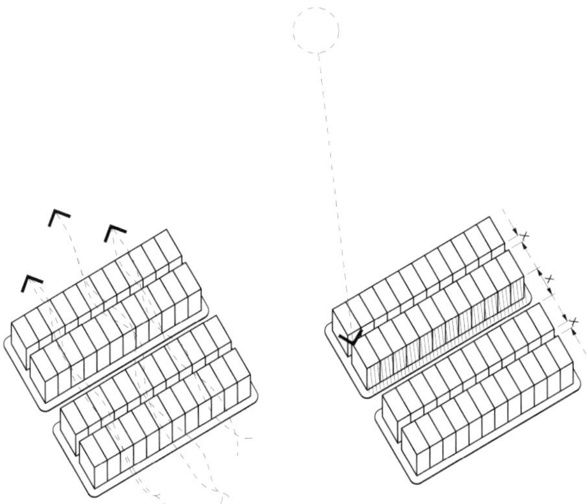

1935 - Public Health (Sanitation) Ordinance

The 1935 Public Health (Sanitation) Ordinance—the last public health-related ordinance to be implemented before the Second World War—separated the oversight of building control and public health and sanitation into two distinct departments, giving authorities in each department updated and more specific means of regulation. It thus generated the first Buildings Ordinance that resembles the modern framework for building regulation in Hong Kong.

The 1935 Buildings Ordinance aimed at controlling building dimensions, structure, and materials, all of which were rapidly changing at the time. The development of this ordinance coincided with the rise of advanced structural engineering and the widespread adoption of new building materials such as steel and reinforced concrete. Elevators and fire escapes were being introduced, as well as vertical extension to buildings.

Some key points of the Buildings Ordinance include the regulation of building heights and lift requirements (s.87/s.44) and precise requirements that building sections be tapered and upper-level verandas and balconies be set back gradually to admit more natural light (s.61). Staircases were now required to have a tread of at least nine inches and a rise no greater than seven inches (s.43). Tenement houses could no longer exceed a maximum height of three storeys and a maximum floor-to-floor height of four metres, unless they were built with fire-resistant materials. The ordinance introduced an official procedure to approve fire-resistant construction materials. Another public safety-related requirement was that the kitchen had to be located in the back of the building, next to a covered yard.

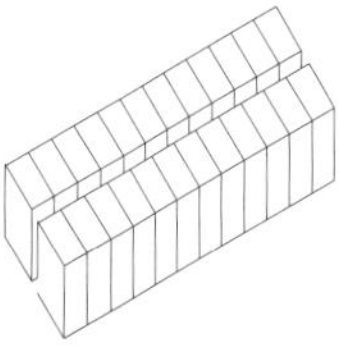

1953 Shek Kip Mei Great Fire and the Birth of Mass Public Housing in Hong Kong

After the Second World War and the Chinese Revolution of 1949, waves of refugees and immigrants from Mainland China fled to Hong Kong, spurring the construction and occupation of informal settlements. The largest settlement of this kind was established at Shek Kip Mei, a shantytown composed of squats made of wood and thin metal sheets. On Christmas Eve in 1953, a fire swept through Shek Kip Mei, raging through the settlement's narrow passages and leaving more than 53,000 people homeless overnight. The tragedy prompted the government to launch an initiative to construct several multi-storey buildings to house immigrant populations in need of accommodation. This marked the birth of mass public housing in Hong Kong.

The housing estates built in the aftermath of the fire, known as Mark I housing, conformed to a general typology: they were generally five- to eight-storey, H-shaped residential blocks, though occasionally they were I-shaped or L-shaped, depending on the terrain. The typical Mark I estate was designed to allot 24 square feet (2.2 m^2) per adult and half that amount for per child (under 12 years old). In reality, however, these cubicles were often occupied by more than one family. Communal spaces for toilets, showers, and washing areas were provided, usually in the centre of the building. There were no individual kitchens or bathrooms and no electricity in individual residential units. The rooftop areas were often built with classrooms, to serve as schools providing basic education.

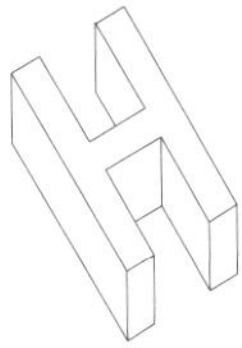

Within one year of the disaster, the Hong Kong government constructed eight Mark I housing blocks in Shek Kip Mei. That same year, 1954, the government enacted a new Housing Ordinance, which established a department known as the Resettlement Department. This department would eventually evolve and merge with other governmental offices to become the Hong Kong Housing Authority, which today serves as the main provider of public housing in Hong Kong.

Gradual improvements to public housing can be traced in the development of Mark I housing, which evolved sequentially to form Mark II, Mark III, Mark IV and Mark V housing blocks. Private washrooms and corridors were introduced in Mark III estates, and toilets in individual units were eventually provided in Mark IV housing blocks, as exemplified in Block 22 of the Tung Tau (I) Estate built in 1965.

1955 - Formalization of the Buildings Ordinance

In 1955, the government enacted a version of the Buildings Ordinance known as Chapter 123. Its objective was 'to provide for the planning, design and construction of buildings and associated works; to make provision for the rendering safe of dangerous buildings and land; to make provision for regular inspections of buildings and the associated repairs to prevent the buildings from becoming unsafe; and to make provision for matters connected therewith.' Chapter 123 accomplished a significant consolidation of existing building regulations in Hong Kong, and it introduced several tenets of building regulation that are still observed in the Buildings Ordinance used today.

The 1955 Ordinance was the first statute to regulate site density and site coverage by specifying a maximum permitted plot ratio, and it established a system of site classification based on the widths of abutting streets. The ordinance also introduced window requirements for all habitable rooms, including kitchens, in order to provide natural lighting and ventilation. Architects and housing developers quickly reacted by minimizing partitions of interior space in apartment units, and over the decades, whole building plans evolved in response, often taking on a cruciform shape to maximize perimeter space and allow for multiple bedrooms to fit into a single residential unit.

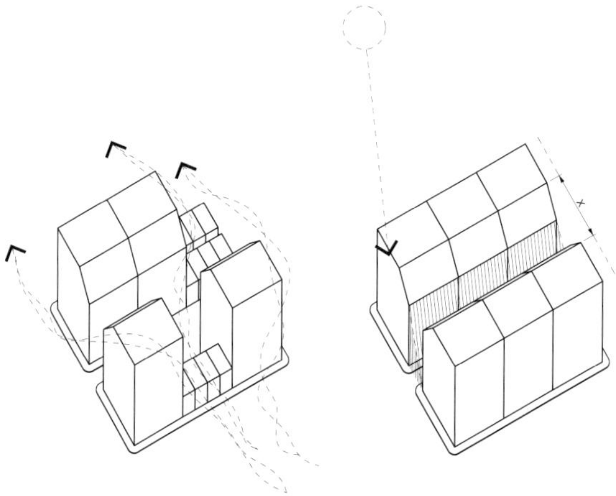

1956 - Building (Planning) Regulation

The Buildings Ordinances underwent an important change in 1956 with the introduction of a supplementary document known as the Building (Planning) Regulations (B(P)R). The Building (Planning) Regulation established the terms 'site coverage' and 'plot ratio' to serve as precise controls over housing development. To more clearly differentiate plot ratio and site coverage, the B(P)R introduced a system to categorize sites into three classes—A, B, and C—defined by how much density the developed building is allowed to accommodate. The general principle is that the more street access the site has, the taller and denser the building can be.

According to the site classification clause in B(P)R Chapter 123 Clause18A (1), 'Class A' sites are defined as those that abut a specified street no less than 4.5m wide or on more than one such street; 'Class B' sites are defined as corner sites that abut two specified streets, neither of which is less than 4.5m wide; and 'Class C' sites are defined as corner sites abutting three specified streets, none of which are less than 4.5m wide. The basic rationale behind the classification of sites is to give higher development potential to construction sites with multiple means of egress, on the premise that these sites are qualified as safe even in the case of a fire or an emergency.

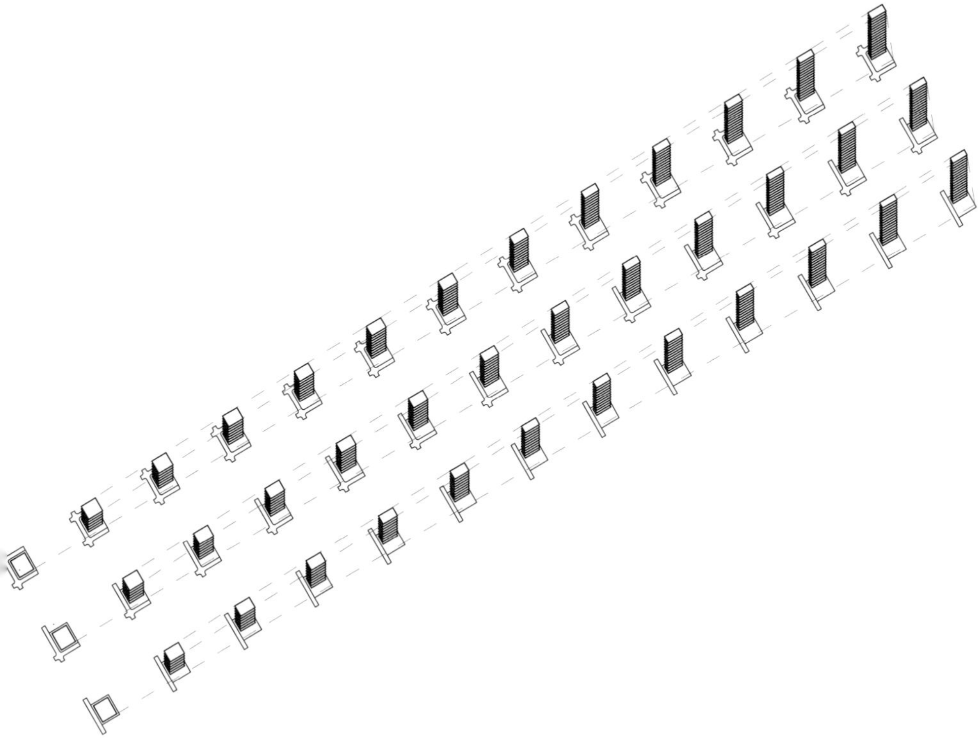

Every residential structure in Hong Kong is either on a class A, B, or C site with different implication to site coverage and is required to have an open space at the rear, partly at the rear and partly at the side, or at a level of not less than 150mm below the floor of the lowermost storey for the purpose of ensuring that every building has some clear space around it. Following the B(P)R classification system, the more access the site has, the higher the plot ratio of the building, and the denser it can be built.

Though the classification system was designed to offer guidelines to ensure public health and safety, most private developers now automatically calculate the allowable site coverage and plot ratio of their properties, using these guiding measures to build to the maximum allowable density, thereby ensuring maximum profit. Thus, while the classification of sites had no direct influence on the layout of buildings, private developers responded to the classification system with a limited set of plot-ratio-maximizing typologies—including double-H, trident, and cruciform plan buildings, and eventually podium buildings.

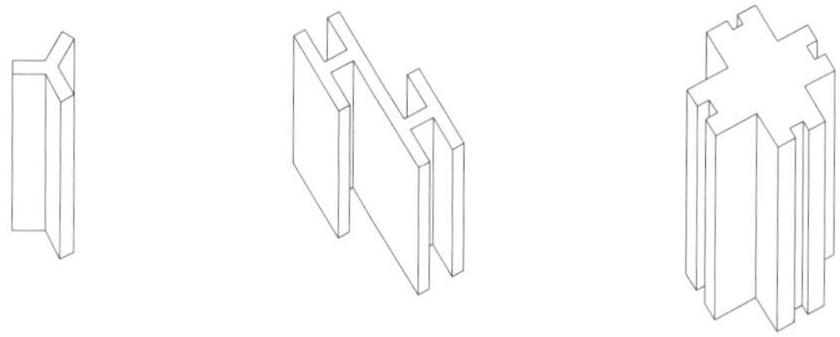

1962 – Changes in Public Housing Design: The Slab Block Typology

Slab-block buildings, such as the Ma Tau Wei Estate and Choi Hung Estate, were introduced in the Hong Kong cityscape in 1962. Utilizing new technology such as lift access on every third floor, slab blocks could rise eight to 15 storeys high. Long corridors running the length of each floor became a characteristic feature of this building.

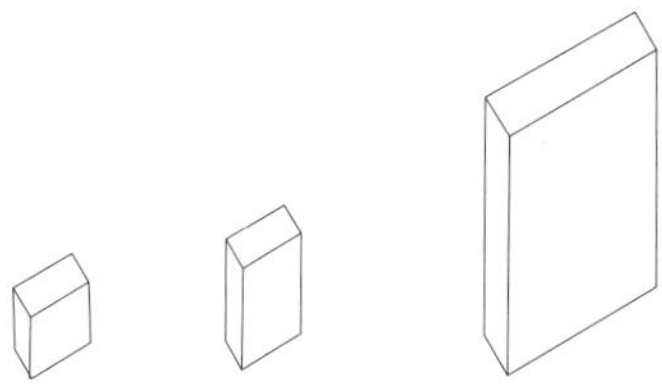

1970 – Increased Verticality in Public Housing: The Twin-Tower and Twin-H Typologies

Unceasing demand for housing prompted the design and engineering of taller public housing buildings in Hong Kong. The twin-tower typology, for example, reached 20 storeys or more and incorporated a central void to improve airflow. Blocks in the Wah Fu (II) Estate (completed in 1970) and some blocks in the Oi Man Estate (completed in 1974) exemplify this type of housing design. Further diversification would take place through the late 1970s, with the advent of the twin-H design floor plan. These buildings rose to 27 storeys. Both twin-towers and twin-H housing blocks were equipped with lift access on every floor, and private balconies, kitchens, toilets, and air conditioners in individual flats.

1972 – Landslides

In 1972, two major landslides—the Po Shan Road landslide and Sau Mau Ping landslide—caused a combined total of 100 casualties and, in the case of Po Shan Road, left two buildings completely destroyed. This incident prompted the local community to build a retaining wall to prevent future landslides. After several more landslides in the late 1970s, the government modified the B(P)R to include new control mechanisms to minimize the impact of landslides on developed land. As a result, improved drainage systems, real-time groundwater pressure monitoring systems, and innovations in foundation design were all implemented. Concern that the entire Mid-Level residential area could be imperilled prompted the passing of additional building requirements for specially designed foundations and piling systems. The residential towers in Mid-Level represent the fortified typological variants that developed from these events.

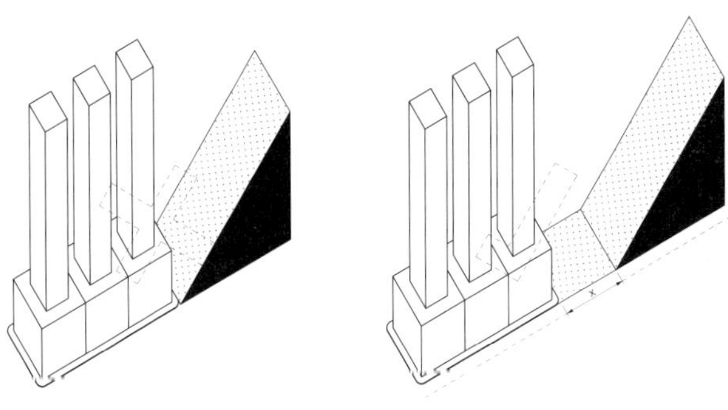

1976 – Land Scarcity, Lack of Housing, and the Rise of the Podium Typology

In 1976, a new Building (Planning) Regulation S.20(3) was enacted to permit non-domestic parts of a building to cover up to 100 percent of the site area, given that these non-domestic parts did not exceed 20m above ground level. The regulation immediately generated a new urban form — the ‘podium tower,' characterized by large podiums that dominate their sites and serve as a non-domestic base supporting an outcropping of thin residential towers. Around this time, the indoor shopping mall came into prominence, accompanying the development of an integrated mass transportation system that connected seamlessly with large commercial facilities. Indoor car parks and clubhouses within living complexes were also introduced and are now commonplace amenities. Podium towers have since become one of the most prominent building typologies in Hong Kong, as they allow developers to maximize gross floor area.

It is important to bring both the advantages and disadvantages of the podium tower into perspective. The podiums used for clubhouses create a new type of residential community characterized by its abundance of amenities. These amenity-rich housing complexes offer unique facilities that require private membership for access. For a culture that values prestige and tenure ownership, this exclusivity is much favoured in the market. However, the excessive provision of these facilities, intended as a means for developers to maximize exempted GFA, is a waste of energy and natural resources and cannot be considered a sustainable or responsible business model. From the point of residents, facilities provide many in-house amenities such as sports halls, swimming pools, and libraries, all of which enhance quality of life. Yet an increase in maintenance and management fees inevitably accompanies these new amenities.

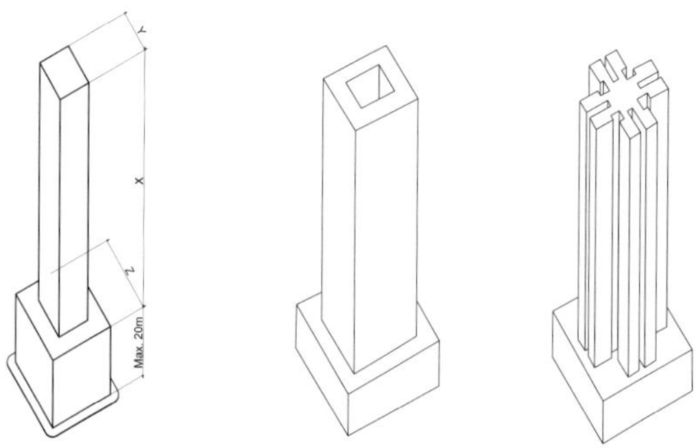

The podium tower typology (popularly known as the 'cake-and-candles' typology) is seen most acutely in private developments that include clubs that house amenities such as gymnasia, bowling courts, band rooms, barbeque areas, indoor children's playgrounds, piano rooms and more. Most of this has, arguably, improved housing quality in Hong Kong. The counter argument is that these provisions lead to waste and maintenance issues, and more immediately, they generate an unfavourable type of gated community.

1980 – New Town Developments

In the 1980s, the government started to identify new areas to develop housing, schools, retail areas, and community services for Hong Kong's growing population. Land reclamation projects were initiated and remote areas such as Sha Tin were selected for development into new towns. Brand new urban planning schemes with larger plots made it possible to develop housing typologies with larger floor plans.

Sha Tin New Town exemplifies this initiative to expand the city with satellite towns, which strive to give Hong Kong residents a balanced, relatively self-sufficient community where they can work, play, grow, and learn. Sha Tin represents a typical new town planning scheme in which a central shopping hub is surrounded by a group of public and private residential towers and integrated with new transportation infrastructure. The linearly arranged development contours along the natural valleys of the Shing Mun River, working within the constraints of existing topography and railway lines. Higher density residential buildings and industrial buildings are distributed on the valley floor, while lower-density housing and reclamation areas occupy higher ground.

1994 – Refining Calculations of Gross Floor Area

The 1994 Practice Notes Issue No. 4/2014, titled 'Accountable and Non-accountable Gross Floor Area (GFA) under Lease' states that in Regulation 23(3)(a) of the Building (Planning) Regulations (B(P)R), gross floor area (GFA) is defined as the area contained within the outer surface of the external walls of a building measured at each floor level. Any portions of this area not floored over should also be included in GFA calculations. According to Regulation 23(3)(b), however, when calculating total GFA, the Buildings Authority may disregard floor area occupied solely by machinery and also equipment for lifts, air conditioning, or heating systems of any similar service. The phrase 'any similar service' has generally been interpreted to include fire control centres, water tanks, electrical switch rooms, meter rooms, transformer rooms, generator rooms, pump rooms, telephone equipment rooms, cable riser duct rooms, CO2 rooms, hose reel closets, sewage treatment plant rooms, and smoke extraction systems.

These specifications for non-accountable GFA were intended to offset the strain on resources that developers faced in their efforts to provide necessary building equipment and service spaces. Since the area is one of the elements that the Building Department cares very much about, all the building elements that can take up space will be calculated. However, it was recognized that some building elements such as plant rooms and escape stairs are necessary so they are accepted in the calculations. In particular, the horizontal area of staircases, lift shafts, and vertical ducts should normally be measured for GFA together with the floor through which they pass, with the exception of refuge floors.

According to these exemption specifications, many electrical and mechanical spatial provisions can be considered qualifications of non-accountable GFA. Developers have interpreted the exemptions to argue that staircases, lift shafts, and lobbies passing through non-domestic GFA accountable areas and leading to domestic towers can be considered qualifications for non-accountable GFA. This loophole has led to the profusion of large main lobbies, excessive mechanical rooms, and other oversized provisions in newly developed residential towers. In response, the government has attempted to refine and tighten this clause in recent years. While no specific new typology was created, the GFA exemptions increased the proliferation of the cake-and-candles phenomenon and prompted the government to crack down with increased scrutiny and new regulations.

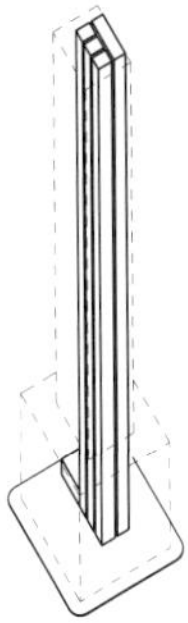

2001 – Air Pollution, SARS Outbreak, and Urban 'Heat Islands'

In recent decades, large-scale residential developments have dominated housing production across Hong Kong. Most private developments in Hong Kong have adopted the profit-maximizing formula of extremely large, site-covering podiums topped with multiple residential towers. In most cases, the massive presence of these podium towers has created an unfriendly environment for pedestrians, denigrating the streetscape and urban relationships. Furthermore, the 'wall effect' created by these podiums and their linking residential blocks has raised concerns about a 'heat island effect' in the inner city. The buildings join to form huge screens that block wind from passing through to the outer edge of the city, resulting in extremely high temperatures in the streets of the inner city, especially during Hong Kong's hot summers.

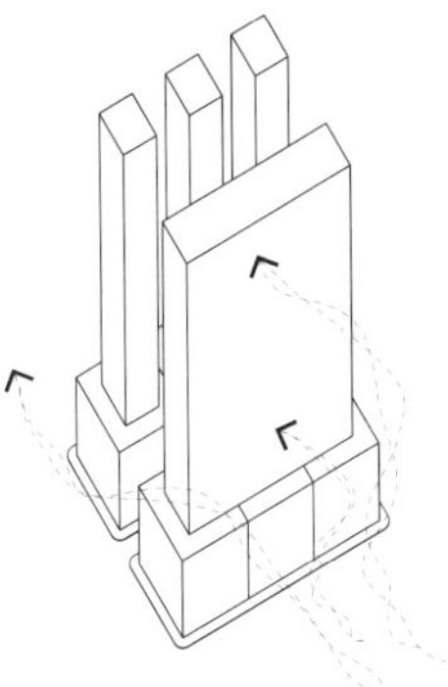

Since 2001, the government has issued a series of Green Sustainable Practice Notes meant to combat this wall effect and improve air circulation in the city by promoting the construction of green and innovative buildings. The Building Departments initiated a series of new PNAP known as the Joint Practice Notes (JPN), with objectives to:

(a) Adopt a holistic life cycle approach to planning, design, construction and maintenance;
(b) Maximize the use of natural renewable resources and recycled/green building material;
(c) Minimize the consumption of energy, in particular non-renewable types; and
(d) Reduce construction and demolition waste. (JPN 1)

Some features of the Joint Practice Notes (JPN) that aim to improve air circulation in the city and improve the environmental conditions of the street include: Maximum Façade Length (Lp) and the Mean Width of Adjoining Street Canyon (U)

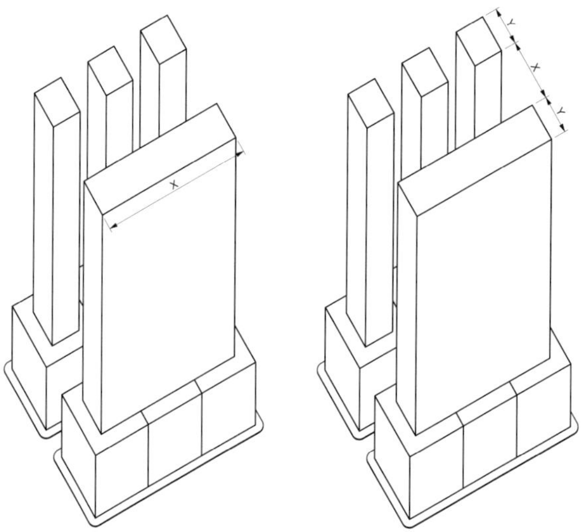

According to the new sustainability guidelines (PNAP 151 and 152), ‘continuous projected façade length’ is defined as the total projected length of the façade of a building or a group of buildings, providing that distance between buildings is less than 15 meters (JPN 1). This abstract concept is applied to encourage the creation of more space between buildings, referred to as ‘street canyons’. Following the ‘Mean Width of Adjoining Street

Canyon' clause, buildings are subject to setback requirements that ensure that buildings are not constructed too close together. The rationale is that the wider the canyon, the more natural air and ventilation will circulate between the buildings.

Width of Adjoining Street Canyon (U): To improve air ventilation within building blocks, one must secure a minimum distance from the external wall of the proposed building to the boundary lines of the site(s) across the street. Buildings on large development sites are required to be separated by intervening spaces. The vertical space of street canyons cannot be obstructed, with exceptions made for signboards, minor projecting features, and open-sided features such as balconies, utility platforms, covered walkways, and trellises. In recent years, new sustainability guidelines are beginning to give more open spaces and set back requirements.

With the outbreak of SARS in 2003 and increased emphasis on public hygiene, natural ventilation within the city became a critically important issue. Interior cross ventilation, direct sunlight into units, and sanitary fitments that help keep air clean became highly recommended housing design features. New guidelines and new Codes of Practice, such as the 'Explanatory Materials to the Code of Practice on Wind Effects in Hong Kong 2004' and the 'Code of Practice on Wind Effects in Hong Kong 2004' promote the generation of greener and more sustainable models. It has yet to be seen how they will directly and indirectly influence the future design of Hong Kong buildings.

2001 – Lack of Urban Green

Several new clauses and new Practice Notes, such as the 2001 'Communal Sky Garden for Residential Building' Practice Note (PNAP 258, now PNAP App-122), have been passed to ensure that more green elements are incorporated into the design of residential towers. In 2001, the Building Authority modified Joint Practice Note No. 1 to mandate the provision of green space for recreational use. The modification pushed for the creation of communal sky gardens on refuge floors and podium rooftops. To ensure safe accessibility and privacy, the regulation states that 'sky gardens and podium gardens are to be designated for the exclusive use of the owners, tenants and their visitors only'. The communal sky gardens that have emerged in response have proven to be great amenities for residents to enjoy outdoor space.

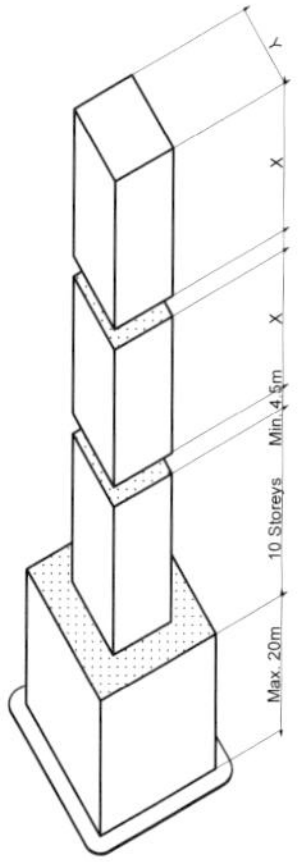

Most developers and architects have opted to place green spaces in the middle of the tower, in order to break up the monotonous sense of verticality. The maximum number of sky gardens allowed in a tower is equal to or less than the number of residential storeys divided by 20. Sky gardens must have a clear height of no less than 4.5m, and they have to be situated at least ten storeys above any other sky garden or podium garden in the same building, unless strong environmental reasons are given to justify exceptions. These height requirements are intended to ensure sufficient headroom for breeze circulation.

2011 – New Sustainable Building Design Guidelines

In 2011, a new series of Practice Notes revolutionized the construction of private residential towers in Hong Kong. There had been rising public concern about the quality and sustainability of the built environment, and factors such as building bulk and height, quality of air ventilation, greening measures, and energy efficiency in buildings came under scrutiny. In 2009, the Council for Sustainable Development, in collaboration with the government, launched a public engagement process called 'Building Design to Foster a Quality and Sustainable Built Environment', The exercise pointed to a need for new measures to foster a sustainable built environment.

One new measure, called 'The New Sustainable Building Design (SBD) Guidelines' (and referred to in Practice Note for Authorized Persons, Registered Structural Engineers and Registered Geotechnical Engineers (PNAP) APP-151 and 152), established three key building design elements that could be more precisely regulated to enhance environmental sustainability: building separation, building setback, and site coverage of greenery. The objectives of the SBD Guidelines were to achieve better air ventilation, enhance the environmental quality of shared living space and provide more greenery, particularly at pedestrian level, and to mitigate the heat island effect.

Along with (PNAP) APP-151 and 152 came a set of complex calculations and diagrams provided for the calculation of building setbacks, percentages of greenery coverage outside of buildings, and even air ventilation assessment (AVA). To incentivize developer compliance with (PNAP) APP-151 and 152, the Building Authority stipulated that it would apply GFA exemptions to green spaces and nonessential plant rooms and services in new building developments. Most of the clauses within these two new PNAP aimed to enhance the quality and sustainability of the built environment.

PNAP 151 also attempts to control bundling bulk and the excessive provisions of amenities in podium towers, by exercising tighter control on the allowance of bonus or exempted GFA. Developers had until April 2011, as stipulated by the Buildings Department, if they were to consider clubhouse podium concessions, which triggered a huge backlog on submissions during that time. With these efforts to curb common real estate development practices for maximizing GFA, the amenity-rich podium typology became less popular. Developers began to look for other means to gain GFA, leading to the hastened adoption of an existing building typology—the curtain wall residential tower.

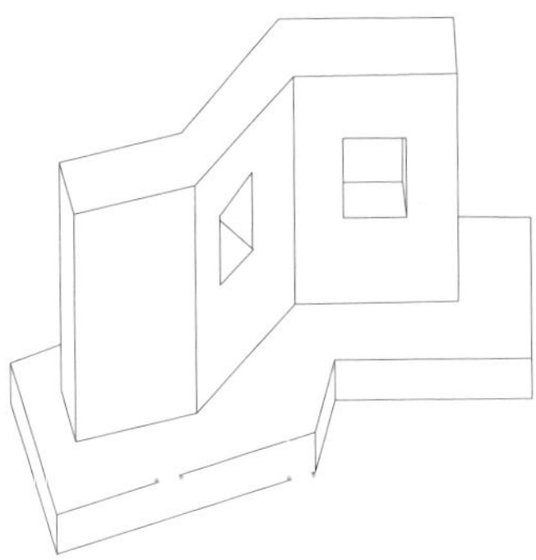

Post-2011 – Curtain Walls Used in Residential Towers

Though curtain-wall technology has existed since the 1970s, Hong Kong was slow to adopt the use of curtain walls in residential towers. Most of the residential blocks have window-walls, and curtain walls were typically reserved only for commercial towers. However, in response to the government's attempt to tighten controls on bonus and exempted GFA, developers found a loophole in building curtain wall towers. In Hong Kong, there are precise regulations on the use of curtain walls, windows, and window-wall systems. Regulations on the structural framing, key structural details, fabrication, and installation of curtain walls are stated in Practice Note for Authorized Persons, Registered Structural Engineers and Registered Geotechnical Engineers APP-37. According to Practice Note APP-37, however, a 300mm gap is allowable between the curtain wall and the external structure. Developers caught onto this small loophole and quickly began developing a type of curtain-walled residential tower designed to allow them to profit on the peripheral GFA 300mm beyond their built structures. Once the buildings are erected, the 300mm gaps are filled to be used as functional interior areas that are saleable to potential buyers for a significant profit. This phenomenon prevails in the new housing market, and the proliferation of curtain-walled residential towers has created new issues such as glare, unsafe curtain wall installations, and overall thermal transfer value issues that exacerbate the excessive generation of heat in interior spaces of residential buildings.

Conclusion

With the emergence of Buildings Ordinance and the constant introduction of new supporting documents, it is clear that Hong Kong building regulations have constantly evolved to keep up with the city's changing needs. The Shek Kip Mei fire in 1953 is widely seen as the historical event that sparked the creation of mass public housing, but it should be noted that there have always been laws to ensure public safety and hygiene and address environmental issues relating to Hong Kong's living conditions. Tracing the lineage of Mark I housing up through the Mark VI generation of housing estates, one can observe how Hong Kong public housing evolved from rudimentary housing blocks that outlined small living spaces without private kitchens or toilets, to more developed housing estates that provide private kitchens, toilets, corridors, and lifts. Other types, such as the Twin-H type, added design features such as central voids for more ventilation and air conditioning vents.

On the other hand, privately developed housing in Hong Kong has mostly been developed by corporates and real estate developers. With the high prices and limited amount of developable land in Hong Kong—and the high potential profits of the real estate market—developers have responded naturally by making every attempt to capitalize on every inch of space, and maximize profit. The Buildings Authority has reacted by rigorously scrutinizing calculations of permitted GFA, limits on site coverage, and even window sizes, to make sure that private developers do not compromise living quality and building safety.

Over the years, the Buildings Ordinances, with all other supporting regulations, have become prescriptive laws as well as referential guidelines that govern the areas that are permissible for building. As the ordinances and regulations have evolved to accommodate changes in demography and building needs, Hong Kong's privately developed residential towers have slowly evolved in reaction, giving rise to the podium tower typology, in which tall, skinny, residential 'pencil' towers sit on top of 15-meter-high podiums loaded with clubhouse facilities. It is not surprising that so many recent developments in Hong Kong are essentially repeated building profiles with little variation, evincing this 'cake-and-candles' typology and, more recently, since the enactment of JPNAP note No. 1 and 2 on Green and Innovative Buildings, curtain-walled residential towers. Developers are sceptical of attempting designs that could risk yielding less buildable GFA.

Until the Hong Kong government relaxes its strict building controls, or developers are motivated by objectives other than maximizing buildable areas, it is unlikely that we will see any major changes to limited scope of Hong Kong's residential tower design. This historical context is intended to put Hong Kong's current residential mega blocks into a longer timeline and a more informed perspective, so that critics of the status quo can be more open, accepting, and sympathetic to the extreme conditions out of which they emerge.

With limited land and fast economic growth, after WW2 Hong Kong started to build effective public housing projects to solve social and urban tension, responding to its high-density living condition and increasing population. Its public housing policy as well as the development of tall-building housing typology has since been considered one of the very successful housing models worldwide for effectively resolving social issues for housing nearly half of its population. Parallel to the public housing, in the last half century private developers also developed their housing pattern, following the planning and building control mechanism set up for the public housing sector, successfully meeting the booming market demand with similar high-rise typology as their development models, establishing themselves as the few large real-estate enterprises shaping the urban landscape of today's Hong Kong.

Mega-housing Form in New Towns of Hong Kong

Text by Weijen Wang and Ryo Fuyimori

Drawings by Ryo Fuyimori

New Town Developments and Mega-Housing Form

The magnitude of urban issues in post-war Hong Kong needed a strategic development with land use planning as a tool to not only address housing and its related issues but also to manage the land resources of the territory effectively. Facing constant challenges for housing provision in the last fifty years, the Hong Kong Government employs a semi-autocratic approach to meet the demand by establishing an efficient mode for building mega-housing in the urban fringe or reclaimed land, as well as developing new towns with mega-housing projects in the New Territory. With the simultaneous building of infrastructure, including metro-rail, highway and public facilities, this unique mode of high-density mega-housing provision also became an effective measure of urban development as well as land control in the territory. Hong Kong's unique high-density urban form, facilitated by this operational process of Development Control, went through a series of urban experiments since the 1960s before reaching the current model.

While developing large-scale housing estate such as Hah Fu or Choi Hung in the '60s, the government also started to develop newly planned towns such as Kwun Tong and Tsuen Wan as both industrial and housing satellites in the district immediately adjacent to the main urban area. In the 1970s, a territory-wide strategic development plan was established, including the urban area and new towns. In particular, the New Town Development Program of 1973 was set up not only to solve the housing problem but also to facilitate the industrial development by creating new urban land away from the urban centre. At the same time, the programme also intended to reduce urban congestion and to improve the environmental conditions, and the planning conditions were translated into the physical layout of master plans, which directly affected their urban form and adjacent environment. Under this programme, the new town developments from Tuen Mun to Sha Tin and Tai Po, from Yuan Long and Fangling to Tseung Kwan O in the New Territory were all curated through strong control under the government policies, efficiently allocated resources, and public funds for transportation and infrastructure with clear development schedules. The diagram on the evolution of housing typology illustrates the different phases of housing models developed during the 1970s to 2000s in Tuen Mun, one of the earlier generations of new towns in Hong Kong. The analysis shows how the unit and building plans were developed in relation to their planning models, from linear-flat with street blocks in earlier generations to the podium and tower types for the recent decades.

Development Control and its Podium-Tower Model

The mechanism of development control on buildings is administered by various means, including planning control, land control, and building control enforced by legislative, contractual, and administrative measures. These measures of controls, including OZPs (Outline Zoning Plan), LPs (Land Planning), Lease Conditions, and PNAP, effectively shape the way building is produced for Hong Kong's housing. After the eighties, under the new planning and building regulations expected to facilitate high-density living while safeguarding basic healthy and safe living conditions, a building was separated vertically into two components: a podium structure that is used for public and commercial, as well as recreational and building services; and residential towers above the podium deck. The vertical separation of the building was a simple functional resolution to accommodate high plot-ratio assigned to each plot of development land that needs spaces for both domestic individuals and public commerce. This entire mechanism of development controls shaped a building complex into a typical form of a large podium structure and several towers of residential floors above the podium deck. In the New Town, where town planning is individually exercised for each development, they appeared as an integrated mega-form of a specific planning layout composed of its component buildings.

Allowing high plot-ratio of developments with podium of nearly full site coverage and residential towers above, the mega-housing structure facilitates numerous towers based on several prototypical efficient unit-layouts with the extrusion of their floor plans for over 100 meters in height. Such an effective layout allows one tower to easily accommodate a thousand people, while one mega-podium development creates a community of 10,000 and 10 or 20 mega-podium street blocks serve one or two hundred thousand, making it a New Town with one or several Metro stations. With excellent provisions for public facilities including hospitals, libraries, sport grounds, swimming halls, adjacent greenery with hiking and bicycle trails, the planning for maximum density and efficiency through very prescribed building codes created several fast-growing new towns with plan-extrusion over the last few decades. The diagram on Building Forms for different Housing Estate illustrates how typologies of podium and tower accommodate models of shopping with housing communities in the new town of Tseung Kwan O. Diagrams on High-Density Developments in Hang Hau and Tseung Kwan O demonstrate how mega-housing forms of podiums with towers are interconnected through skywalks based on infrastructure provisions including the Metro Station for Hong Kong's New Town.

Mega-Housing as an Open City

Housing is the most important component of urban form, and housing is also urban fabric and public spaces. It is hoped that by identifying the issue of its repetitive and uniform character and by negotiating and revising its current mechanism of planning and development control, the mega-structure of housing developed in Hong Kong can begin to evolve and transform. By establishing smaller communities and a hierarchy of communal spaces within the large-housing system, issues of diversity and porosity on a human scale can be better addressed, in order to develop the mega-housing form into to a city of living organisms, in which parts are organized into a system of community, while they can also be unfolded into an open whole with variety and identity. It is also hoped that, with visions and more 3-dimensional innovations as well as open processes, city and housing of mega-form can be an ongoing process with the capacity for transformation wherein new parts are generated into multiple assemblages from within, allowing itself to be re-fabricated into multiple-layers of grounds with permeable spaces of urbanity in Hong Kong. [9, 10]

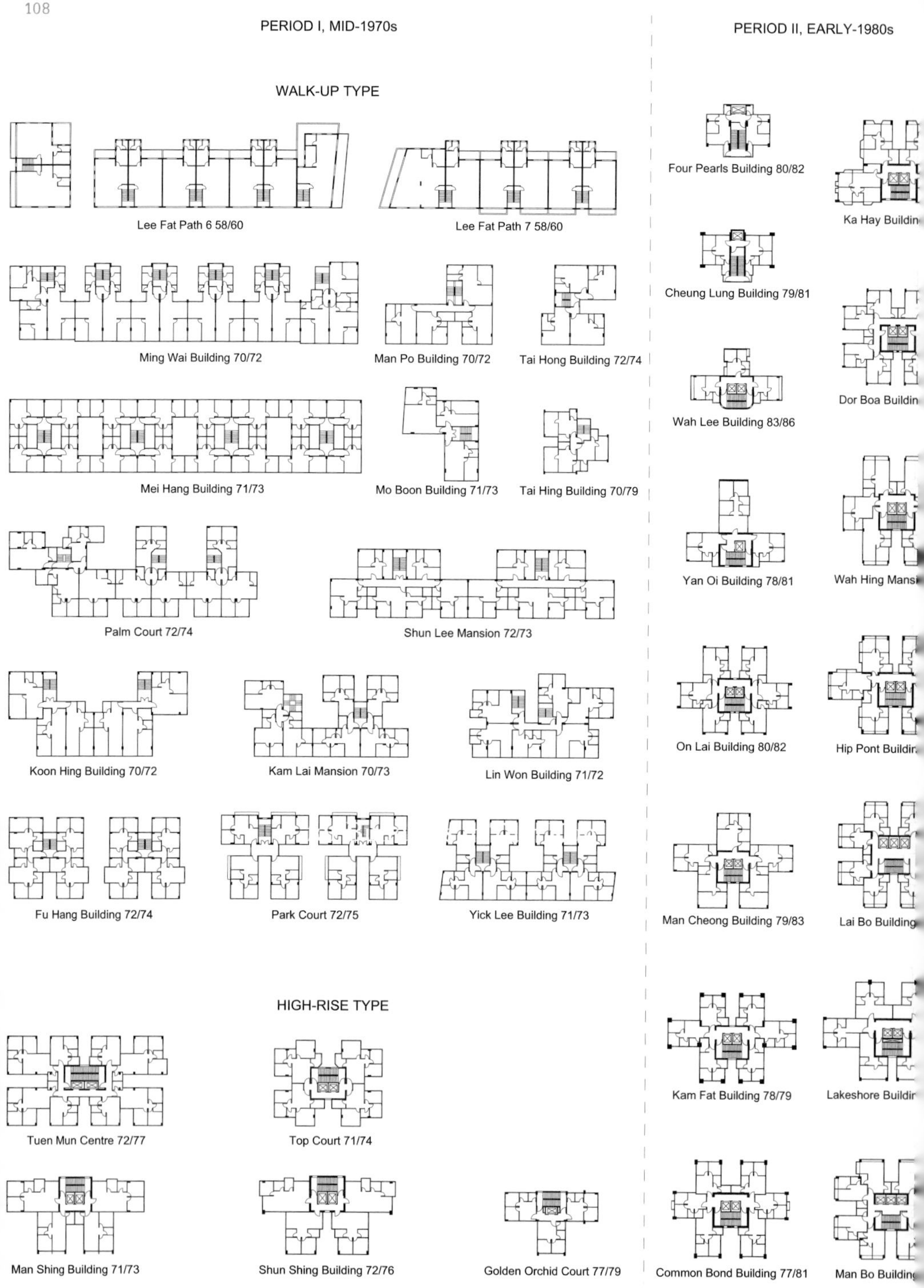

Residential Floor Plans for Buildings in Tuin Kun

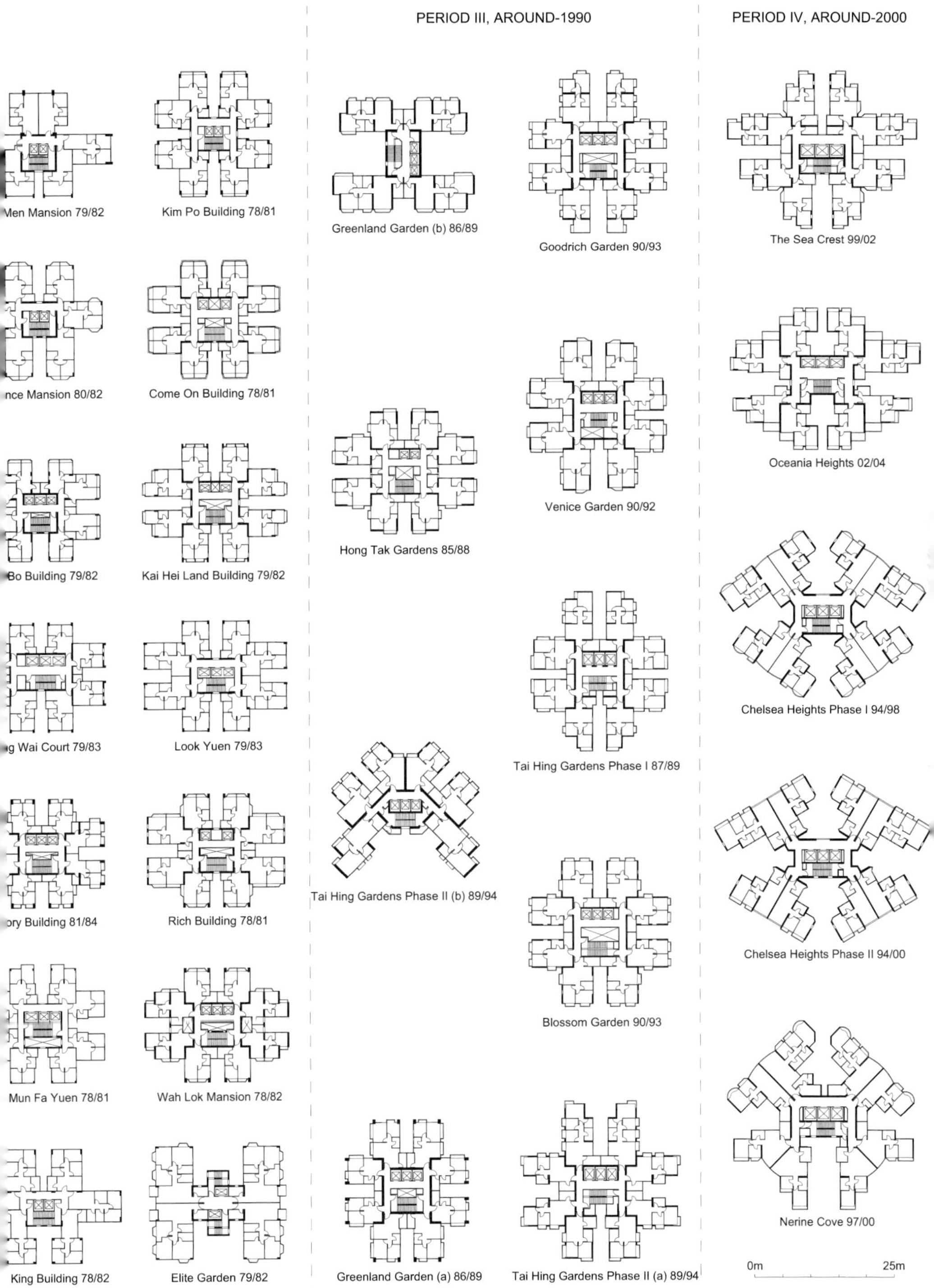
PERIOD III, AROUND-1990
PERIOD IV, AROUND-2000
Men Mansion 79/82
Kim Po Building 78/81
Greenland Garden (b) 86/89
Goodrich Garden 90/93
The Sea Crest 99/02
nce Mansion 80/82
Come On Building 78/81
Oceania Heights 02/04
Venice Garden 90/92
Bo Building 79/82
Kai Hei Land Building 79/82
Hong Tak Gardens 85/88
Chelsea Heights Phase I 94/98
g Wai Court 79/83
Look Yuen 79/83
Tai Hing Gardens Phase I 87/89
ory Building 81/84
Rich Building 78/81
Tai Hing Gardens Phase II (b) 89/94
Chelsea Heights Phase II 94/00
Blossom Garden 90/93
Mun Fa Yuen 78/81
Wah Lok Mansion 78/82
Nerine Cove 97/00
King Building 78/82
Elite Garden 79/82
Greenland Garden (a) 86/89
Tai Hing Gardens Phase II (a) 89/94
0m
25m

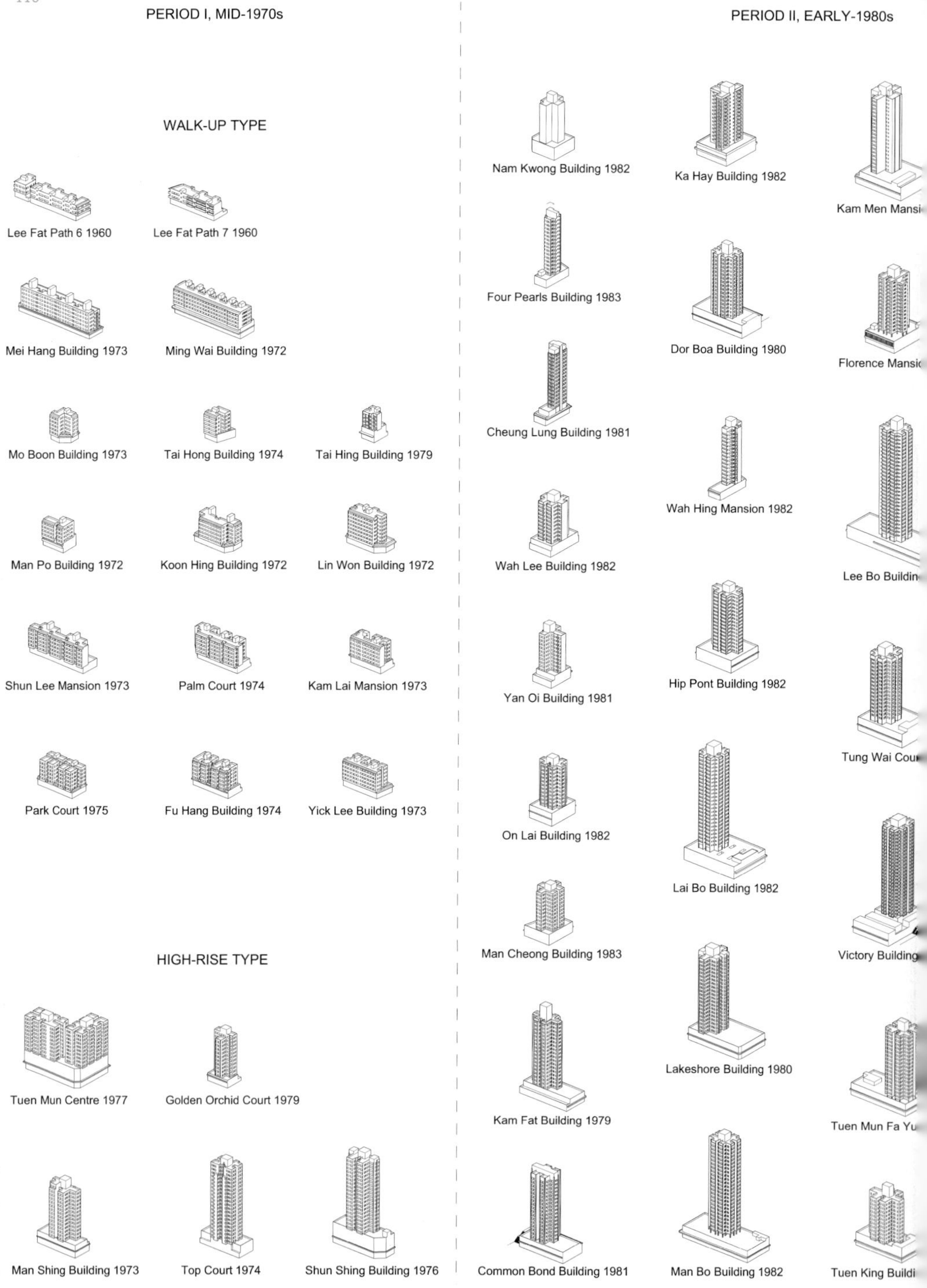

Residential Floor Plans for Buildings in Tuin Kun

Po Building 1981

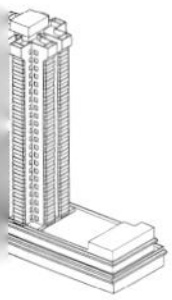

On Building 1981

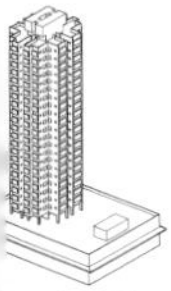

Land Building 1982

ook Yuen 1983

h Building 1981

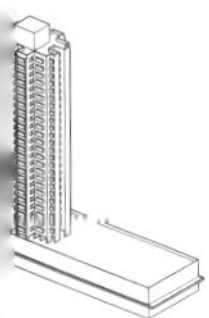

Lok Mansion 1982

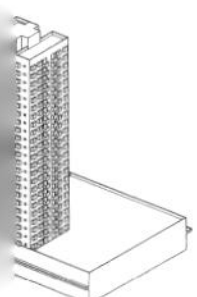

te Garden 1982

PERIOD III, AROUND-1990

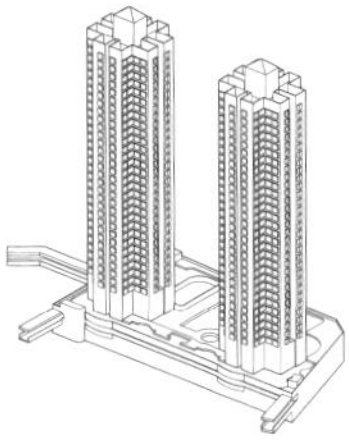

Venice Garden 1992

Blossom Garden 1993

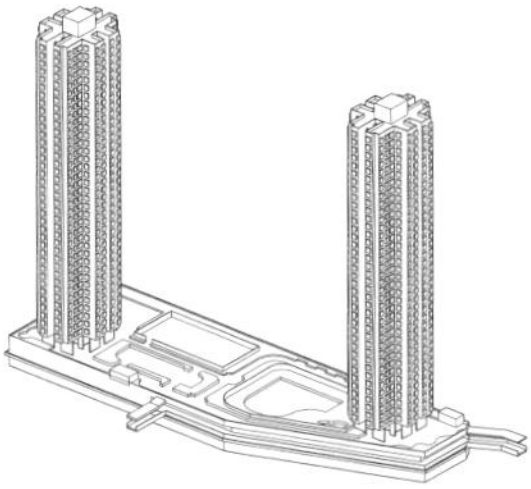

Goodrich Garden 1993

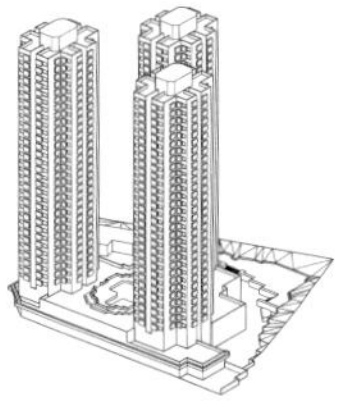

Hong Tak Gardens 1988

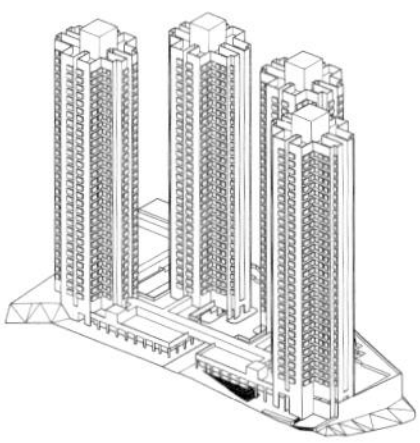

Tai Hing Gardens Phase I 1989

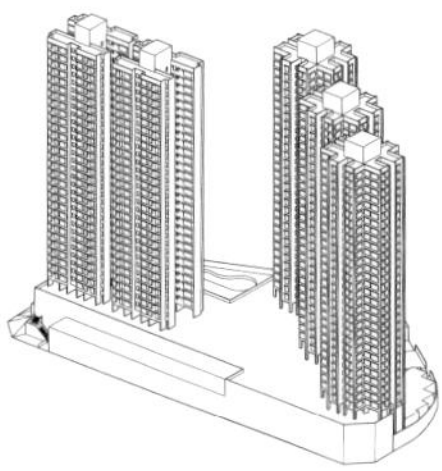

Greenland Garden 1989

Tai Hing Gardens Phase II 1994

PERIOD IV, AROUND-2000

The Sea Crest 2001

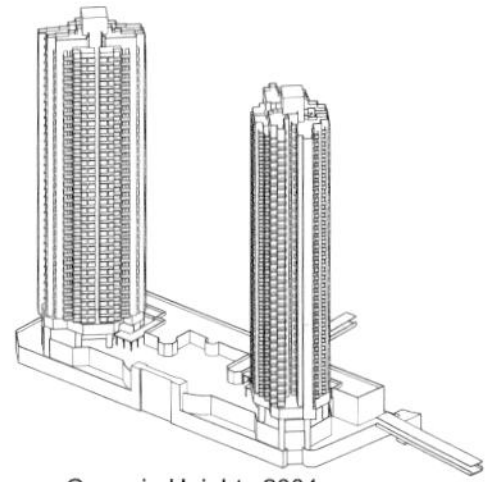

Oceania Heights 2004

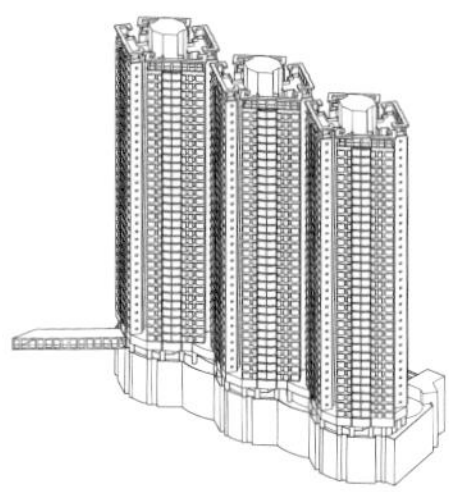

Chelsea Heights Phase I 1998

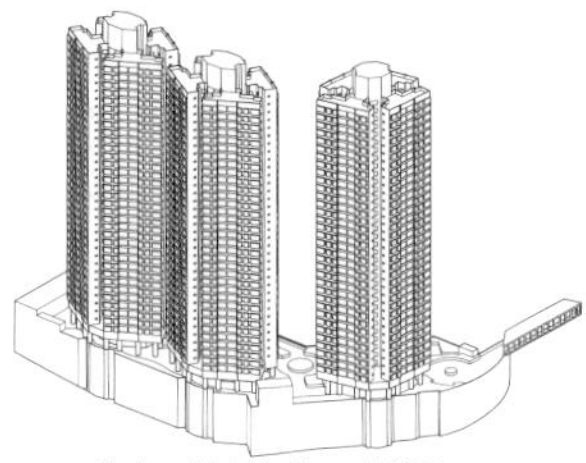

Chelsea Heights Phase II 2000

Nerine Cove 2000

'OU, OTHER SPECIFIED USES'

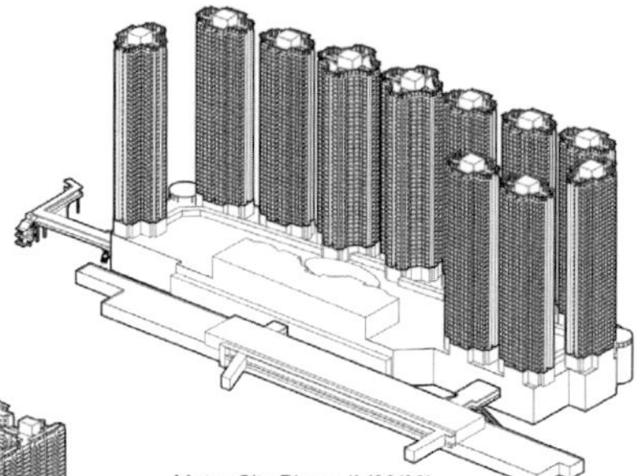

Metro City Phase II (93/99)

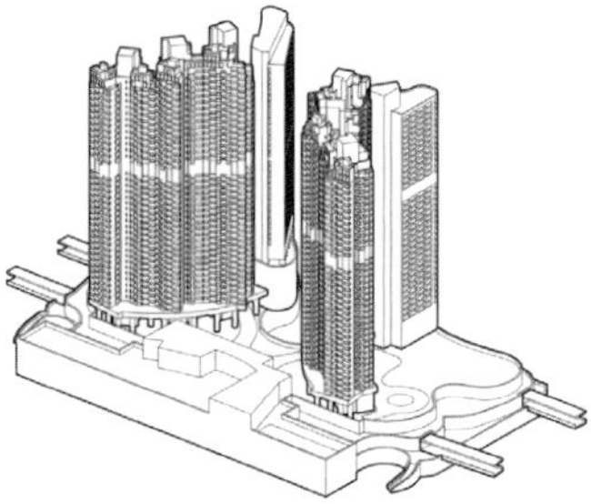

The Wings (98/11)

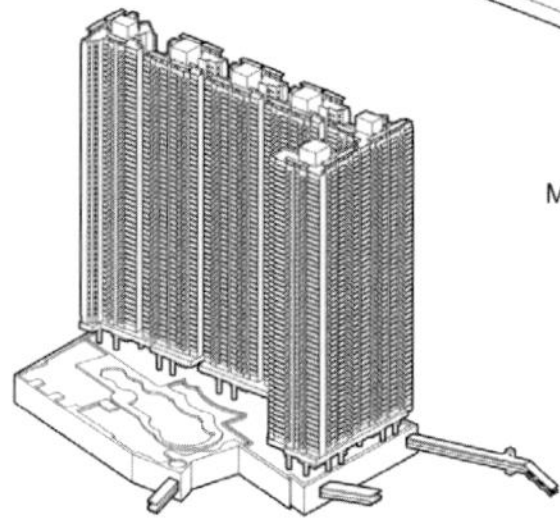

Residence Oasis (02/04)

'C/R, COMMERCIAL/RESIDENTIAL'

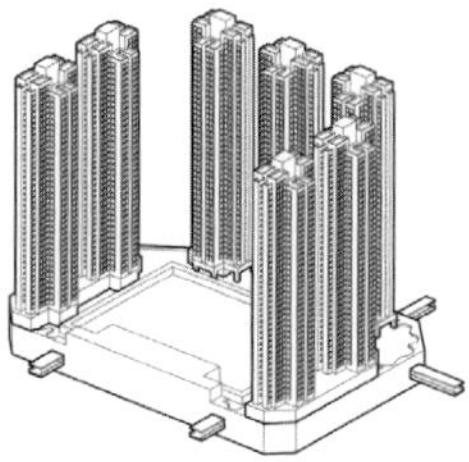

East Point City (93/97)

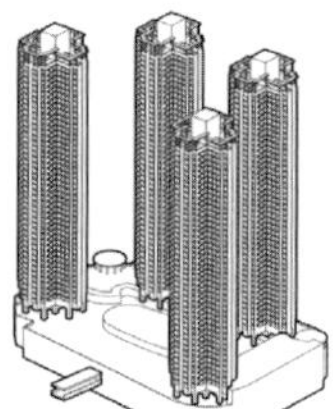

The Metropolis (94/99)

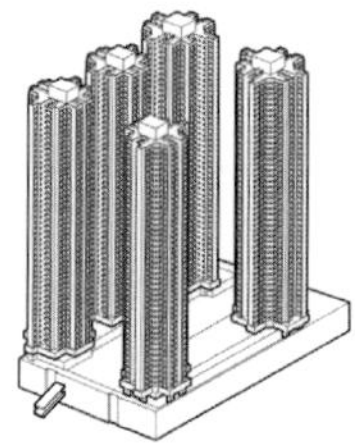

Nan Fung Plaza (95/99)

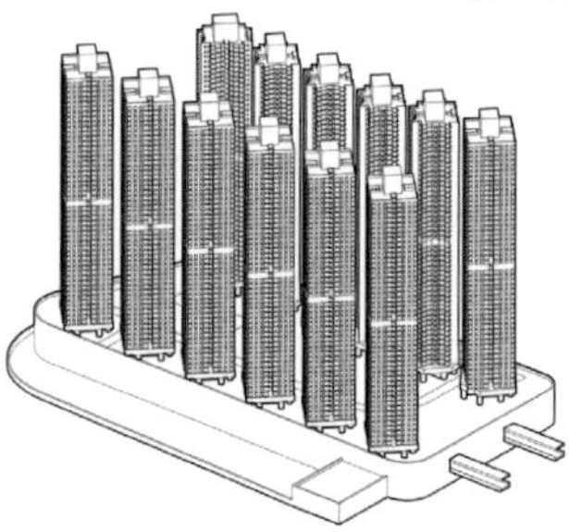

Park Central (97/03)

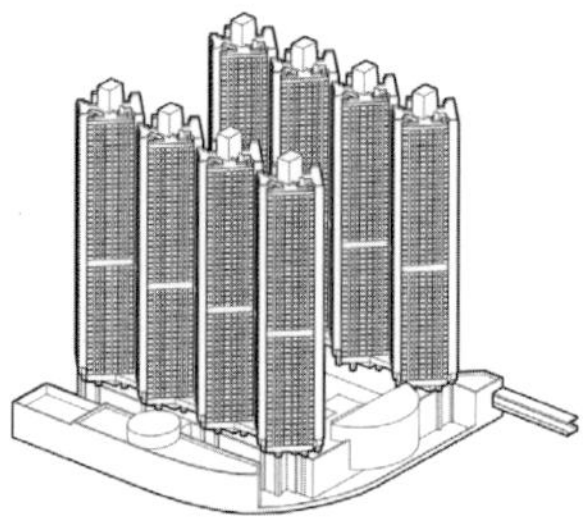

Tseung Kwan O Plaza (97/03)

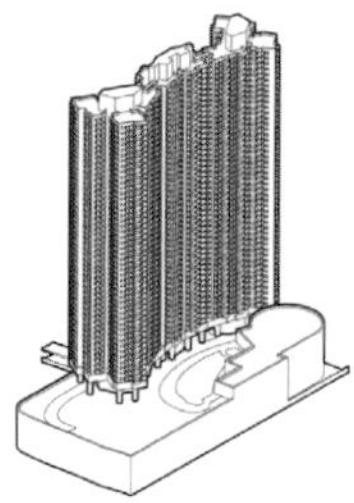

The Grandiose (02/06)

'R(A), RESIDENTIAL (GROUP A)'

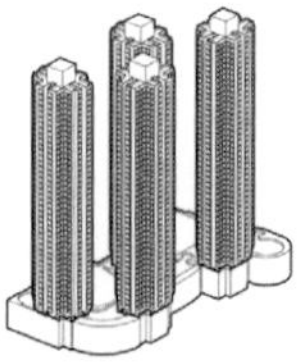

Well On Garden (91/94)

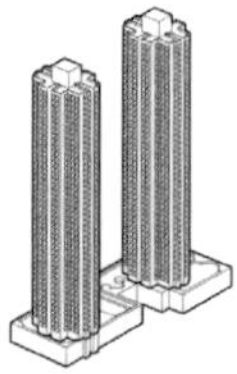

Finery Park (91/94)

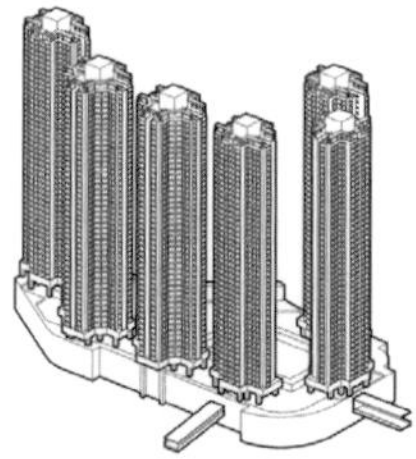

Metro City Phase I (92/96)

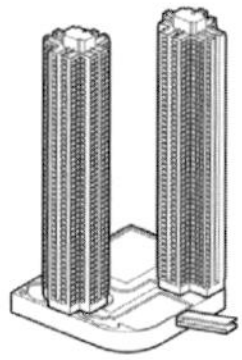

Maritime Bay (95/98)

La Cite Noble (94/99)

Building Form of 14 Housing Estates in Tseung Kwan O

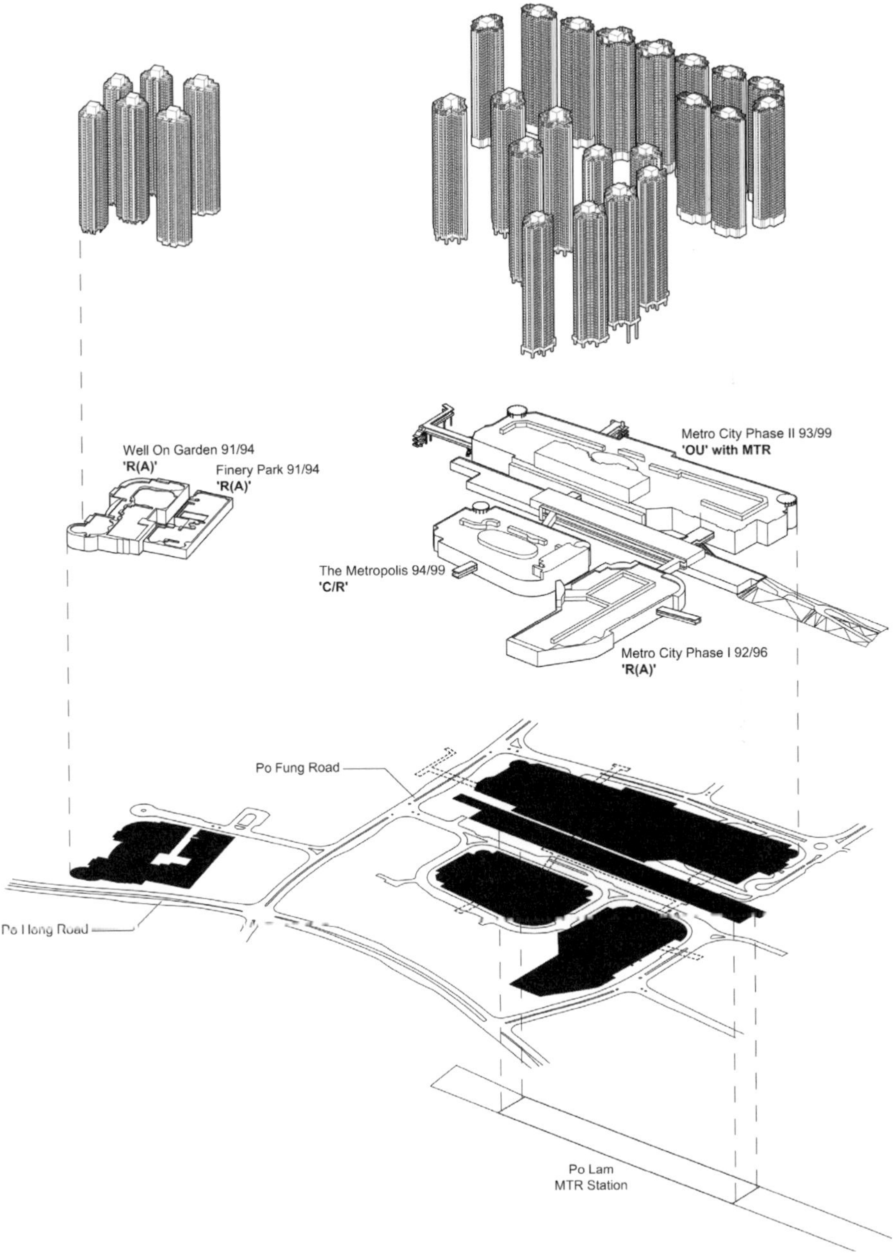

High-Density Private Development Projects in Po Lam

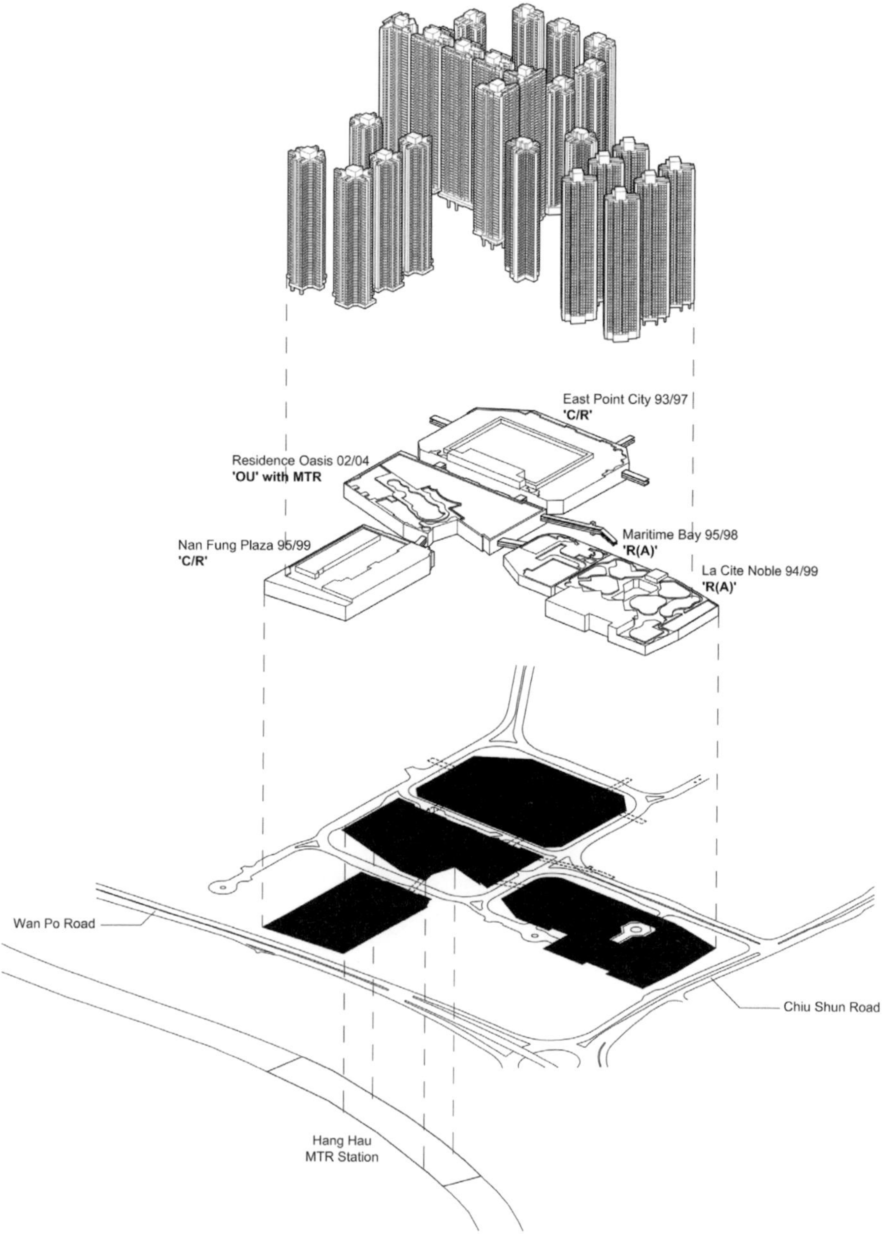

High-Density Private Development Projects in Hang Hau

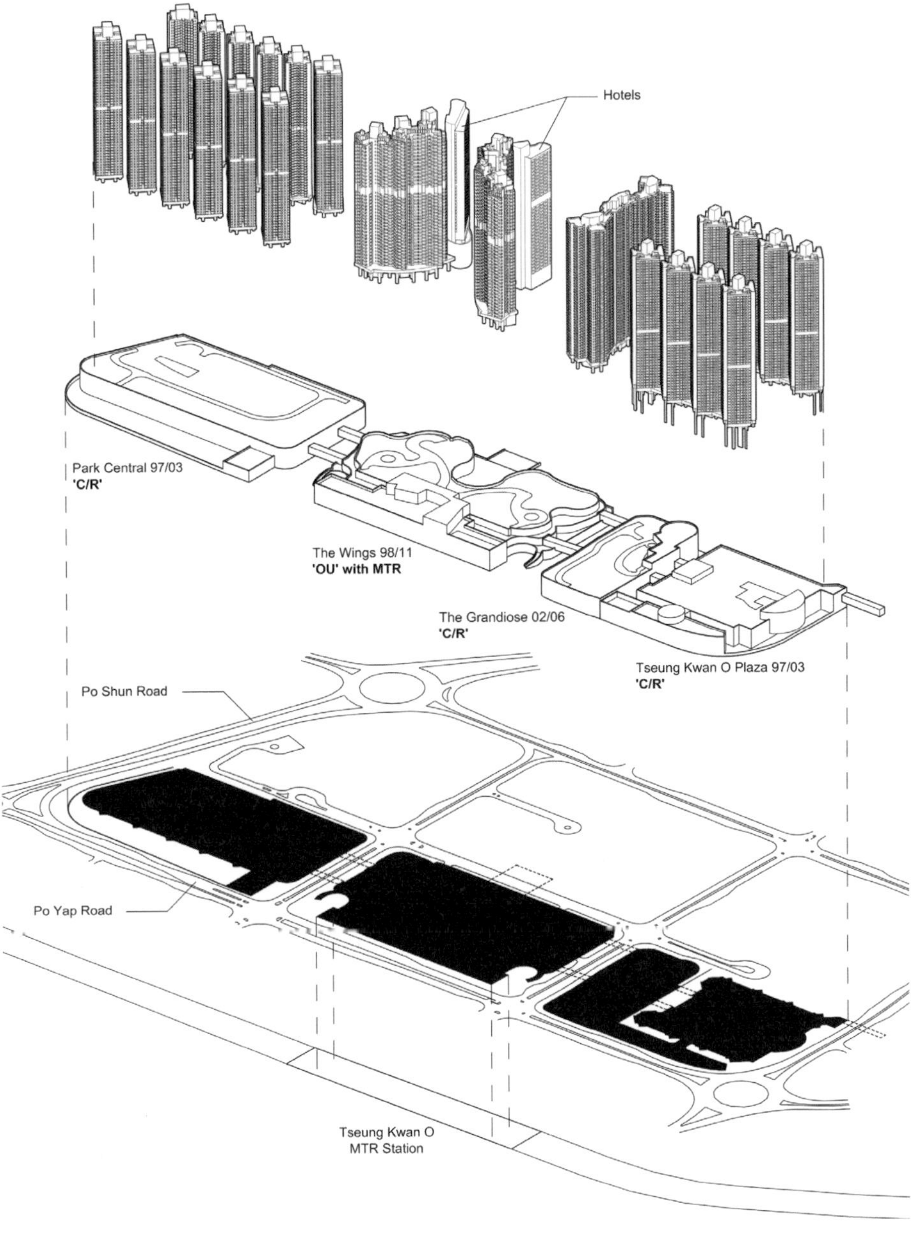

High-Density Private Development Projects in Tseung Kwan O

A wide gap often appears between architecture as it is imagined and architecture as it is built. One can imagine homes with open kitchens and private sky gardens, apartments with sustainable design elements like crossventilation and external peripheral flowerbeds, buildings with communal gardens and recreational areas in intermediate floors, or structures that feature innovations in built form. But in reality, most residential buildings that get built are composed of common characteristics such as a central core, scissor staircases, and bay windows, and they rarely include sustainable features or other expressions of diversity. It is as if, upon stepping into the real world, the architect has forgotten his training. What happened? The following chapter investigates the powerful spell of constraint that has been cast upon the architect in practice and proposes a direction for change.

Design Constraints on Residential Space, and a Possible Breakthrough

Text by Wah Sang Wong

Design Led by Real Estate

In a typical Hong Kong architect's practice, clients expect to maximize the development of every residential project. The architect's plans are supposed to meet the demands of the real estate market. High efficiency is a prime requirement. That means the saleable area (defined as the area sold as private residential units) has to occupy the maximum possible floor area, while the common area (which includes lifts, lobbies, staircases, and service ducts) should occupy a minimum amount of floor area in a given property. Some typical architectural responses to this concept of efficiency are the cruciform floor plan, configured with a central core and an average of eight flats, the scissor staircase, and the prefabricated façade.

Organizing the building's elevator system, staircase, and common corridor into a central core theoretically takes up the least amount of common area and is thus accepted as the most efficient use of space. The even distribution of eight residential flats around the central core allows for more or less equal access to windows, lighting, and ventilation. While this central core design has simplified the use of space, it comes at a cost. With its limited amount of corridor space, the central core plan restricts possibilities for much-needed innovations in sustainable design, which depend on more site-orientated layouts.

Scissor staircases, formed by overlapping two sets of staircases in the same floor plan, serve the logic of the central core design by allowing the core to stay compact. Invented through a clever manipulation of three-dimensional imagery, the scissor staircase theoretically saves half of the area occupied by staircases. However, because of the required distance of access to the residential main doors, the scissor staircases must be situated in the centre of the floor plan, which severely restricts possibilities for the organization of space.

In the past two decades, bay windows have become a ubiquitous feature in residential design. The phenomenon of designing windows that project from an external wall probably originated from efforts to provide more space and light in residential units. However, due to regulations from the Buildings Department, these windows do not produce useful interior space, nor do they necessarily provide more light than conventional windows. In fact, they often admit light from unwanted orientations. In terms of construction, bay windows are difficult to make and maintain, often leading to later defects such as water leakage. Nonetheless, for developers concerned with maximizing saleable area, bay windows are valued because the floor area they enclose is not counted as gross floor area, yet it can be tallied as saleable floor area and sold to residential unit owners at premium prices. They are a clear example of how features not considered accountable for gross floor area are preferred by developers, despite their functional inefficiencies.

In recent years, the government has restricted the use of these bay windows, but another feature—the prefabricated façade—has come into prominence through a similar logic. Prefabricated façades are external walls constructed out of components that are made in a factory and quickly assembled on site. Because prefabrication reduces the amount of pollution on construction sites, the government has encouraged the use of prefabricated façades by exempting the area they delimit from the gross floor area of the development. However, developers have adopted the feature for profit, selling that area as part of the residential home. In certain cases, residential homes are designed with the maximum prefabricated façades on the periphery, again demonstrating how considerations oriented toward real estate have come to determine design choices.

Form Follows Building Regulations

Of course, aside from monitoring and controlling development, building regulations serve to govern matters relating to public health and safety. Developers and architects have to provide lighting and ventilation in residential buildings according to exacting requirements. The typical response of developers is not one of measured consideration for the health and safety of inhabitants, but one of minimum effort to meet requirements. For example, developers often insert deep vertical recesses into buildings to make external walls that provide windows for kitchens, bathrooms, and other rooms, thereby satisfying statutory requirements but not necessarily creating quality living spaces.

Constraints on floor height have also had a significant impact on residential design. Hong Kong's building regulations restrict floor-to-floor height by prescribing a maximum height for stair risers (175 millimetres) and a maximum number of steps in one flight (16 steps). These two parameters restrict floor-to-floor height to 2.8 meters. If higher ceilings are desired, one will have to add a second flight of steps together with a landing, which would allocate more of the gross floor area to a common service space and subtract from the saleable floor area. This is a reluctant concession in real estate-led architectural design.

When architects adopt all the features designed to comply with building regulations and satisfy their clients' desire for maximum saleable floor area, the result is predictable: a standardized elevation of floors and standardized floor plans. The massing, the basic organization of interior space, and many distinctive features are essentially predetermined. Under these circumstances, what further design work can the architect pursue for innovation? Scarcely any!

The Bottom Line of Development Control: Gross Floor Area

From the point of view of the real estate market, the efficiency of a residential building is calculated as the percentage of saleable floor area over the gross floor area of the typical residential floor. According to a research study on the efficiency of residential homes, this percentage ranges from 80 to 90 percent in urban areas. This high percentage can largely be attributed to the use of the central core plan and the scissor staircase, both of which minimize the amount of common area in a typical residential floor, and the calculated use of features such as bay windows and prefabricated façades to claim as much saleable floor area as possible. The ubiquity of these design features points to the fundamental mechanism of development control in contemporary Hong Kong: the measuring of density through gross floor area.

Prior to 1955, the government regulated development through volumetric calculation rather than gross floor area. Building regulations would relate the bulk of a new development to the adjoining streets, taking into consideration the basic use of the building. With the establishment of the Buildings Ordinance and Building (Planning) Regulations in 1955, the focus of the regulations shifted to the density of building development measured by gross floor area. This measure of density considers the floor area within the external wall of a building as gross floor area, with common exemptions to total gross floor area of a site made for required service areas such as mechanical and electrical rooms and car parks. The total gross floor area divided by the site area gives what is known as the 'plot ratio' of the development, which is the measure that is directly regulated by law, and which varies depending on the site conditions and the use of the building. For instance, in an urban site, the plot ratio of a domestic or residential building has a maximum of 10, while that of a non-domestic building is 15.

From the perspective of developers, the gross floor area of a typical floor consists of two kinds of areas: the saleable area of the residential units and the non-saleable common area. It is because the saleable area and the common area both fall under the broadly defined measure of gross floor area that we see such a constrained, real estate market-led architectural responses. The saleable area, the meat of the development, is always maximized, and the common area is always minimized. The effect of this zero-sum game on architecture is a lack of diversity and an inability to implement improved sustainability in residential design.

A New Hope

In 1955, the Buildings Ordinance was established to regulate development by governing the allowable density of buildings. Over the years, additions and amendments have been made, but the basic form of the Buildings Ordinance remains unchanged. Meanwhile, there have been many changes in the realms of technology, living habits, working modes, and economical bases. It is time for development control to be revised.

In 2013, the Hong Kong government enacted a new ordinance called the Residential Property First Hand Sales Ordinance. The 2013 ordinance requires that developers disclose 'saleable floor area', defined as the gross floor area circumscribed within the external wall of a residential unit and the main entrance door, to inquiring buyers. Hence, the exact floor area sold has to be made clear. This step towards transparency and clarification can also lead the way to defining the density of development much more precisely.

To initiate changes to the current building code, one suggestion is to change the measure of density from gross floor area to the more precise measure of 'saleable floor area', which could liberate developers and architects from the pressure to minimize the common areas. Saleable floor area could be subject to strict regulations to control density and manage public safety and health, while a more flexible approach can be adopted for the regulation of common areas, which can be judged on the individual merits of design innovation and sustainability. This relaxing of constraints of gross floor area may lead to an increase of building bulk, but this outcome can ultimately be a benefit if it raises environmental awareness and enhances the quality of residential homes, including their relationship with the city.

This change in the development regulation could be a great step forward, especially if it is motivated by the courage and determination of those in government as well as the understanding and support of the community. If, instead of abstract market forces, an informed community generates a demand for quality living, developers will be pressured to respond. With these conditions, the realization of architecture as imagined by architects and the populations they serve will not be far away.

EXPERIME

NTATIONS

The trend in Hong Kong is that homes are becoming smaller by the day, while their prices are steadily rising. Most Hong Kong residents spend about two-thirds of their monthly income on rent or on paying their mortgages, which significantly affects their quality of life. To purchase an apartment, residents are forced to cut down other basic expenses such as food, clothing, and leisure purchases. Many Hong Kong residents fill their spare time with part-time jobs in order to survive and pay their monthly rent or mortgage. These are just some of the adjustments to social and family life that are necessary for survival. If Hong Kong wishes to become a more liveable and prosperous city, it must start by producing a more diversified housing stock, one that is both attractive to and affordable for low- and middle-income residents.

Diversifying Housing in Hong Kong

Text by Tihamér Salij

The trend in Hong Kong is that homes are becoming smaller by the day, while their prices are steadily rising. Most Hong Kong residents spend about two-thirds of their monthly income on rent or on paying their mortgages, which significantly affects their quality of life. To purchase an apartment, residents are forced to cut down other basic expenses such as food, clothing, and leisure purchases. Many Hong Kong residents fill their spare time with part-time jobs in order to survive and pay their monthly rent or mortgage. These are just some of the adjustments to social and family life that are necessary for survival. If Hong Kong wishes to become a more liveable and prosperous city, it must start by producing a more diversified housing stock, one that is both attractive to and affordable for low- and middle-income residents.

Instead of channelling efforts into the development of micro-sized apartments, as is currently a trend in housing development, the local government should stimulate and encourage design freedom among architects and developers. Together, they could work towards creating more affordable apartments that use design innovation to sustain a minimum size of 80 square meters—enough to accommodate the average-sized family in Hong Kong—and provide spaces that facilitate everyday life in Hong Kong rather than restrict it. Embracing a more diversified residential tower model with various apartment sizes and typologies could lead the way towards a healthier housing market and promote the happiness and well-being of Hong Kong citizens.

To move towards this goal, the Hong Kong government may have to re-evaluate its building regulations and land use policies. Authorities could effect change by abandoning overly prescriptive guidelines and plan for the smarter use of the remaining 60 percent of unbuilt land that is owned by the government. They could loosen restrictions and facilitate the redevelopment of vacant industrial buildings and warehouses into residential buildings. In addition, if both the government and private developers were required to forfeit just ten percent of their profits, this money could be reinvested into housing development to allow for larger average apartment sizes. Such reform could give way to more creativity among architects and developers, which, in turn, could benefit the city and its housing supply. Hong Kong could become a more liveable city for its citizens, and its liveability would attract new citizens, as well as investors and new industries.

In this regard, it would be wise to formulate a visionary housing development plan for the next ten to twenty years, one that actively involves all stakeholders, such as government authorities, policymakers, developers, environmentalists, sociologists, engineers, architects, as well as potential users representing all layers of society. No government should survive on income from high land premiums. Hong Kong needs a long-term plan that embraces diversity and fosters conceptual and material innovation, a plan that prioritizes the provision of decent, affordable, attractive, and larger living spaces for the broad population of hard-working Hong Kong residents. Such a plan would not only aim to annually supply affordable housing of a varied size and typology, but it would also prioritize nature-inclusive building concepts to improve the quality of Hong Kong's public spaces and cultivate street life by promoting walking, building bicycle networks, creating zones for mixed-use neighbourhoods, and providing and protecting shopping streets with small-sized shops to promote the local economy. Housing developments with cooperative user groups could be encouraged, thereby building and empowering communities that could help shape alternatives to large-scale housing developments with gigantic retail podiums topped by slender, uniformly extruded towers. The provision of affordable and diverse housing has the potential to nurture the well-being of Hong Kong citizens and, in the long term, support micro-economic growth. Rather than spending most of their income on rental costs and mortgages, residents could spend more on food, clothes, and entertainment. Lower- and middle-income residents could enjoy increased purchasing power, benefiting the retail, leisure, and food and restaurant industries. Overall, people in Hong Kong would have more access to economic opportunity.

Hong Kong has a unique potential to become a fertile testing ground for vertical living environments. Its dense population and finite amount of land can inspire creativity and innovation that could have far-reaching benefits, as other cities around the world are growing at similarly rapid rates. The city could become a role model for creative, high-density housing development. Those with a stake in the future of Hong Kong can start by asking some important questions. How can housing development grow out of the standardized design processes that currently suppress diversity? How can architects, together with developers, free themselves from strict planning and building regulations and work towards producing higher quality housing? What values could be added with creative design? Could better housing radically change Hong Kong? And if so, what are the conditions necessary for realizing this kind of housing?

As architects, we can explore these questions in creative ways. What if architecture could better facilitate everyday activities such as cooking, dining, bathing, sleeping, storing, relaxing, cleaning, and serving? What new programmes would emerge from designing sufficient private space for live-in domestic workers, for instance? Or, what if the walls could absorb belongings and function as valuable storage space? What if dining rooms were expanded to facilitate dining with friends and family, with panoramic views? What if apartments could feature fireplaces, around which to gather, dine, and sing? Can we imagine apartments that provide space to grow food? What if all rooms had access to their own private balconies? What if all bedrooms incorporated sky views, and people could regularly experience sleeping under the stars? Could we design apartments that allow their dwellers to swim around the house?

What desires could be supported through such experimental specializations, and what would need to be sacrificed? Some proposed specializations would call for higher ceilings, more window openings, more outdoor spaces, or more screening mechanisms to create privacy. Others would call for fewer walls and different ways of connecting spaces, or better natural cooling. In the process of envisioning these spaces, we should also aim to make them more organizationally efficient than the current standard, by using a more comprehensive definition of efficiency. Can these recalibrations of space lead to better living conditions? Can they offer more natural light and ventilation, better views, or more outdoor space? How would they influence the cityscape?

Experimenting Against the Standard Housing Tower

For this chapter, the cruciform-shaped tower will be used as a benchmark against which we can compare the efficacy of residential towers generated through experimental design processes. Formed by the simple extrusion of a cruciform-shaped floor plan composed of uniformly planned apartments, this type of tower has dominated the city's housing development for more than five decades. In setting this form as a benchmark, it becomes possible to identify specific areas where modifications are made through experimentation, and to evaluate whether these modifications lead to apartment units and towers that perform better or worse than the typical Hong Kong housing tower.

In addition to the specialization of individual apartments, the stacking of apartments into towers has been studied and evaluated using qualitative indicators such as the amount of light, views, natural ventilation integrated into the design and the level of access to outdoor spaces such as balconies or roof spaces. Using this research, we can ask how different ways of stacking apartment units can generate better living conditions. Could certain vertical configurations facilitate change and generate more diversity and a better quality of living throughout the city? Aside from managing a dense metropolis, providing dwelling spaces at astounding heights, and adding up to an attractive skyline, these towers can fulfil another role—they could enhance the complex organism that is the city. Towers with greater porosity could facilitate better wind circulation in the area; or they could generate a substantial amount of energy through the smart use of façades. Towers could be designed to increase biodiversity by supporting a diverse range of local plants and trees at different heights, providing habitats for birds, bats, and insects and purifying the air and producing oxygen. Designed with more creativity and forethought, these towers could become aesthetically appealing and iconic landmarks that enhance the city's liveability.
These towers have the potential to become catalysts for change.

The Typical Hong Kong Apartment

Text by Tihamér Salij

Drawings by Cheng Pok Him BOB, Claudia Mainardi and Sylwia Franczak

Apartment typology is based on work from The Why Factory's 'Towers Beyond Extrusion' studio at the Department of Architecture (Architecture and Urban Design III, ARCH 5001) at the Hong Kong University, during Fall 2014.

Studio Tutors: Prof. Winy Maas, Tihamér Salij, Martine Vledder with Donn Holohan
Students: Au Yeung Chun Yu JOEY, Chan Fong Tong FRED S, Cheng Pok Him BOB, Ching Ka Ho FRED, Henao Granda Jan Esteban, Ho Sheung Hay TERENCE, Hu Xiangdong HOCK, Ko Pak Kan ZETH, Li Zhixin ALLISON, Liu Chuen Yung VINCENT, Ma Yue, Qin Liting TING, Tang Tak Shing KELVIN, Wen Fan, Wu Yucong, Xie Junni, Ffion Zhang, Ho Yin SUNNY CHA, Sai Bond, Man Hei KENNIF, Han PAT

The Typical Apartment

The typical Hong Kong apartment is laid out over a single floor (a simplex) and divided into three bedrooms, two bathrooms, a combined living and dining room, and two balconies, of which the larger balcony is in the master bedroom and the smaller one is connected to the kitchen and combined with a utility platform. For the purposes of this research, the size of a typical Hong Kong simplex is set to 80 square meters, which is considered a relatively large apartment. The apartment has painted walls, a split-type air-conditioning system, and wooden floors. The living/dining room is arranged in an L-shape with a single (bay) window on the living room side. The dining area is windowless, with enough room for a small dining table, and it connects to the kitchen through a door. The typical master bedroom can fit a double bed, a large wardrobe, and a small desk. It has access to a small balcony, which is the best place to enjoy the views and natural breeze, depending on how the apartment is situated. The master bathroom provides a showerhead over a bathtub, a sink, and a toilet, and the guest bathroom includes the same features. The two single bedrooms can each fit a single-sized bed and a small desk. The kitchen usually has space for a combined washer-dryer, a two-hob gas stove, a range hood, a refrigerator with a freezer, and some hanging wall-cupboards.

The typical apartment usually accommodates two adults, two children, and a domestic worker who lives and sleeps in the kitchen space. Its most common defects include a lack of natural ventilation, especially in the bathrooms and the kitchen, and a limited amount of natural light in the living/dining room due to the minimal number of windows. Storage space is usually insufficient, and the balconies are too small to serve any purpose other than providing a platform for standing and enjoying the view or for drying a small amount of laundry. The standard apartment layout ignores some of the basic needs and routines of its users, and as such it provides an inadequate response to the simple question of how parents, children, and domestic workers can carry on with their daily lives.

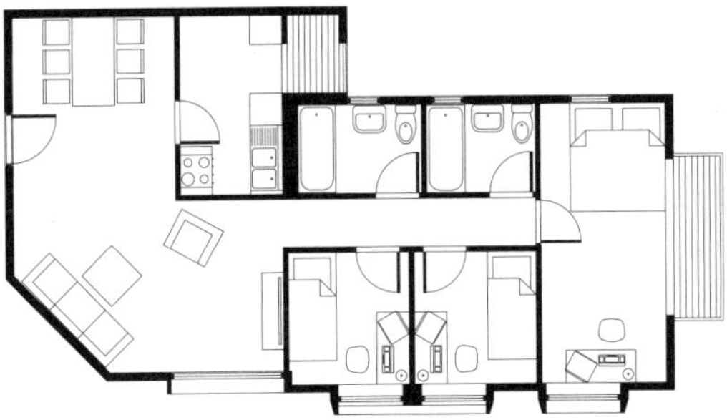

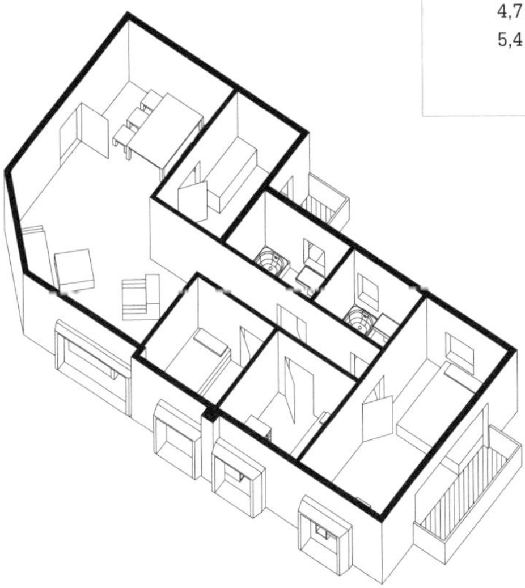

Apartment Layout, 1:200

The following proposals explore possibilities for generating diversity and improving the quality of the typical 80 m^2 Hong Kong apartment. We start with the premise that everyday activities such as cooking, dining, bathing, sleeping, storing, relaxing, cleaning, and serving could be better supported within the parameters of an 80 m^2 apartment. Rather than accept a uniform standard in which none of these activities have the appropriate space and design features to thrive, what if we diversified the organization of space to support specific daily functions? How can we evaluate the efficacy of these specialized spatial arrangements? What will they improve, and what will be sacrificed for it? What will be discovered in the process?

Specializing Apartments

Text by Tihamér Salij

Additional research by Tihamér Salij with Martine Vledder

Drawings and images illustrated by Tihamér Salij and Claudia Mainardi with Sylwia Franczak

Apartment typologies are based on work from The Why Factory's "Hong Kong Tower Revolution" studio at the Department of Architecture at the Hong Kong University, during Fall 2013,
and of The Why Factory's "Towers Beyond Extrusion" studio at the Department of Architecture at the Hong Kong University, during Fall 2014.

Photo collage impressions illustrated by The Why Factory: Tihamér Salij and Claudia Mainardi the students of The Why Factory's "Hong Kong Tower Revolution" studio at the Department of Architecture at the Hong Kong University, during Fall 2013,
and by the students of The Why Factory's "Towers Beyond Extrusion" studio at the Department of Architecture at the Hong Kong University, during Fall 2014.

Hong Kong Tower Revolution, Architecture and Urban Design III (ARCH 5001), Hong Kong University.
Studio Tutors: Prof. Winy Maas and Tihamér Salij
with Sander Mulders and Arend van Waart
Students: Au Wing Yi, Chak Tsz Kin, Chan Chung Man, Chan Ian Yin Yan, Chan Pui Yin, Chau Shek Lun, Cheng Ching, Ip Kai Hong, Liu Kemeng, Mok Wang Chee, Tang Ho Yin, Kong Ho Ching, Kwok Ka Ching, Lau Xin Yee, Lee Kin Wai, Li Mei Yu, Lung Man Ching, Ma Ching Yi, Suen Wing Yin, Sze Ivy, Sze Ying Ying, Yeung Cho Yui, Yeung Ho Man

Towers Beyond Extrusion, Architecture and Urban Design III (ARCH 5001), Hong Kong University
Studio Tutors: Prof. Winy Maas, Tihamér Salij, Martine Vledder with Donn Holohan
Students: Au Yeung Chun Yu JOEY, Chan Fong Tong FRED S, Cheng Pok Him BOB, Ching Ka Ho FRED, Henao Granda Jan Esteban, Ho Sheung Hay TERENCE, Hu Xiangdong HOCK, Ko Pak Kan ZETH, Li Zhixin ALLISON, Liu Chuen Yung VINCENT, Ma Yue, Qin Liting TING, Tang Tak Shing KELVIN, Wen Fan, Wu Yucong, Xie Junni, Ffion Zhang, Ho Yin SUNNY CHA, Sai Bond, Man Hei KENNIF, Han PAT

Specialization aims to improve select rooms and select functions of the Hong Kong apartment. As such, spaces dedicated to certain other functions will, to some degree, have to be sacrificed or even cancelled. This flexibility is what allows architects to experiment with apartment designs that have more useful outdoor spaces, spatially distinctive bathrooms, dreamy bedrooms, smart corridors, high-class dining rooms, chef's-special kitchens, extraordinary living rooms, comfortable maids' rooms, increased storage space, and even newly created accessory spaces, such as study rooms. Each specialization of an apartment generates a unique typology with its own formal configuration. In addition, each specialization provides an opportunity to improve factors such as natural ventilation, light, views, and access to outdoor space.

What follows is an exploration of ten apartment specializations, each with an analysis of the spatial qualities desired, as well as two sample layouts executed within the spatial limit of 80 m^2.

The Balcony Zone

The basic definition of a balcony is a railing-enclosed platform that projects from the side of a building to give direct access to outdoor space. Larger and more useful outdoor spaces, such as patios or roof terraces, are very rare in Hong Kong due to their high cost. In all cases, these spaces present design challenges in terms of privacy and accessibility.

According to the Hong Kong building code, balconies theoretically function as 'green features', in that they provide additional space for planting and consequently help minimize noise and air pollution in the city. They are often the only form of outdoor space provided in Hong Kong housing units, and they often span just two square meters, which is the minimum size prescribed by the Hong Kong Buildings Ordinance. It is common to only have one balcony per unit.

Despite being so small and often badly designed, balconies support a wide range of activities besides having plants: from drying laundry to cooking to providing a small space for relaxation. But in most cases, the balcony is too small to use. With better-designed balcony spaces, there is the potential to create higher quality relaxation spaces for residents. The balcony could become an integral rather than an ancillary part of the apartment and support the activities and functions of actual dwelling.

The proposals shown here explore the overall benefits of maximizing outdoor space, in one case through an enlarged balcony space and in the other through the creation of a platform that connects all other functions of the apartment.

The Cleansing Zone

Before 1903, there were basically no sanitary fitments provided in Chinese tenement houses. The Buildings Ordinances enacted in 1903, 1935 and 1955 gradually increased requirements for the integration of latrines and sanitary fitments in Hong Kong housing. Moreover, changes in lighting and ventilation requirements for toilets and bathrooms have clearly influenced the evolution of residential building plans. The standard location of toilets and bathrooms on apartment and building floor plans began to shift, affecting the external façade by resulting in narrow tubular voids in buildings that function as shafts of light and ventilation punched with windows with unattractive views. This is the genesis of the cruciform-shaped floor plan. Since the widespread adoption of mechanical ventilation and artificial lighting, starting around 1997, residential tower design has started to deviate from the cruciform shape, making room for slightly more variety.

Despite the addition of basic regulations on bathroom and toilet design, the quality of bathrooms and toilets has remained the lowest priority in housing design in Hong Kong. The low regard for bathroom and toilet design ignores the reality of how these spaces are used. Despite their typically small dimensions, they are the private wellness areas of our homes, the sites of important daily life activities such as cleaning ourselves, relieving ourselves, brushing our teeth, shaving, styling our hair, applying makeup, and washing and drying laundry. Bathrooms and toilets should be furnished with a certain amount of open space to support the relaxation of the body and mind.

Because apartment units in Hong Kong have such limited space, laundry is usually done inside the bathroom or kitchen. Laundry is often hung to dry inside the bathroom, where a dehumidifier is placed, or it is arranged on clothes hangers and clothes-drying racks in other rooms such as the living/dining room. It is not uncommon for people to use the bathroom or toilet as a dressing room, given the access to a mirror, running water, and private space. All of these basic activities could be better supported.

The Sleeping Zone

Besides providing a place to sleep, bedrooms are spaces where one can expect a little bit of privacy. This is very important to maintain a healthy coexistence among family members. Most bedrooms in Hong Kong are just large enough to fit a bed and a small desk. It is therefore common to use bunk beds to provide enough sleeping space for the family, which often means that children and parents sleep together in a stacked configuration. Sometimes even three generations of family members—children with their spouses, parents, and grandparents—sleep together in one bedroom, with improvised curtain systems to secure the barest amount of privacy. Intimacy has become a major problem, stemming from Hong Kong's cramped living conditions. In addition, if there is a window in the bedroom, it often looks directly out into an adjacent apartment. Given these circumstances, the need for privacy in the bedroom is hardly satisfied.

The Corridor Zone

In the typical Hong Kong apartment, corridors are limited to the functions of separating and connecting other, more useful spaces in the apartment. Because of their perceived secondary nature, they are often designed with poor lighting and insufficient ventilation. In general, they are treated as the dark spots of the apartment, mere subtractions of precious square meters. They are deprived of the chance to add positive qualities to domestic space.

What if corridors are considered as spaces that can contribute positive qualities to the apartment, such as more views or more natural ventilation? Alternatively, what apartment configurations could be imagined if we moved the corridor to the outside the apartment, transferring its circulatory function to the balcony?

The Dining Zone

Eating and sharing meals is an important aspect of daily life. In Hong Kong, especially, people typically spend a lot on food, especially on eating out. Gathering around a table and sharing food and conversation is an essential social activity in this city.

In the typical Hong Kong apartment, the dining room is often combined with the living room in a continuous L-shaped space. Often designed without a window, dining areas lack sufficient light and have no views.

Furthermore, it is often too small to comfortably fit all family members around a table that is large enough to hold all the food, drinks, and, in some instances, the porcelain crockery and crystal glassware that are kept for certain dining occasions. Dining together with family and friends is unthinkable in most Hong Kong homes. As a result, dining often takes place in the living room, in front of the television set.

The Cooking Zone

The average-sized kitchen in Hong Kong has enough room to accommodate one and a half person. With such limited space, cooking often feels like a chore, and getting together with friends for a home-cooked meal is not an appealing choice of activity. That type of socializing often takes place outside, in restaurants, which are abundant in Hong Kong. However, there is still a demand for space to cook and dine in a private, home-like setting. Rental kitchen spaces, equipped with everything from pots, pans, cooking utensils, spices, refrigerators, cooking surfaces, ovens, microwaves, and bars, speak to the desire shared among some Hong Kong residents to cook and dine together as if they were at home.

Besides being too small, apartment kitchens in Hong Kong often lack sufficient natural light, natural ventilation, and proper storage space. In most cases, only one small window, facing the centre core of the building, is provided, just to satisfy building code.

How can space be organized to support cooking and dining at home and make these social activities pleasant and relaxing again?

The Living Zone

The living room is usually located at the entrance of the apartment, where it is used to greet people and socialize with family and friends. Many activities take place in the living room, including sitting, reading, watching television, listening to music, playing games, or taking short naps to recover from work. Living rooms in Hong Kong apartments are often crammed with belongings, indicating a lack of adequate storage space. They are sometimes divided with simple curtains to allow for some privacy. They also can serve as an additional bedroom for family members or domestic workers. Burdened with too many functions, living rooms in Hong Kong do not offer much privacy, nor do they provide sufficient space for the activities that take place there.

The Services Zone

Foreign domestic workers make up a critical demographic of Hong Kong society, fulfilling a demand for domestic laborers. Working six days a week for an average salary of about HK$4,000 a month, the majority of domestic workers in Hong Kong have to accept a very low quality of life. They are legally obliged to live with their employers, often in very poor conditions. Even though some families want to pay domestic workers enough to support their ability to live independently, they face fines, bans, and imprisonment for violating employment laws, and the domestic workers risk imprisonment and deportation to their home countries.

Cramped conditions often force domestic workers to sleep together in one room with the children they are employed to look after. Others sleep in storage spaces, or in the kitchen, which is often designed for this purpose. If government policy were to change, how can the space of the home be organized to create more privacy and provide a higher quality of life for both the domestic worker and the employing family?

The Storage Zone

Creating adequate storage space is a huge challenge in Hong Kong apartments. Rarely do apartments have dedicated storage rooms or spaces. In recent years, the need for better storage has led to the emergence of self-storage units, many of which now occupy old industrial buildings throughout the city. Their numbers are rapidly growing, becoming a noticeable new industry and non-traditional form of real estate investment. Most storage spaces are rented by the month, and they offer extra services such as 24-hour pick-up and delivery services, giving rise to new businesses from which landlords, investors, and small enterprises benefit.

If storage spaces are provided in Hong Kong apartments, they typically measure about two to four square metres and are directly connected to—and only accessible through—the kitchen. Besides storing groceries, household tools, clothes, and other necessities, these micro-sized spaces often function as sleeping rooms for domestic workers.

How can the demand for storage space be addressed within the confined space of the apartment? What organization would allow for enough storage space without having to sacrifice space dedicated to other functions and activities?

The Study Zone

Hong Kong society and its education system put extreme pressure on its young students. As such, it is important to design proper, quiet study spaces in apartments that are conducive to reading, learning, and studying. Young people between 16 and 25 suffer most from the lack of adequate study spaces at home. Although public libraries provide some space for studying, students are generally limited to the space provided by their schools and universities.

The more convenient option would be to seriously consider the integration of study spaces in the layout of homes. Good working spaces at home would also support flexible working hours and give family members the option to work from home. Students could then spend less time away from home, and families could organize their lives in a more convenient way, mitigating stress and leading to improved general well-being.

More Outdoor Space: The Wrap-Around Balcony

This apartment layout maximizes the amount of outdoor space by arranging small rooms in a hutong-like setting, with each room surrounded by a minimum of 90 cm of outdoor space. As in a traditional hutong, this apartment features courtyard-like corridors for connecting spaces as well as facilitating communal gatherings, which foster harmonious living among the family. These in-between spaces allow regular access to outdoor space. Besides integrating the social values of the hutong, this apartment layout supports better ventilation and provides more natural light and views to every room.

With up to 42.55 m^2 of accessible outdoor space, this apartment layout creates more room for activities such as drying laundry, growing plants, barbecuing, and engaging in other recreational activities. Levels of natural ventilation, natural light, and number of views are also improved.

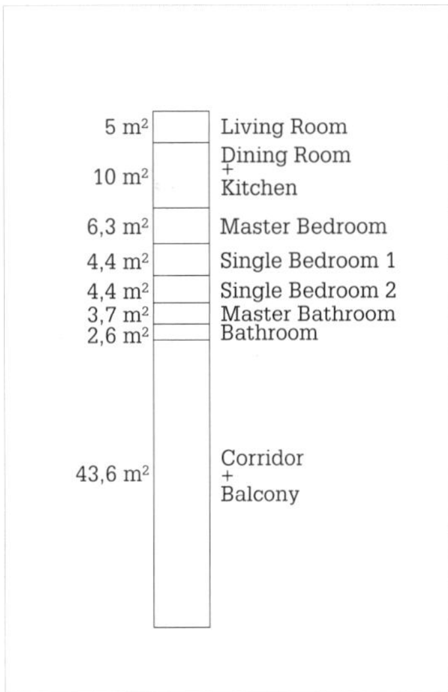

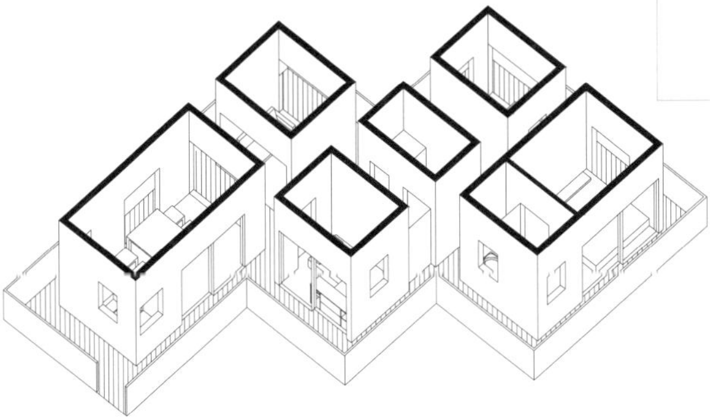

Apartment Layout, 1:200

More Outdoor Space: Seven Private Balconies

This apartment provides a private balcony for all rooms, giving each room additional space for activities. While the bathrooms have additional space for drying laundry, other rooms such as the bedrooms have their own extensions for leisure, such as sunbathing, or reading outside. The kitchen and dining room, which are combined, have an outdoor space sufficient for barbecuing or having small social gatherings. Together, the balconies provide access to multiple impressive views and create more opportunities for privacy, in addition to enhancing each room so that it can better serve its specific function.

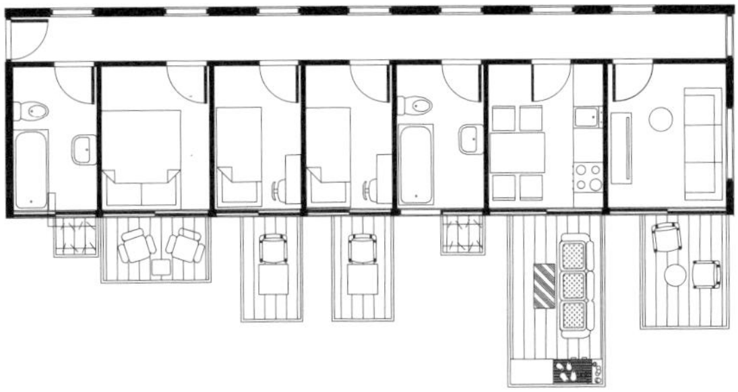

7,8 m²	Living Room
10,9 m²	Dining Room + Kitchen
5,4 m²	Master Bedroom
4,6 m²	Single Bedroom 1
4,6 m²	Single Bedroom 2
5,6 m²	Master Bathroom
5,7 m²	Bathroom
15,4 m²	Corridor
20 m²	Balcony

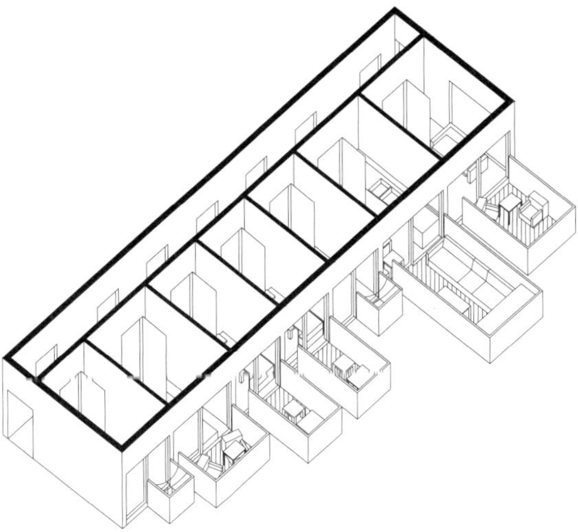

Apartment Layout, 1:200

Exclusive Bathrooms: Bathing in Nature

This apartment facilitates natural wellness and cleansing routines by making the bathroom—or bathing lounge—the heart of the interior, where it is directly accessible from all rooms. In Chinese philosophy, humankind and nature can exist in a harmonious balance. The bathing lounge incorporates principles of Feng Shui in its organization to bring the dweller into a state of tranquillity. Natural ventilation is integrated into all of the rooms, with enhanced ventilation in the bathroom. The bathroom is also combined with an outdoor space in the form of a wooden deck. Bamboo plants placed on the deck provide shade from direct sunlight and create privacy. This outdoor space has a leisure-like atmosphere, evocative of a natural hot spring, where one can bathe and replenish a sense of wellness in a natural setting. Each room looks out on natural features of the balcony and thus embodies the desire of a living in nature. The bathroom also provides additional space for laundry.

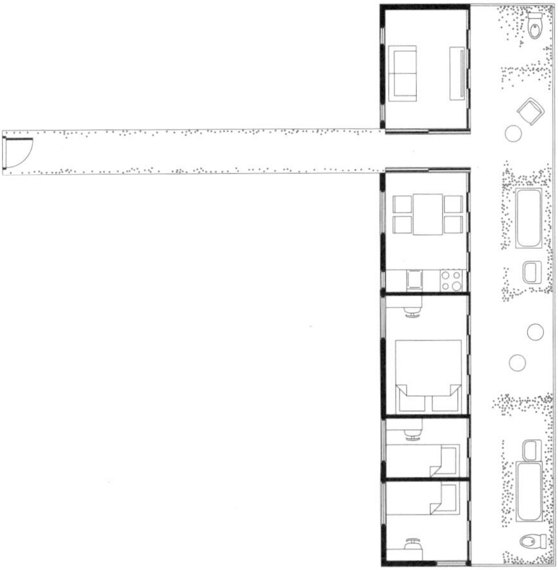

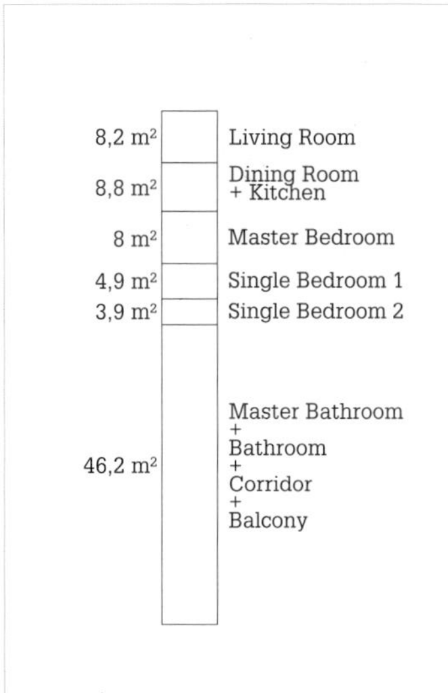

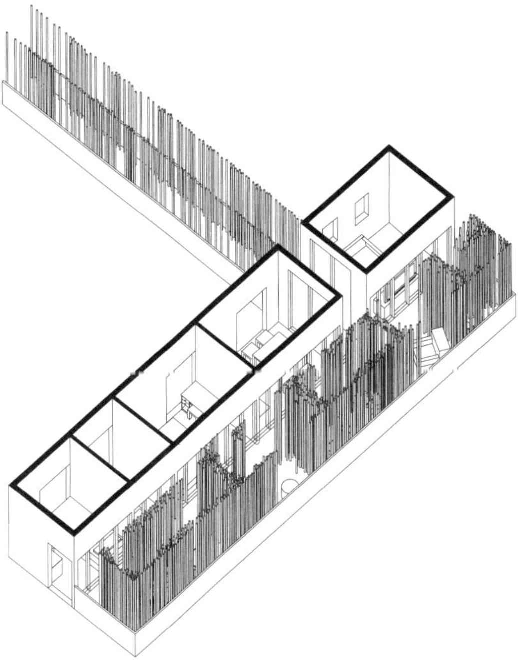

Apartment Layout, 1:200

Exclusive Bathrooms: Swimming around the House

Defying expectations for an 80 m^2 home, this apartment provides a swimming pool that surrounds all rooms, allowing occupants to swim around the house. The balcony space merges with the bathtub and becomes one giant heated pool of about 30 m^2. Windows function simultaneously as doors that give each room direct access to the pool. A small wooden deck connects the rooms at each side of the apartment, thus functioning as open corridors.

To conserve water, pool water is recycled, which involves treating the water to allow it to re-enter the pool or using it to flush toilets, so that it re-enters the public water system. The walls and ceilings of the apartment hold water tanks to store grey water. The water-filled walls also cool down the apartment, lowering energy costs typically spent on air conditioning.

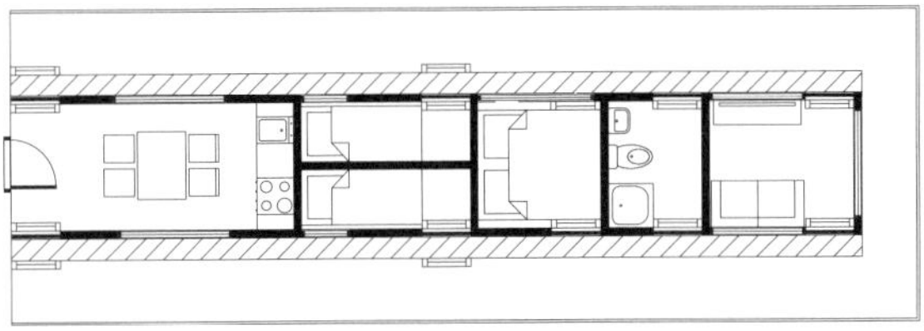

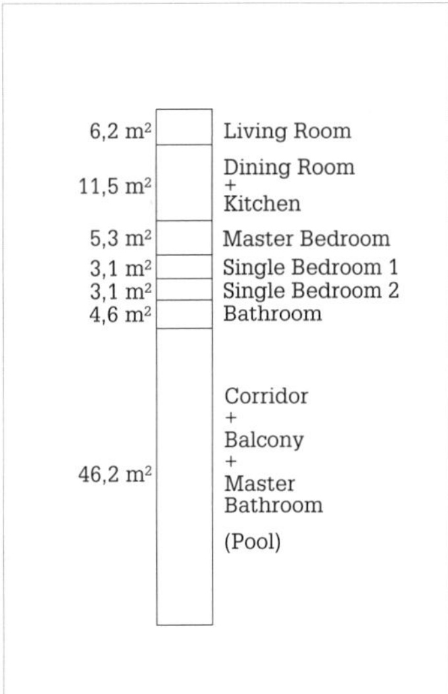

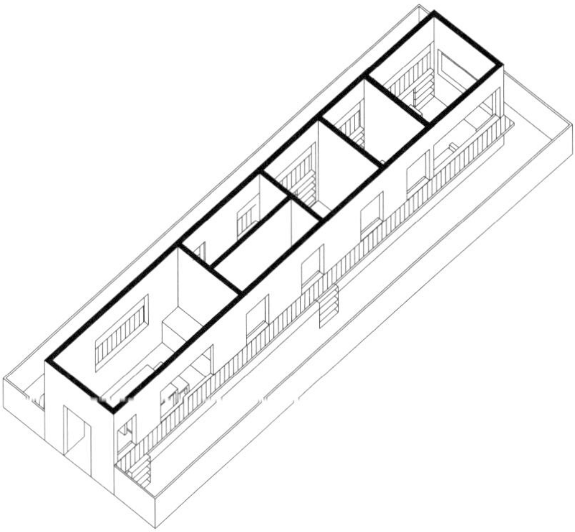

Apartment Layout, 1:200

Dreamy Bedrooms: Sleeping under the Stars

This apartment design was developed from the idea that each bedroom could have maximized views, including beautiful sky views. All bedrooms are completely surrounded by glass curtain walls and topped by a glass ceiling that is slightly angled to allow rainwater to drip to the ground. Bedrooms are endowed with full panoramic views and views of the starry sky at night. This configuration also increases natural ventilation and natural light.

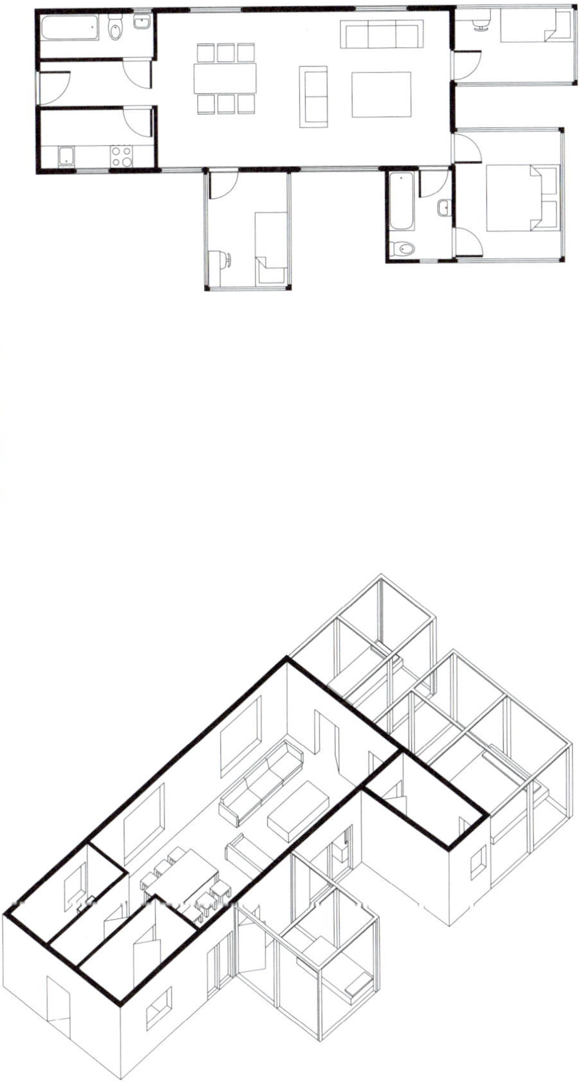

Apartment Layout, 1:200

Dreamy Bedrooms: Sleeping on Top of Each Other

This rectangular apartment layout minimizes the size of the bedrooms to the dimensions of the beds, allowing the balcony and living room to gain additional floor area. The bed of the master bedroom is stacked on top of two single beds. Bedrooms are condensed into cosy capsules, separated by a sound-proofed wall to ensure privacy. The capsules are equipped with a dimmable light system, a sound system, a television, and other small features such as a folding table and cup holders.

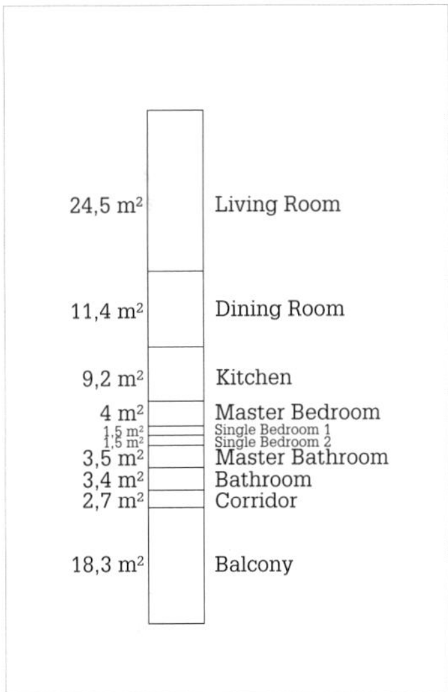

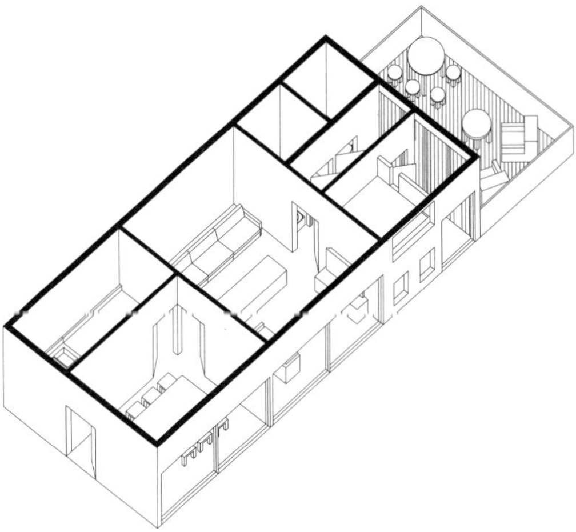

Apartment Layout, 1:200

Smart Connecting: Sky Bridges

In this configuration, all rooms are connected by small outdoor passageways, which function as hybrid balconies and corridors. Turning corridors into balcony spaces increases the surface area of the façade and maximizes natural ventilation and daylight in each room. The apartment becomes a complex, atom-like structure with enhanced privacy, better natural ventilation, and customized views in each of the rooms. The configuration looks hermetic and monolithic, with small window openings on multiple sides of all rooms.

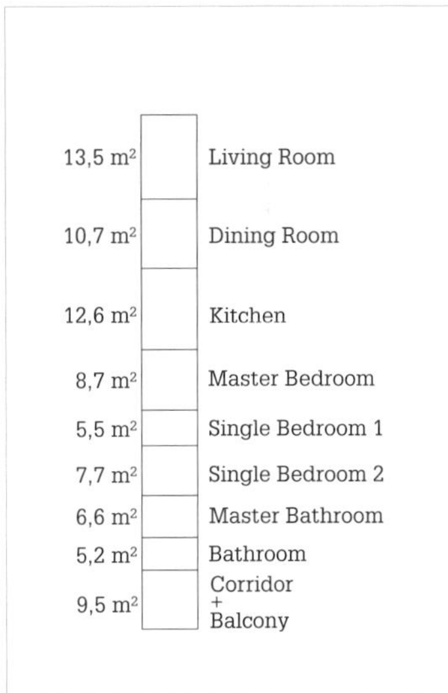

Apartment Layout, 1:200

Smart connecting: Flexible space

What if the corridor were completely eliminated? Without corridors, this apartment layout lends itself to greater flexibility, adapting to different activities by enabling different configurations of space. The interior is divided evenly into a set of sixteen units, each with an area of 5 m^2, that can be separated and closed off by curtain walls that can also dampen sound. Although the kitchen, bathrooms, and toilets are fixed in place, there are still multiple ways to convert the space. The apartment becomes a giant loft where inhabitants can experience varying degrees of openness and enclosure.

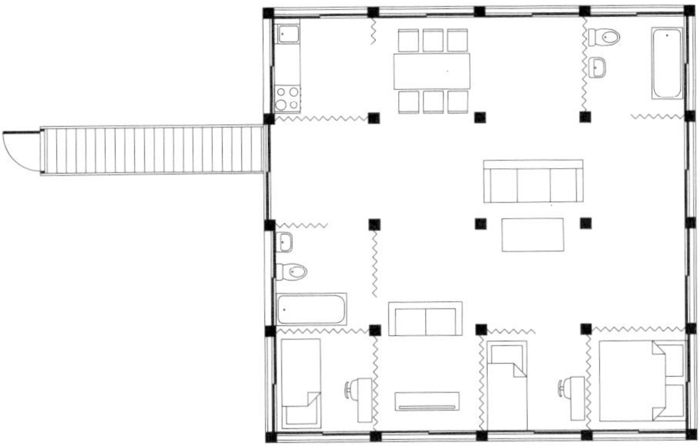

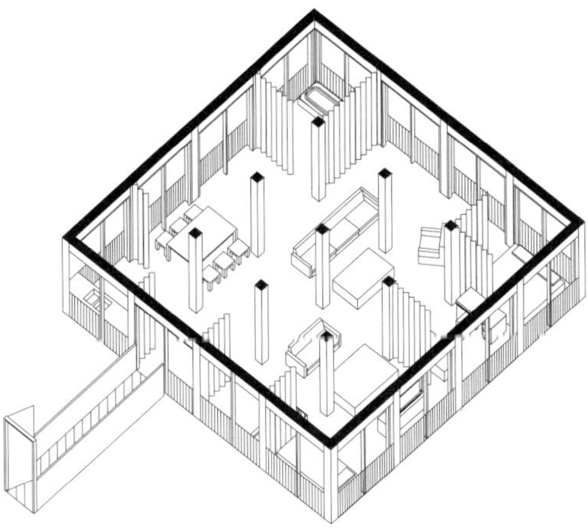

Apartment Layout, 1:200

High-Class Dining: Dining with Panoramic Views

Dining with a great view is typically an exclusive experience, reserved only for top restaurants in Hong Kong. To enable panoramic-view dining in the space of the apartment, this layout isolates the dining room from the other rooms. An L- shaped corridor gives access to all the rooms along one side of the apartment, with the living room at its corner end leading finally to the sequestered dining room. This arrangement frees up the most amount of surface area around the perimeter of the dining room, which is glazed with glass curtain walls. The curtain wall is optimized for high thermal performance and protection against extreme weather conditions such as strong winds or heavy rains.

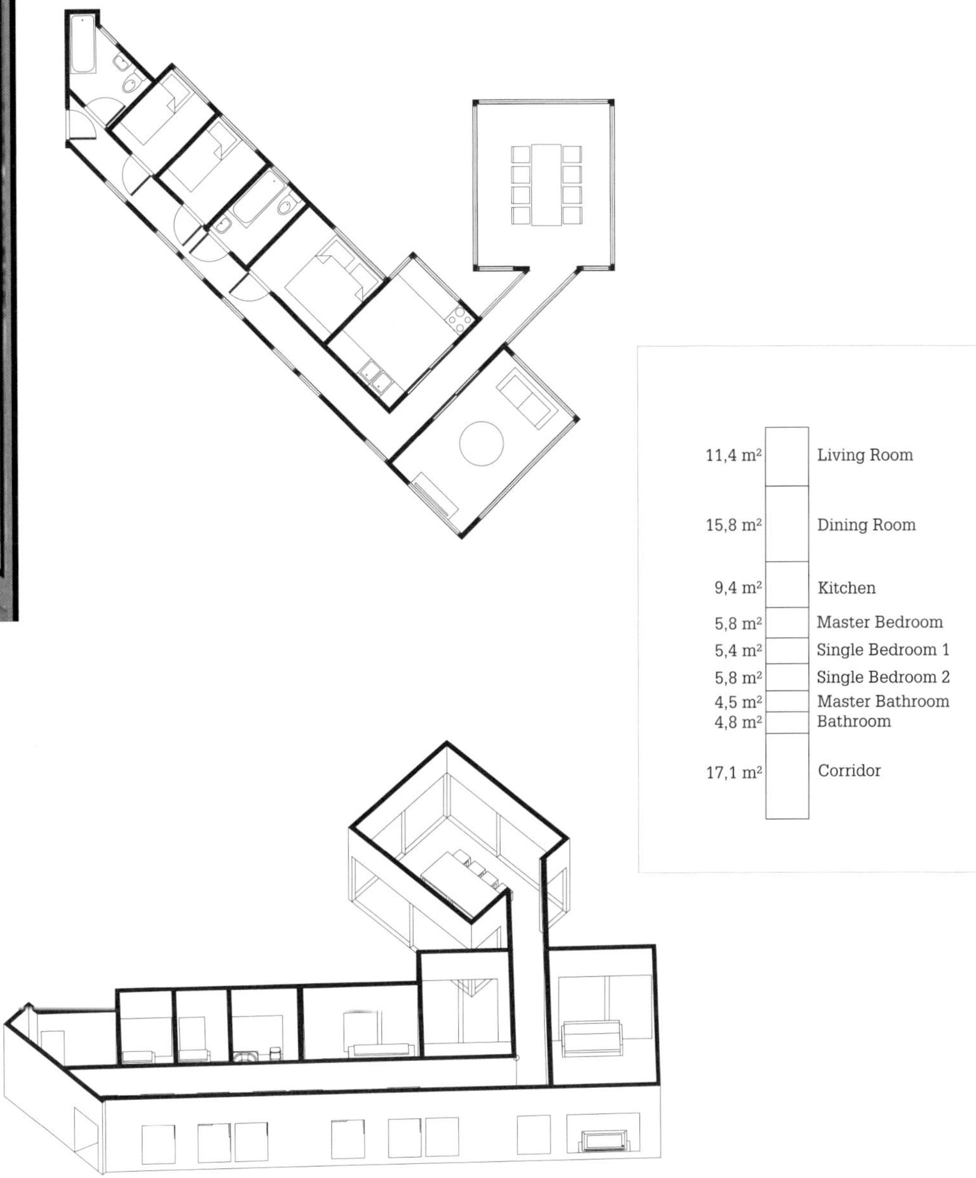

Apartment Layout, 1:200

High-Class Dining: Picnicking Sky-High

For this apartment organization, picnicking is reintroduced into the urban setting. The dining room is merged with the balcony space, creating the perfect area for socializing and getting together in a fresh-air environment. This apartment facilitates two types of outdoor dining. The balcony attached to the kitchen becomes the main area for breakfast, lunch, and dinner, while the balcony extending from the living room functions as a space to enjoy smaller snacks and tea. Both picnic areas are covered with soft, green flooring made from grass and moss. This apartment creates pleasurable outdoor dining experiences with great views and an intimate atmosphere, alleviating the current need to escape to the few neighbourhood parks in the city

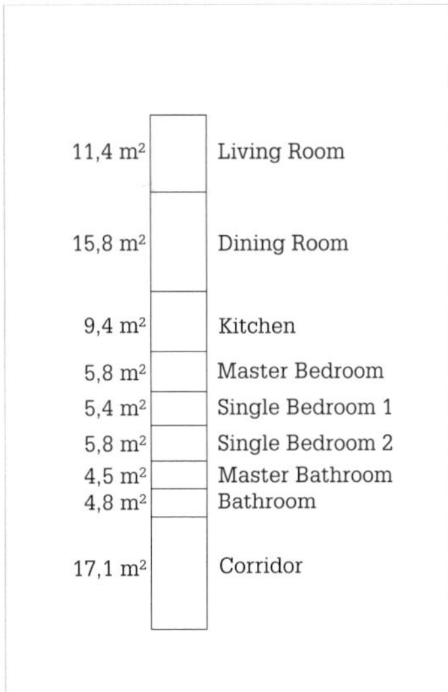

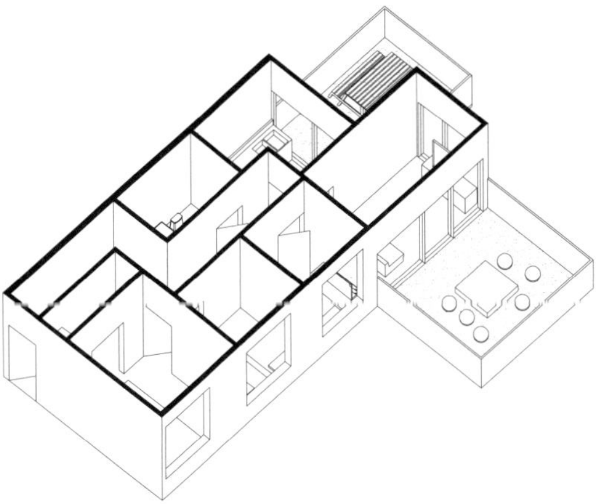

Apartment Layout, 1:200

Chef's Special: Enjoying Home-Grown Food

This apartment design envisions a home covered by a 'green skin', a feature that enables dwellers to do some gardening and grow their own vegetables, fruits, and herbs. With both indoor and outdoor growing areas, leafy vegetables such as lettuce and kale or herbs such as oregano, basil, or mint can be planted indoors, as they need less sunlight, while fruiting vegetables such as tomatoes or bell peppers could be grown outside, where they can receive direct sunlight. The apartment becomes a green oasis, a small-scale farm producing just enough food for a household of two adults and two children.

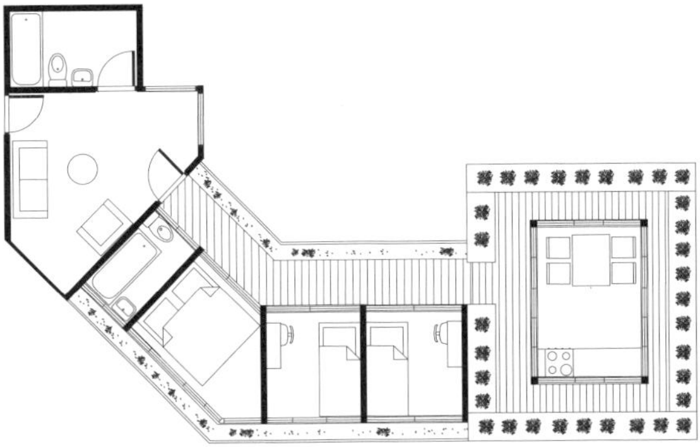

10,2 m²	Living Room
25,6 m²	Dining Room + Balconies
7,7 m²	Kitchen
9 m²	Master Bedroom
4,8 m²	Single Bedroom 1
5,2 m²	Single Bedroom 2
2,8 m²	Master Bathroom
5 m²	Bathroom
9,5 m²	Corridor

Apartment Layout, 1:200

Chef's Special: Cooking with a Natural Breeze

In this layout, activities such as cooking and dining can extend onto the balcony and corridor space. This hybrid living space occupies almost a quarter of the floor area, making the apartment an optimal site for enjoying the daily activities of cooking and eating in an environment enriched with great views, sufficient ventilation, and ample natural light. The large, multipurpose living room is connected on one side to the bedrooms, which are positioned to catch most of the views and the sunlight from the open space. Activities relating to cooking and dining take place in the open centre of the apartment and are thus perceived as integral to family life.

15,1 m²	Living Room
19,2 m²	Dining Room + Kitchen + Corridor + Balconies
10,5 m²	Master Bedroom
8,4 m²	Single Bedroom 1
8,4 m²	Single Bedroom 2
7,4 m²	Master Bathroom
5,4 m²	Bathroom
5,6 m²	Corridor

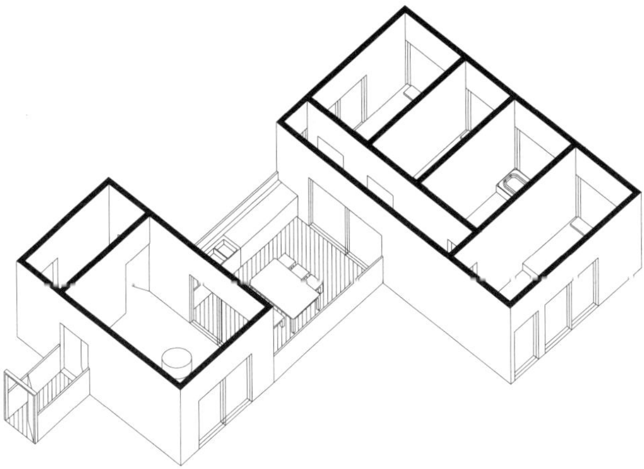

Apartment Layout, 1:200

Extraordinary Living: The Observatory

An apartment with a circular floor plan and a domed roof has the advantage of structural stability without the need for interior walls, allowing for an essentially panoramic view of the entire space of the apartment. Privacy would have to be created by introducing additional features.
Because of its structural soundness, this circular structure can be constructed out of lightweight materials, keeping construction costs at a minimum. The dome allows air to circulate more freely around the home, which increases natural ventilation while mitigating wind pressure. Temperature is maintained more consistently in the open space of the apartment, which allows for more efficient heating and cooling and less energy consumption by air conditioners. Another advantage is that the circular plan creates a spacious, open interior completely surrounded by windows. With a circular organization, one can easily change the room's layout according to different desires and activities, or in response to a growing or shrinking family. The shape redefines the home as a place where all activities and functions are bound together with unusual intimacy, which could elicit creative responses depending on the dynamic of the occupants.

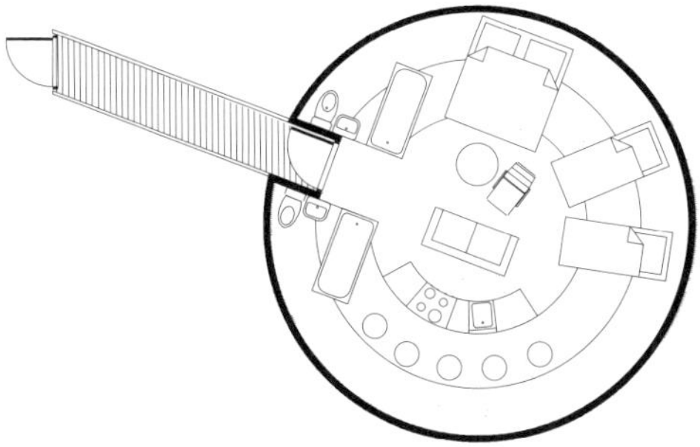

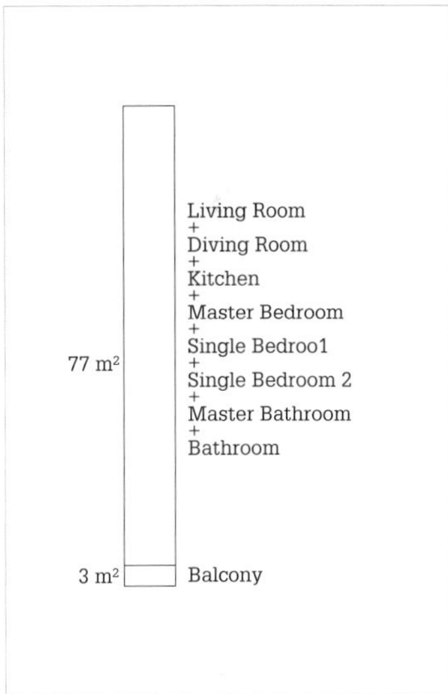

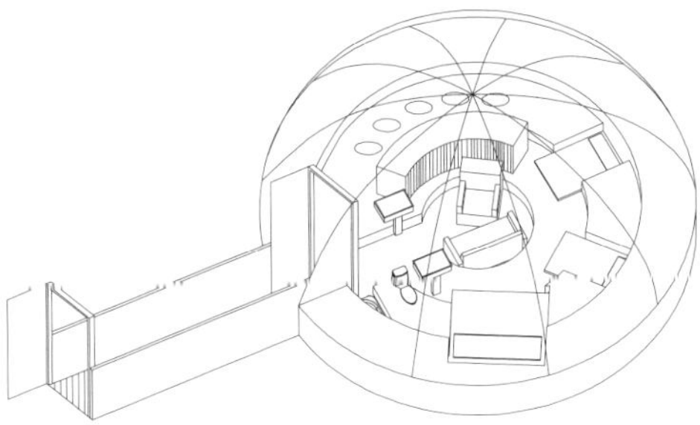

Apartment Layout, 1:200

Extraordinary Living: Separated Living Activities

While open space has its advantages, so does fragmented space, which provides distinct rooms for each individual activity, such as reading, listening to music, playing the piano, studying, watching television, dining, sleeping, cooking, bathing, washing, or fitness. This fragmented arrangement maximizes privacy and allows for different activities to take place at the same time, with minimal interference and thus greater focus, presence, and efficiency.

5,6 m²	Music Room
4,2 m²	Yoga Room
3,2 m²	Indoor Bike Room
5,2 m²	Reading Room
4 m²	Study Room
6 m²	TV Room
1,6 m²	Washing Machine Room
4,5 m²	Dining Room
4,5 m²	Kitchen
6 m²	Master Bedroom
4,2 m²	Single Bedroom 1
4,2 m²	Single Bedroom 2
5,5 m²	Master Bathroom
4,3 m²	Bathroom
13,8 m²	Corridor
3,2 m²	Balcony

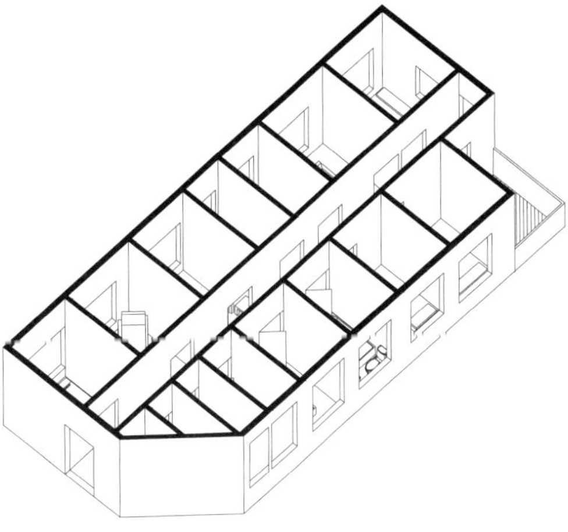

Apartment Layout, 1:200

Space for Domestic Help: The Maid's Private Paradise

How can an 80 m^2 apartment be organized in such a way that domestic workers and the families that employ them are given the maximum amount of privacy to foster a healthy sense of independence from each other? One approach is to divide the apartment into two compartments, each with its own entrance. Domestic workers would thus have their own domains, composed of a kitchen, a storage space, a bedroom, and a bathroom, all organized within 22 m^2 of space. All rooms in this compartment are interconnected by sliding doors, to enable flexible circulation and improve convenience while supporting increased privacy. The remaining space, divided into three bedrooms, a combined living and dining room, and a bathroom, would be designated for the family. All bedrooms in this apartment open onto the outdoor balcony-corridor through glass doors that allow for sufficient sunlight and good views.

26,3 m²	Living Room + Dining Room
5,5 m²	Kitchen
3,7 m²	Storage
7,4 m²	Maid Bedroom
9,8 m²	Master Bedroom
6,9 m²	Single Bedroom 1
6,9 m²	Single Bedroom 2
3,9 m²	Maid's Bathroom
3,9 m²	Bathroom
5,7 m²	Balcony + Corridor

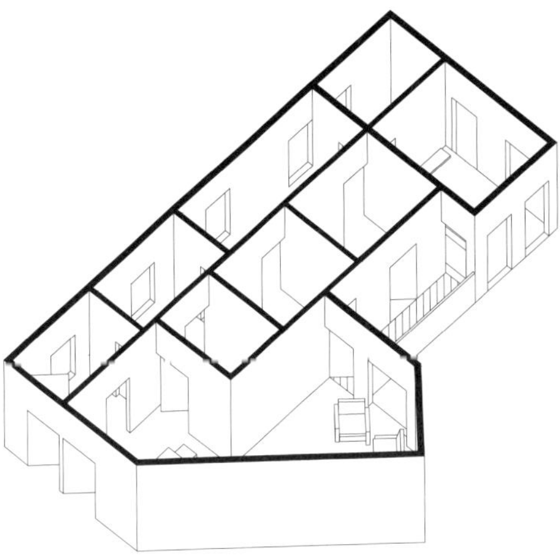

Apartment Layout, 1:200

Space for Domestic Help: Meet the Maid Everywhere

Another way of providing a more comfortable sense of home for domestic workers is to essentially accept them as members of the family. This extension of family bonds is already a commonly practiced concept. However, the typical apartment layout to support it has not yet evolved. By combining living, dining, and cooking areas with the maid's room, this rather conventional apartment shape puts the maid literally in the centre of the home and family life.

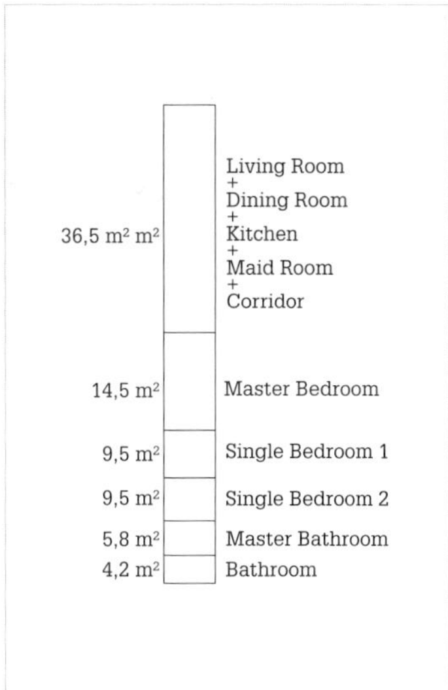

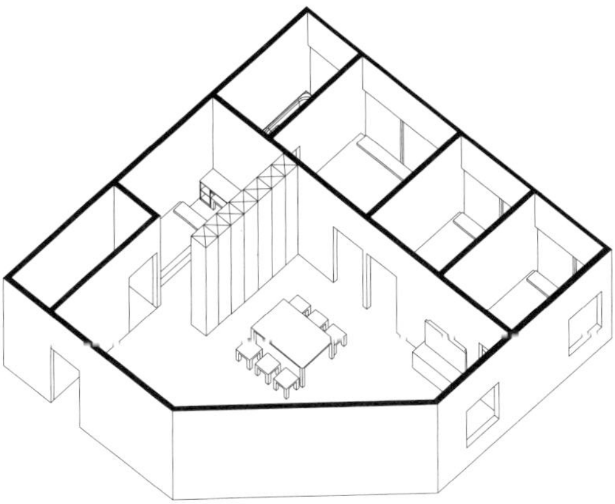

Apartment Layout, 1:200

More Storage: The Central Super Store

This apartment responds to a desire for extra storage space consolidated into a single room. This apartment has a large storage room at the entrance of the apartment. It is the biggest room, and it also absorbs the functions and fixtures of the kitchen and dining room. A compact cooking island and a large dining table for six to eight people is surrounded by a comprehensive system of cupboards with roll out shelves, racks, and variously sized cabinets, which turn the room into an organized super store.

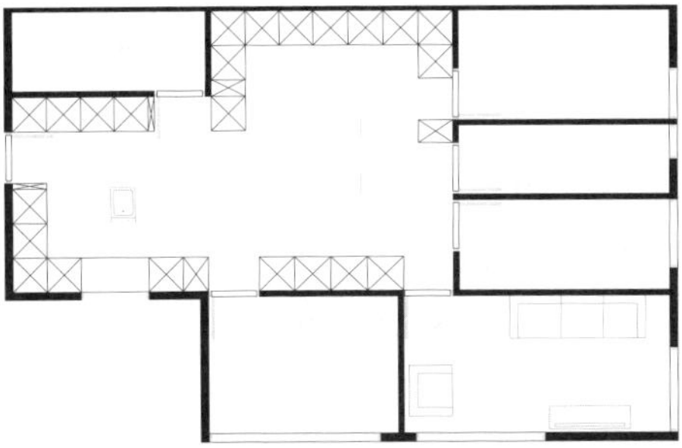

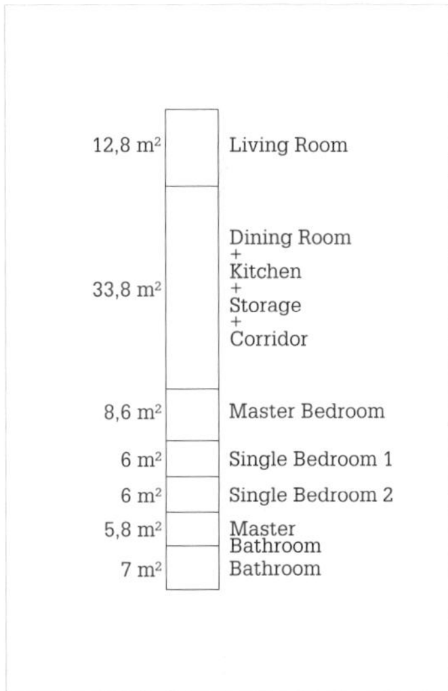

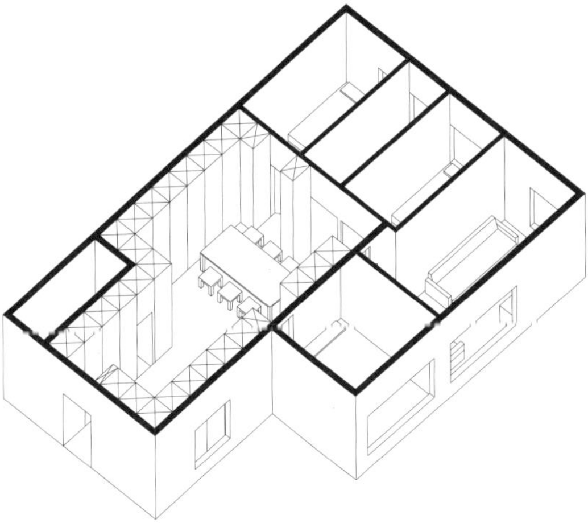

Apartment Layout, 1:200

More Storage: Hiding Belongings in the Walls

This apartment offers hidden storage by using smart walls that can hide furniture and other belongings. The entire apartment takes on the form of a huge walk-in closet, without feeling claustrophobic. These camouflaged storage spaces allow occupants to maintain a sense of openness and order in the living space. By storing infrequently used items in the surrounding walls of each room and using customized, multipurpose furniture that combines storage with multiple functions into one module, one can make more efficient use of the space one has.

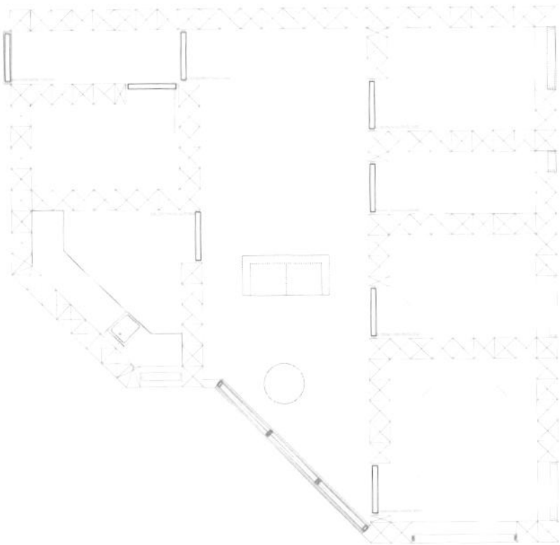

29,8 m²	Living Room + Dining Room + Corridor + Storage
8,9 m²	Kitchen+Storage
13 m²	Master Bedroom+Storage
8,1 m²	Single Bedroom 1+ Storage
8,1 m²	Single Bedroom 2 + Storage
4,2 m²	Master Bathroom + Storage
7,9 m²	Bathroom + Storage

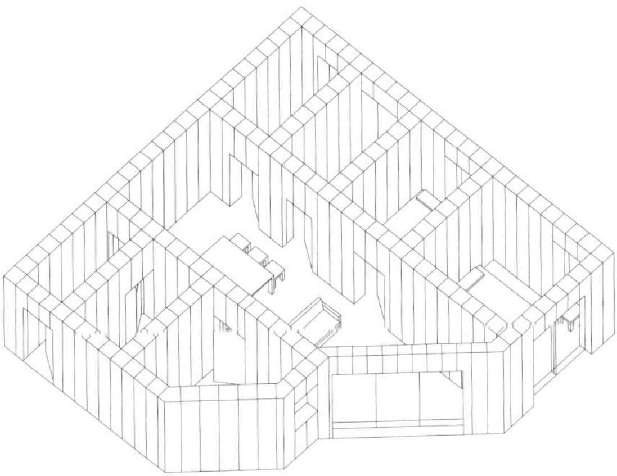

Apartment Layout, 1:200

Top Study Conditions: Books Everywhere

This apartment layout is designed for people who enjoy curling up with a good book. It celebrates the pursuit of enrichment through reading by displaying books in a library-like setting. A good library is defined by not just its books but also its ability to create cosy spaces for relaxation and the absorption and contemplation of knowledge. In this apartment, the corridor is expanded to encompass activities such as reading and studying. It is organized into a rectangular shape, to which other rooms are docked. The library becomes the central spine of the apartment. Every room has direct access to the library, boosting the prominence of reading in the home and making it an easier and more fulfilling source of pleasure.

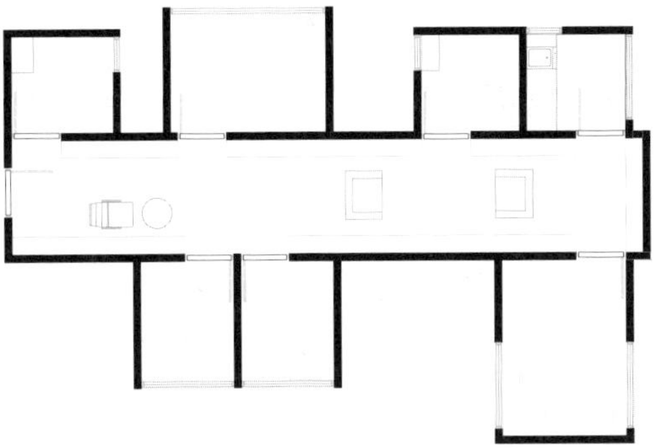

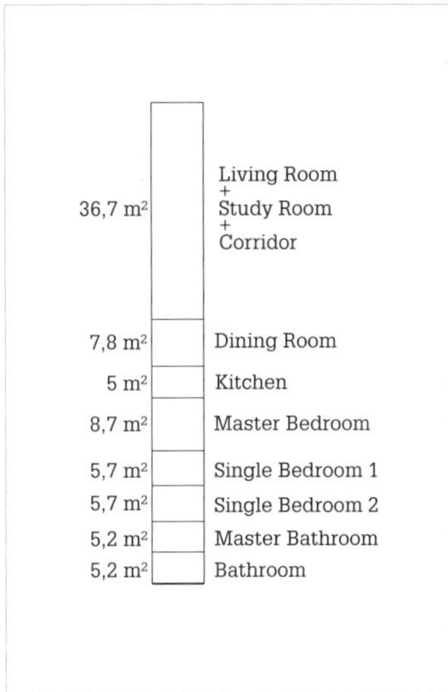

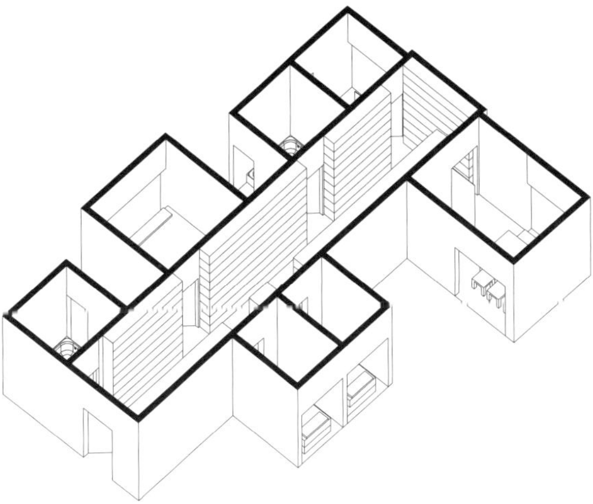

Apartment Layout, 1:200

Top Study Conditions: Secluded and Quiet Studying

A study room needs to have a tranquil atmosphere, one that is quiet yet also imbued with the right level of stimulation, in order to support certain learning processes. This apartment configuration creates ideal conditions for studying by providing a silent space with panoramic views and maximized daylight. The large space of the study room, which is made the centre of the home, is isolated from other functions of the apartment. Connected through a long corridor, the study room functions as a retreat, a satellite space with views on all sides.

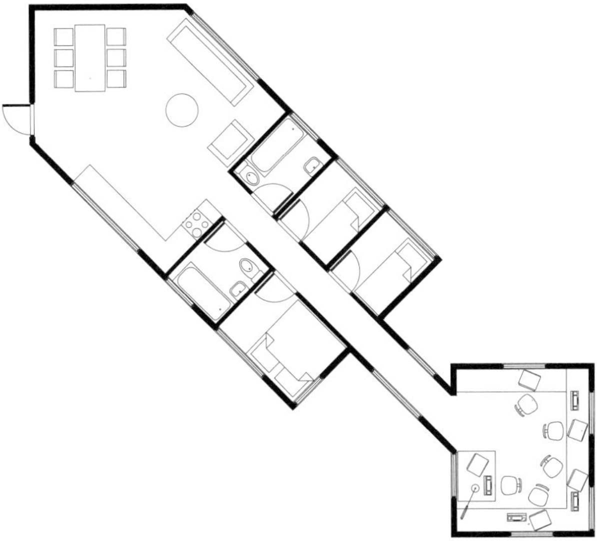

31 m²	Living Room + Dining Room + Kitchen
17,4 m²	Study Room
6,5 m²	Master Bedroom
4,4 m²	Single Bedroom 1
4,4 m²	Single Bedroom 2
4,4 m²	Master Bathroom
4,2 m²	Bathroom
7,7 m²	Corridor

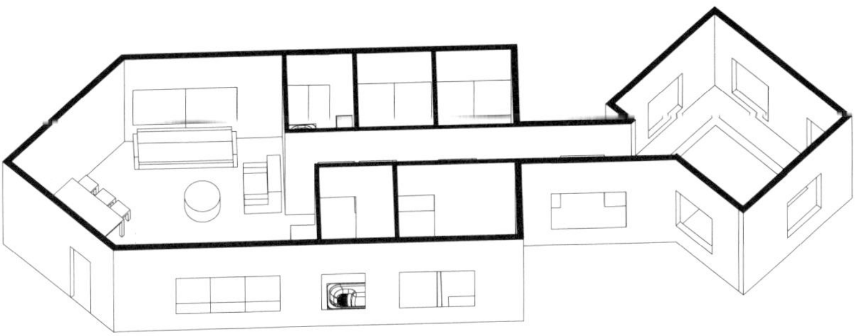

Apartment Layout, 1:200

In order to understand the qualitative differences between these specialized apartments and typical Hong Kong apartments, a precise scoring system is necessary. Comparing apartment layouts in a systematic way will allow us to recognize the limitations of their designs and consider modifications for further improvement.

Rather than continuing to place disproportionate emphasis on cost and location, as is done in the current real estate market, our scoring system was developed with consideration for more comprehensive qualifying criteria.

Tower Scoring System - Measuring Apartment Qualities

Text by Tihamér Salij

Additional research by Tihamér Salij, Arend van Waart, Sander Mulders

Drawing by The Why Factory: Cheng Pok Him BOB

Scoring system as developed during The Why Factory's 'Hong Kong Tower Revolution' studio at the Department of Architecture (Architecture and Urban Design III, ARCH 5001) at the Hong Kong University, Fall 2013

Studio Tutors: Prof. Winy Maas and Tihamér Salij with Sander Mulders and Arend van Waart
Students: Au Wing Yi, Chak Tsz Kin, Chan Chung Man, Chan Ian Yin Yan, Chan Pui Yin, Chau Shek Lun, Cheng Ching, Ip Kai Hong, Liu Kemeng, Mok Wang Chee, Tang Ho Yin, Kong Ho Ching, Kwok Ka Ching, Lau Xin Yee, Lee Kin Wai, Li Mei Yu, Lung Man Ching, Ma Ching Yi, Suen Wing Yin, Sze Ivy, Sze Ying Ying, Yeung Cho Yui, Yeung Ho Man

Examining Factors

Each room of the apartment was evaluated in terms of factors commonly used to calculate sales and rental prices. Aside from land value, construction costs, and location, six other qualitative factors determine the square-meter price of an apartment: (1) view, (2) direct light (sunlight), (3) indirect light (daylight), (4) ventilation, (5) room efficiency and size, and (6) quality of accessible outdoor space, typically in the form of a balcony. Each room or functional area of an apartment was measured in terms of its contribution to the provision of these six factors. The scores were added up to a total average score, which became an index for judging how the apartment and the tower performed in comparison with the standard Hong Kong apartment and residential tower. Scores above the benchmark score of 100 indicated an improvement to the typical apartment and residential tower, while scores below 100 indicated a decrease in quality in terms of the six qualitative factors.

View

Besides land price, location, and proximity to MTR stations, shops, and schools, the view from an apartment contributes significantly to its value. There is a remarkable difference in price between apartments with sea views, city views, and mountain views. The price per square meter of an apartment with a sea view, compared to a similar apartment with a mountain view, is easily tripled or quadrupled. Sky views are currently the most valued, followed by sea views and mountain views. Their values are precisely calculated, taking the quality of the view into consideration. Any room in the apartment with a mountain, sea, or sky view and a viewing angle of 20 degrees or above is boosted in value. Units with long-distance views score higher than units with short-distance views. The viewing distance of units within the same building facing different orientations are compared.

Under Building Planning Regulation Cap.123 Clause 31(1)d, no part of the building should have a viewing distance under 15 meters. The longer the viewing distance, the higher the score is. Views accessible from outdoor spaces (such as balconies and rooftops), living rooms, bedrooms, and dining rooms yield higher scores, while views provided in bathrooms and kitchens yield lower scores.

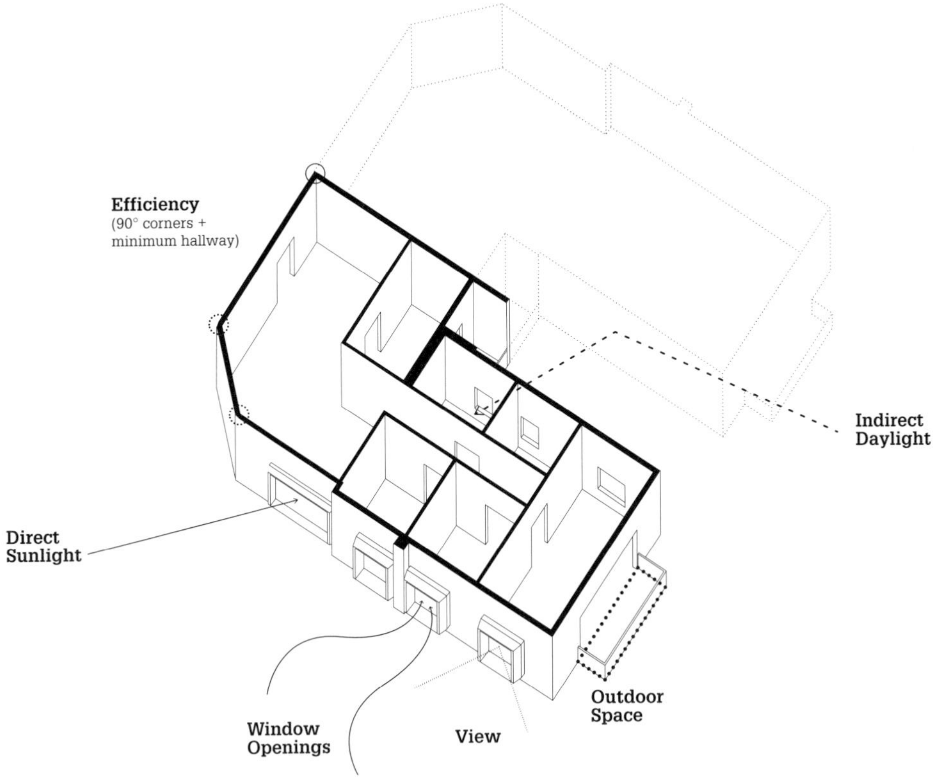

Direct Light (Sunlight)

Sunlight from the south is the most favoured kind of light in Hong Kong. In the summer, direct sunlight is less desirable because of the heat it brings with it; conversely, in winter, direct sunlight helps raise the indoor temperature. Rooms and functions are arranged according to users' needs and preferences for direct sunlight with respect to season and exposure time.

Indirect Light (Daylight)

Indirect sunlight, or daylight, refers to the amount of light that reflects off neighbouring surfaces and enters into the apartment unit within three deflections. Natural light is provided this way, without the accompanying heat of direct sunlight, therefore the effect of daylight on the temperature of interior spaces is considered negligible. The above table indicates the preferred levels of daylight, represented by degrees of brightness, measured by percentage, in each room or area. For example, the balcony is prioritized after the living room and dining room, where it is preferred to have an indirect sunlight level of over 50 percent.

Natural Ventilation

Increased natural ventilation through window openings adds to the value of a Hong Kong apartment. The more window openings an apartment has, the higher its score. In our scoring system, equal value is given to ventilation in all rooms except the storage space, which does not need an openable window for ventilation. Under Building Planning Regulation Cap.123 Clause 31, aggregate window area must total to at least 6.25 percent of the internal floor area of the room. Windows must be able to be opened to provide natural ventilation.

Efficiency

Efficiency here is measured as the amount of floor area that can be used for living activities as opposed to circulation. Apartment units with more floor area delimited by 90-degree corners are considered more efficient, as more 90-degree corners indicate more usable space and less transitional space, usually articulated as hallways and corridors. In theory, these circulation features detract from floor area that could be used for more versatile living spaces, without adding to the quality of living.

Generally, it is more efficient to have apartment units without separate hallways, to minimize the time and space devoted to facilitating transition from room to room. For instance, if the living room is positioned in the centre of the flat, hallways are not necessary for the transition from room to room. This layout would increase the percentage of usable area in the apartment and thereby enhance the efficiency of the layout.

Accessible Outdoor Space

Access to private outdoor space is always a selling point for any real estate development in Hong Kong. Balconies, roof terraces, and utility platforms that are directly accessible from the apartment unit all add value to the apartment design and enhance its score. Rooftops from neighbouring units will also increase the score, if there is direct access to them from the apartment. In addition to the presence of balconies, roof terraces, and utility platforms, qualities such as the view and light provided by these outdoor spaces are factored into the calculation of scores.

Scoring Location

To evaluate how proposed apartments compare with apartments in a typical residential tower, they will be compared against the apartment units of a specific, representative standard tower. This benchmark tower occupies a 40-by-45-metre plot of land in North Point, Hong Kong Island. This plot of land will also serve as the hypothetical site for the proposed towers.

North Point is a mixed-use urban area in the Eastern District of Hong Kong. It is the northernmost point of Hong Kong Island, adjacent to Causeway Bay and Quarry Bay, and its waterfront looks out to Kowloon Bay. Fortress Hill, a developed, hilly area to the west of the Causeway Bay Community Centre, occupies the western end of the North Point area.

The 1,800 m^2 site is situated on relatively flat ground, with sloping mountains on the south side and Victoria Harbour to the northeast. It is currently zoned as 'commercial and residential' (C/R), with a building height limitation of 110 to 120 metres, and in some instances up to 140 metres, depending on restrictions defined by specific land leases. The maximum plot ratio in North Point is set to 10.

North Point lacks large-scale shopping malls, but the area is teeming with supermarkets, restaurants, wet markets selling meat and produce, and small shops that offer items at affordable prices, making this area popular among local Chinese. Victoria Park, the largest park in Hong Kong, is within a short distance, with the northeast entrance to the park located at Tin Hau and the new central branch of the public library also located in the vicinity.
The main streets surrounding this site are Marble Road and King's Road, both of which are serviced by tram rail. Marble Road hosts a busy street market, which occasionally brings in heavy pedestrian traffic. North Point is scattered with local secondary schools. A Chinese International School and a Hong Kong Japanese School are also located in this area, making it appealing to international citizens. Apartments here have views of the sea, the mountains, and sometimes both, depending on their orientation.

How Does the Uniform Residential Tower with Typical Apartments Score?

Text by Tihamér Salij

Drawings by The Why Factory: Cheng Pok Him BOB, Claudia Mainardi, Sylwia Franczak

Image illustrated by The Why Factory: Claudia Mainardi

The Standard Tower with Typical Apartments

The benchmark tower located in North Point contains 192 apartment units, each with an area of 80 m^2. With 24 floors, the tower reaches a height of 84 metres on a plot with the size of 1,800 m^2. It has a plot ratio of 9.87, which is slightly less than the maximum plot ratio for this area.

Every floor of the tower is essentially identical, with eight apartment units on each floor. As is typical in a standard Hong Kong housing tower, the floor plans of the units are generated from a single prototype that is mirrored and flipped around the central core.

This tower is set as a benchmark, with a total score of 100 points. Certain individual apartment units within this standard tower score higher than others. The top scoring apartments in this tower, located on the 23rd and 24th floors, score as high as 128. Some of the north-facing apartments have sea views, contributing to higher scores. Only the apartments on the highest floor have access to the open space of the rooftop, which has the size of about 640 m^2.

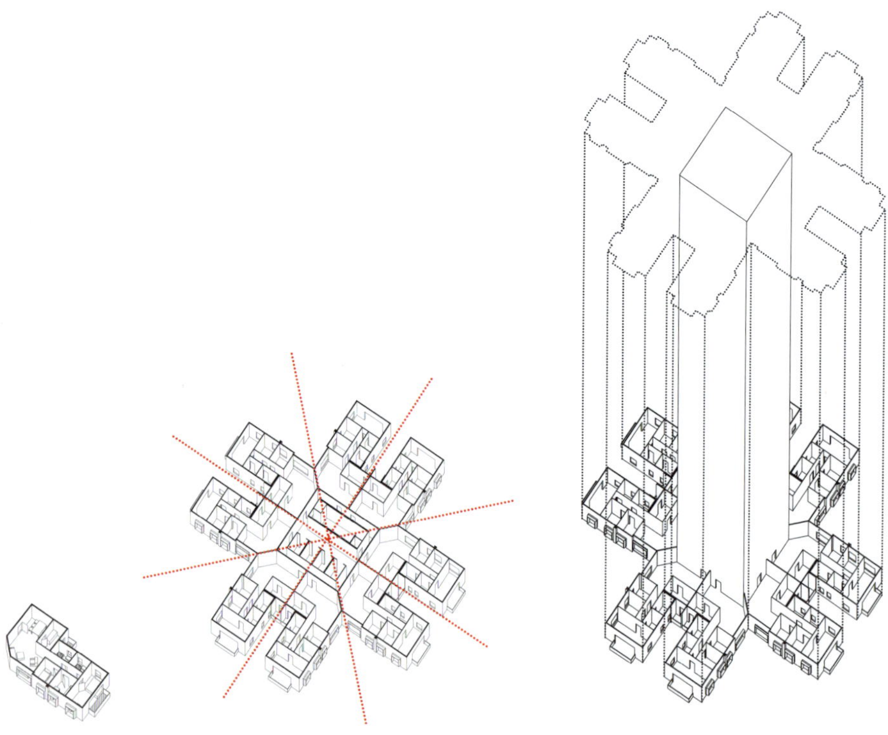

Average-scoring units are exemplified by the mountain-view apartments located on the 15th, 16th, and 17th floors. The lowest scoring apartments, with 85 points, are located on the first and seventh floors, scoring poorly due to their limited city views and minimal levels of sunlight.

On average, the uniform tower with typical apartments scores 44.41 points for view, 21.6 for light, 11.16 for ventilation, 22.52 for efficiency, and an abysmal 0.31 points for available accessible outdoor space. It has no great views, hardly any sky views, and no extra study spaces or storage spaces. Domestic workers living in these apartments are forced to sleep in very tiny spaces in the kitchen, as they have no decent or private spaces of their own.

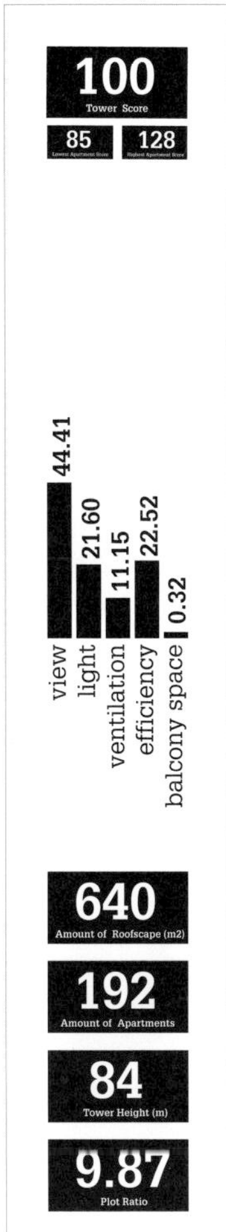

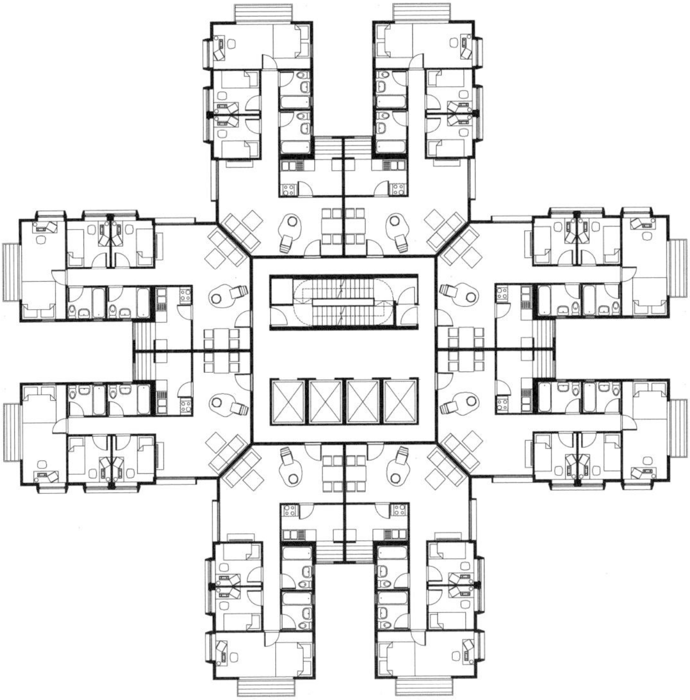

Tower floor plan, 1:400

How Do Uniform Towers with Specialized Apartments Score?

Text by Tihamér Salij

Drawings by Claudia Mainardi and Sylwia Franczak
Additional research by Tihamér Salij and Arend van Waart

Apartment typologies used for the tower configurations are based on work from The Why Factory's "Hong Kong Tower Revolution" studio at the Department of Architecture at the Hong Kong University, during Fall 2013, and from The Why Factory's "Towers Beyond Extrusion" studio at the Department of Architecture at the Hong Kong University, during Fall 2014.

Hong Kong Tower Revolution, Architecture and Urban Design III (ARCH 5001), Hong Kong University.
Studio Tutors: Prof. Winy Maas and Tihamér Salij with Sander Mulders and Arend van Waart
Students: Au Wing Yi, Chak Tsz Kin, Chan Chung Man, Chan Ian Yin Yan, Chan Pui Yin, Chau Shek Lun, Cheng Ching, Ip Kai Hong, Liu Kemeng, Mok Wang Chee, Tang Ho Yin, Kong Ho Ching, Kwok Ka Ching, Lau Xin Yee, Lee Kin Wai, Li Mei Yu, Lung Man Ching, Ma Ching Yi, Suen Wing Yin, Sze Ivy, Sze Ying Ying, Yeung Cho Yui, Yeung Ho Man

Towers Beyond Extrusion, Architecture and Urban Design III (ARCH 5001), Hong Kong University
Studio Tutors: Prof. Winy Maas, Tihamér Salij, Martine Vledder with Donn Holohan
Students: Au Yeung Chun Yu JOEY, Chan Fong Tong FRED S, Cheng Pok Him BOB, Ching Ka Ho FRED, Henao Granda Jan Esteban, Ho Sheung Hay TERENCE, Hu Xiangdong HOCK, Ko Pak Kan ZETH, Li Zhixin ALLISON, Liu Chuen Yung VINCENT, Ma Yue, Qin Liting TING, Tang Tak Shing KELVIN, Wen Fan, Wu Yucong, Xie Junni, Ffion Zhang, Ho Yin SUNNY CHA, Sai Bond, Man Hei KENNIF, Han PAT

The extrusion of a simple floor plan is typically seen as the easiest way to build the maximum number of residential units on a small piece of land. Even Hong Kong's cultural and commercial high-rises, which can have exuberantly styled façades, often disguise this fundamentally conservative design concept motivated by the maximization of programme and the repetitive stacking of generic spaces. Time and again, developers of both private and public residential buildings have applied this formula of extrusion. Is there room for innovation and improvement within this constricting framework? If, for the time being, we have to accept this monotonous approach as the norm, what qualitative improvements are possible?

The specialized apartments generated through our design experiments not only explore specific ways to reorganize living space, but they also effectively improve qualities such as light, ventilation, efficiency, and access to outdoor space. That is to say, even if these specialized floor plans were subsumed by the development principles of cookie-cutter repetition, simple mirroring, and vertical extrusion, they may still make meaningful interventions to housing design and effectively improve the quality of life of Hong Kong residents. The question is, just how much variety, and what precise qualitative improvements, can be gained by these specialized apartment designs? Would towers developed from the uniform extrusion of these experimental typologies score higher when measured against the uniform tower with typical apartment layouts?

The Wrap-Around Balcony Tower

The tower composed of apartments surrounded by balcony space scores 76 points higher than the standard tower with typical apartment floor plans. Even when uniformly extruded into a tower, most of the wrap-around balcony apartments perform better than most of the typical apartments in the reference tower, in terms of the factors being evaluated. The top scoring apartment gains 216 points, whereas the lowest scoring apartment, with 160 points, still scores higher than the benchmark score of 100. Although the accessible rooftop area decreases from 640 m^2 to 460 m^2, the profusion of private balcony spaces with views compensate for the decrease in score caused by the reduction of rooftop space.
Even higher scores could be obtained by varying apartment sizes and connections to the core, which would improve light levels and increase the amount of accessible rooftop space. If open spaces are integrated and connected to form a continuous stream of alleys, this tower has the potential to cultivate a lively sense of neighbourhood, redolent of a traditional hutong.

176
Tower Score

160 Lowest Apartment Score | **216** Highest Apartment Score

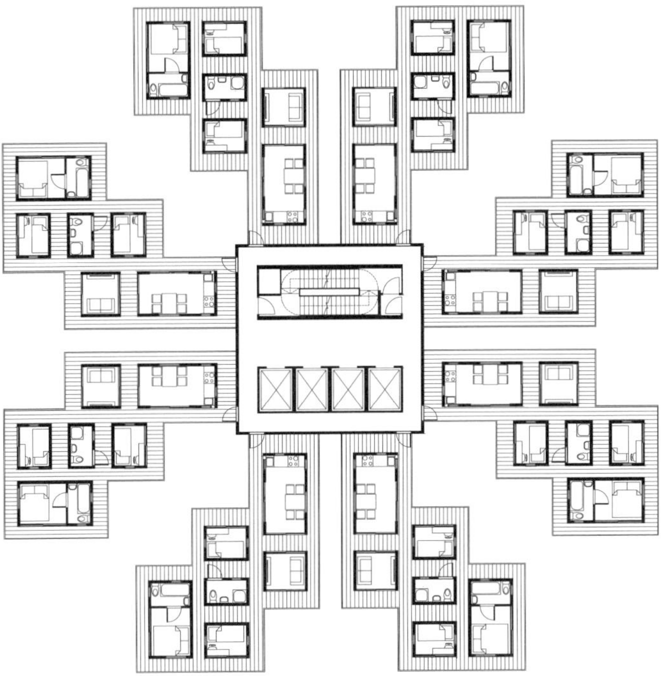

Tower floor plan, 1:100

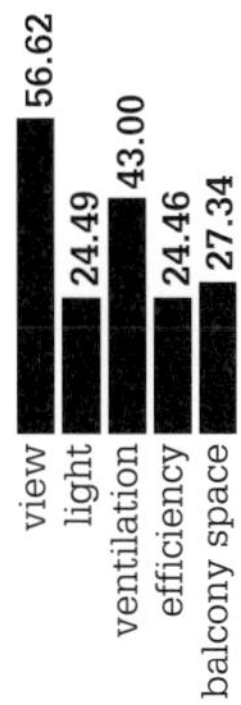

460
Amount of Roofscape (m2)

192
Amount of Apartments

84
Tower Height (m)

9.87
Plot Ratio

The 1,344 Private Balconies Tower

The tower with 192 single-balcony apartments scores 41 points higher than the standard tower with typical apartments. It offers better views, increased levels of daylight, more natural ventilation, and greater efficiency, through the maximization of functional, non-circulatory living space. Further improvements could be made by slightly varying the order of room functions and balconies based on the specific preferences of inhabitants. Varied balconies would potentially allow more sunlight into the apartment's living spaces. A similar effect could be achieved by attaching the apartments to the core at different points.

141
Tower Score

125
Lowest Apartment Score

174
Highest Apartment Score

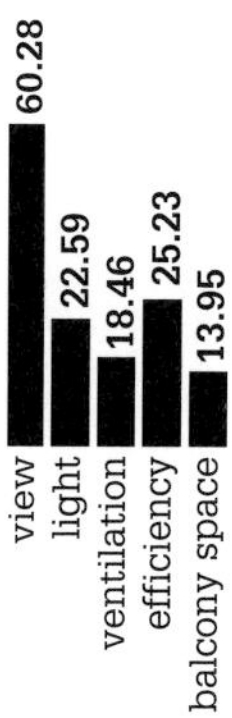

620
Amount of Roofscape (m2)

192
Amount of Apartments

84
Tower Height (m)

9.87
Plot Ratio

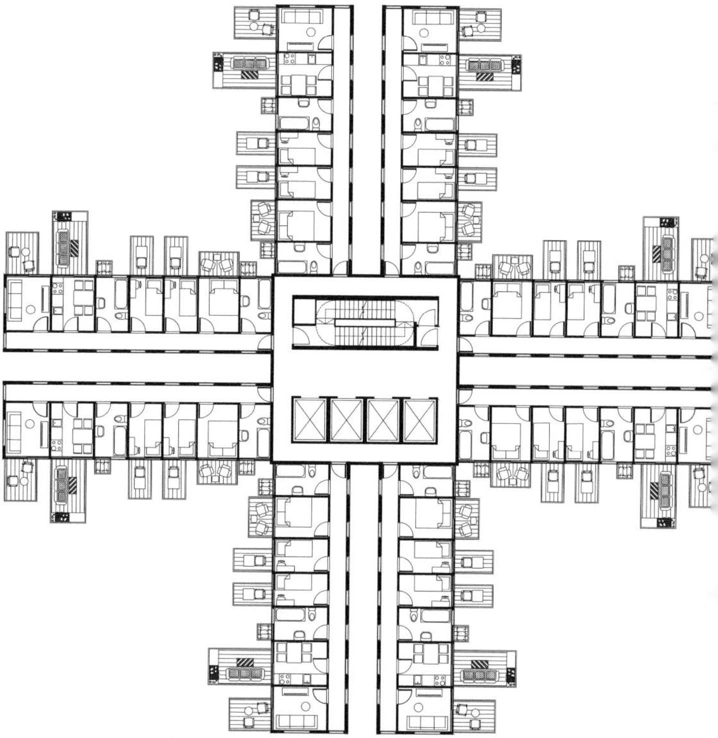

Tower floor plan, 1:400

The Bathing in Nature Tower

With a score of 181, the bathing in nature tower emerges as the top-scoring tower in this selection of uniformly extruded towers. Most apartments in this tower offer better views, more daylight, higher natural ventilation, and maximized efficiency in all rooms. The walls of bamboo plants that screen the balconies contribute significantly to the high performance of this design, by transforming the balcony into a versatile feature that ensures privacy and manages the temperature of the interior. Large vertical voids bring in extra light and ventilation to apartments on lower floors, which is one reason why even the lowest scoring apartment achieves a remarkably high score of 160 points. If the outdoor corridors could vary slightly in length, the apartments could potentially score higher on factors such as increased daylight, increased sunlight, and more sky views.

181
Tower Score

160
Lowest Apartment Score

213
Highest Apartment Score

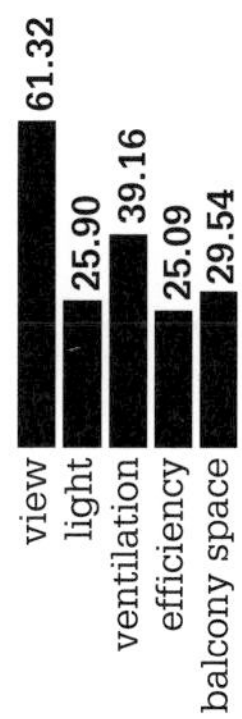

428
Amount of Roofscape (m2)

192
Amount of Apartments

84
Tower Height (m)

9.87
Plot Ratio

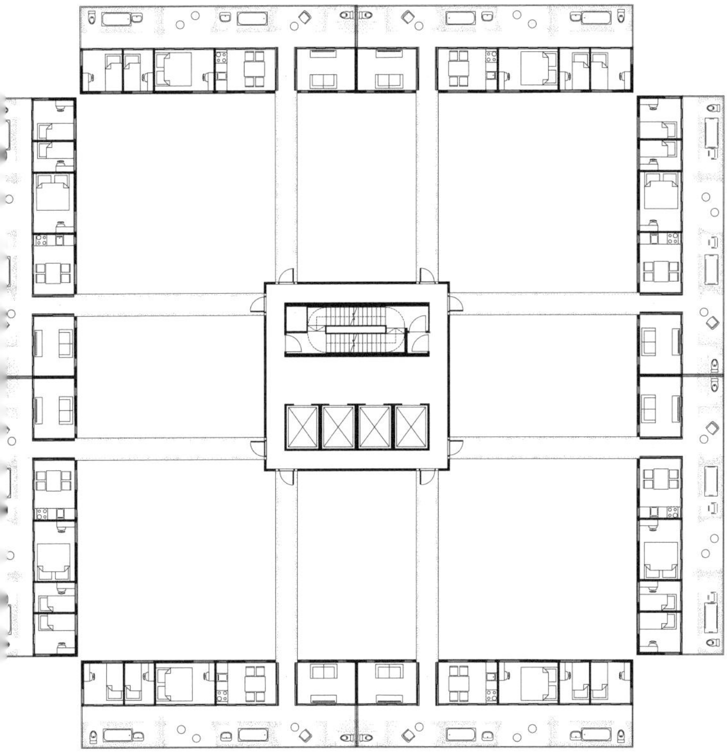

Tower floor plan, 1:400

The Swim Around the House Tower

Featuring 192 private pools, this tower has a score of 157, gaining points on factors such as view and the amount and quality of outdoor space. There is potential for added value if one experiments with merging pools on the same floor to form more spacious swimming areas. By inserting additional pool spaces at the corners of the tower core, each floor could have an exceptionally large shared pool with a continuous swimming route of about 140 meters wrapping around each floor. The highest scoring apartment in this tower has a score of 192 points, while the lowest scoring apartment has a score of 139 points.

157 Tower Score

139 Lowest Apartment Score | **192** Highest Apartment Score

435 Amount of Roofscape (m2)

192 Amount of Apartments

84 Tower Height (m)

9.87 Plot Ratio

Tower floor plan, 1:400

The Sleeping Under the Stars Tower

This tower scores a total of 130 points, gaining points for its exceptional views. While only the upper eight apartments have the desired full sky view through the glass ceiling, apartments below the top floor enjoy sky views at an angle, through a set of glass curtain walls. Nonetheless, all the apartments, even when replicated and flipped around a central core and vertically multiplied through extrusion, score higher than the apartments in a typical tower. The lowest scoring, ground-level apartments score higher than the average scoring apartments of the tower used for reference. If the apartments could be variously organized and re-shaped to enable better access to sky views for all units, the score for views could be even higher than the received 61.28 points.

130
Tower Score

107 Lowest Apartment Score | **154** Highest Apartment Score

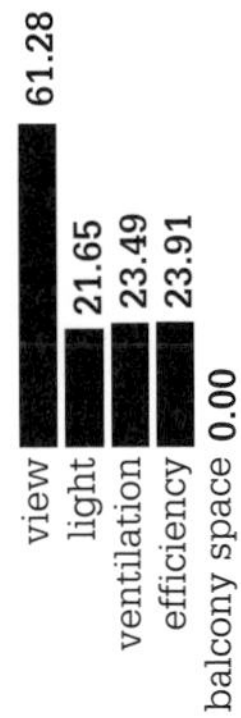

612
Amount of Roofscape (m2)

192
Amount of Apartments

84
Tower Height (m)

9.87
Plot Ratio

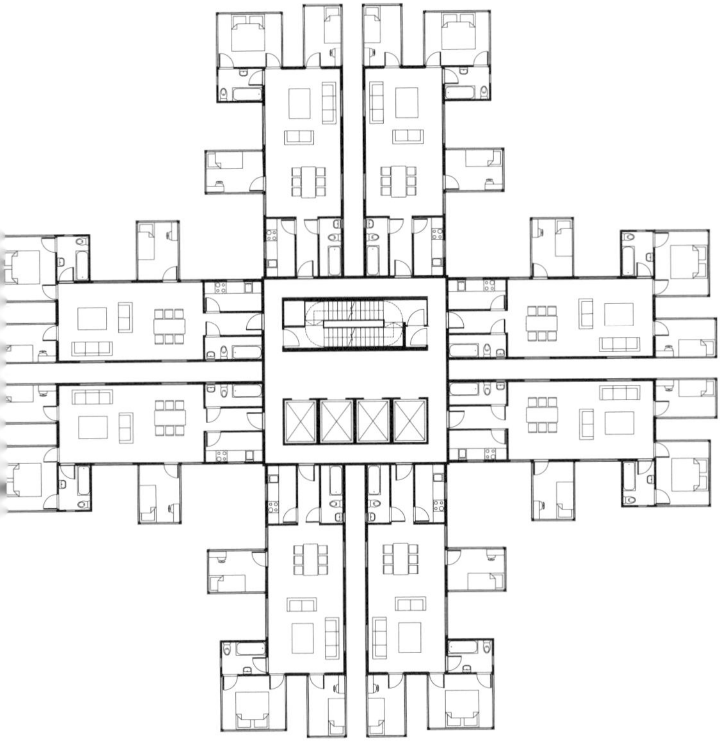

Tower floor plan, 1:100

The Compact Sleeping Tower

This tower scores 121 points, with its lowest scoring apartment totalling 103 points and its highest scoring apartment totalling 155 points. If the balconies are merged and shared among neighbours, inhabitants of this tower could have access to an extraordinary outdoor space of about 36 m^2 in size. Apartments in this tower score relatively high on view, with 51.72 points.

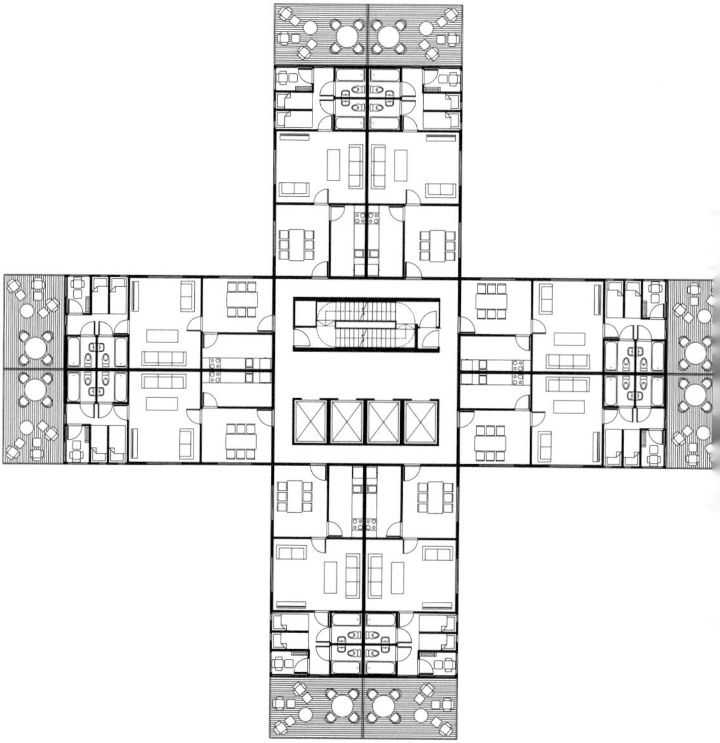

Tower floor plan, 1:400

The Sky Bridge Tower

This formally complex tower features an exceptional amount of negative space. With its many sky-bridges, this tower is characterized by a high degree of porosity, boosting natural ventilation with a high score of 45.7 points. In total, the apartments in this tower score an average of 124 points, with the lowest scoring apartment totalling 108 points and the highest scoring apartment totalling 154 points.

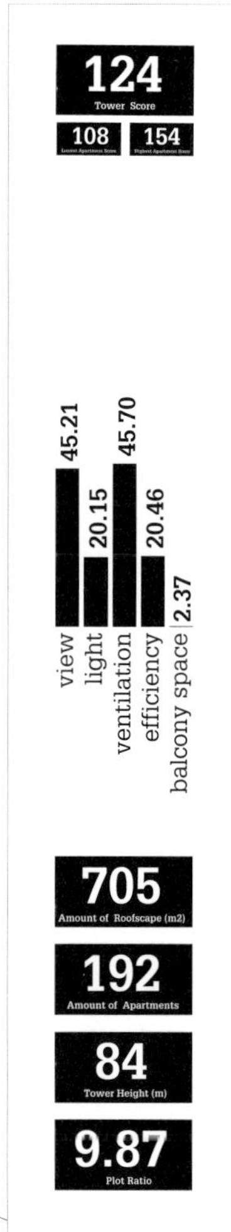

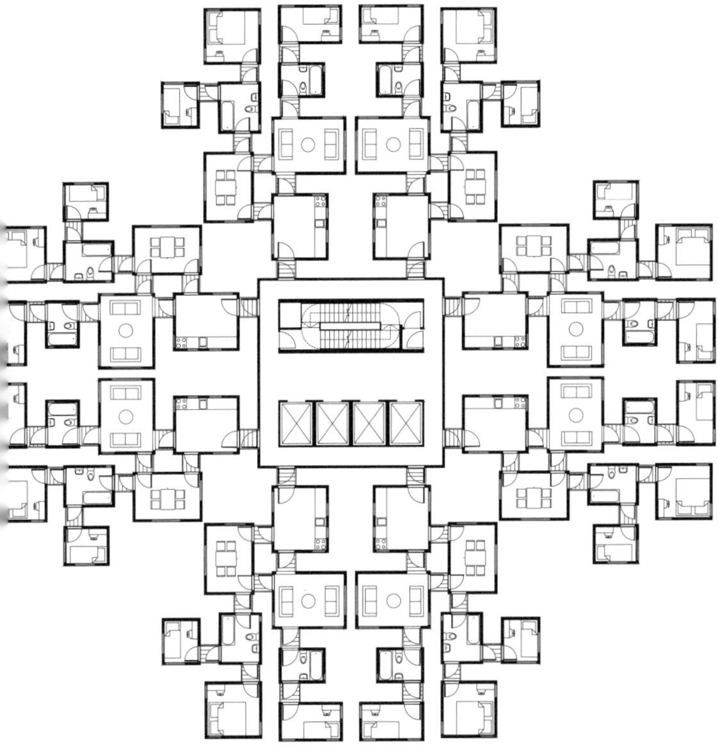

Tower floor plan, 1:400

The Flexible Space Tower

With an average score of 47.68 points for ventilation and 51.84 points for view, the apartments in this tower score no lower than a remarkable 160 points, which is significantly higher than the highest scoring apartment in the typical residential tower. If the lengths of the sky-bridge at the entrance of each apartment could be varied, the apartments could enable access to neighbours' roof spaces below, which would increase accessible outdoor space and increase the total score.

179
Tower Score

160
Lowest Apartment Score

207
Highest Apartment Score

600
Amount of Roofscape (m2)

192
Amount of Apartments

84
Tower Height (m)

9.87
Plot Ratio

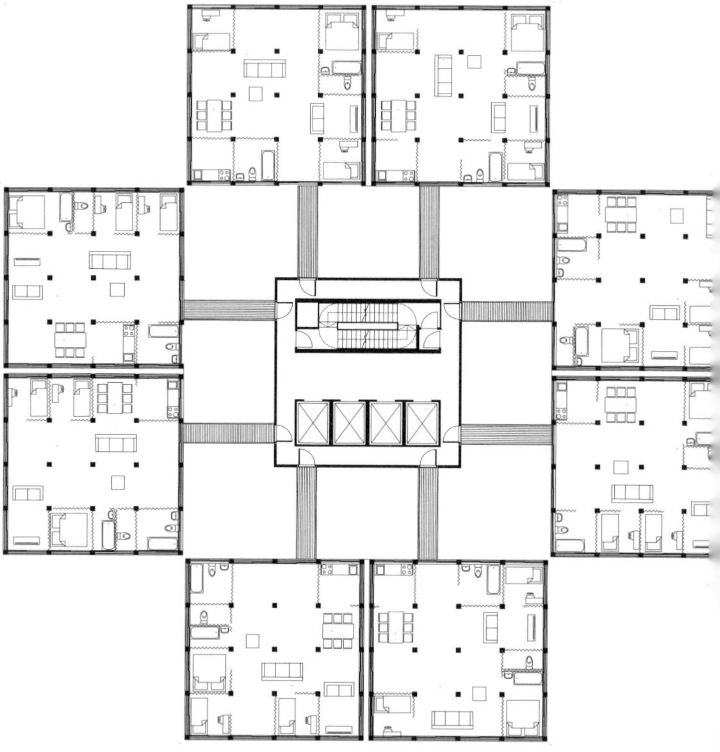

Tower floor plan, 1:400

The Dining with Panoramic Views Tower

The concept here was to maximize scores on view for all 192 dining rooms in this tower, which gave the tower itself a total score of 134 points. Although the apartments have no balcony spaces, the lowest scoring apartment, with 117 points, scores only a little less than the highest scoring apartment in the reference tower. With 58.21 points for view, this tower scores exceptionally high for providing great views in areas where they can be well appreciated: the dining and living rooms.

134
Tower Score

117 **167**

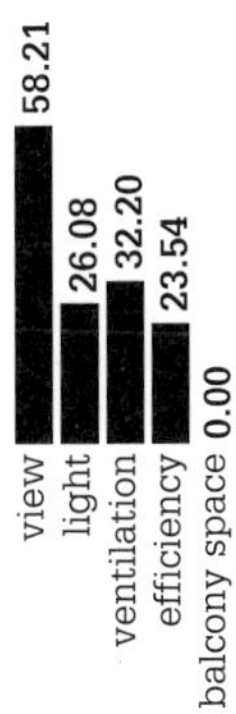

740
Amount of Roofscape (m2)

192
Amount of Apartments

84
Tower Height (m)

9.87
Plot Ratio

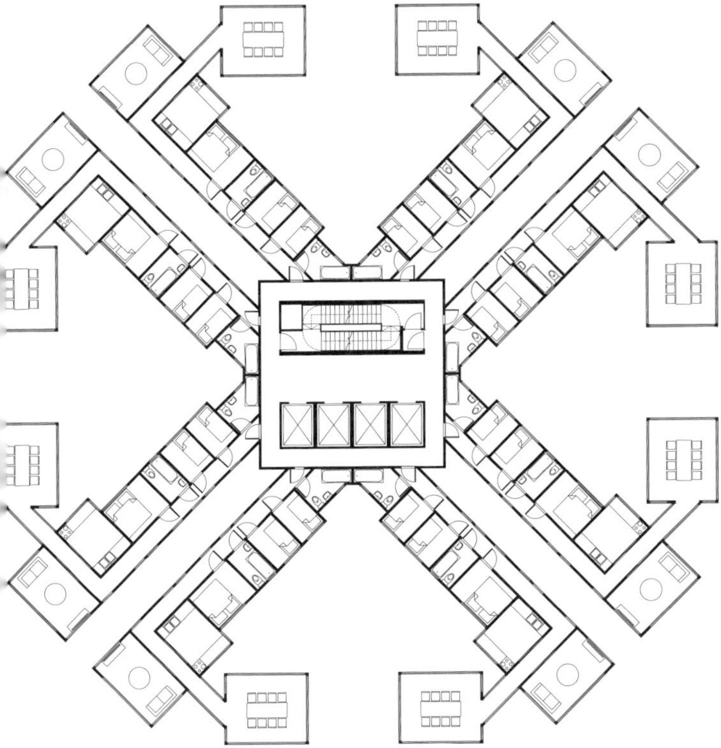

Tower floor plan, 1:400

The Picnicking Sky-High Tower

Apartments in this tower generally score high, with an average score of above 130 points. This tower could score even higher if the large balconies featured in these apartments could be arranged with greater variety, so that they are staggered and oriented to allow for better views for all apartments and less shadow cast over the apartments below. This concept could also evolve into a more playful design with 'green' extensions. The tower earns 55.58 points for view. The highest scoring apartments, with 185 points, are located on the upper floors.

148 Tower Score

130 Lowest Apartment Score

185 Highest Apartment Score

625 Amount of Roofscape (m2)

192 Amount of Apartments

84 Tower Height (m)

9.87 Plot Ratio

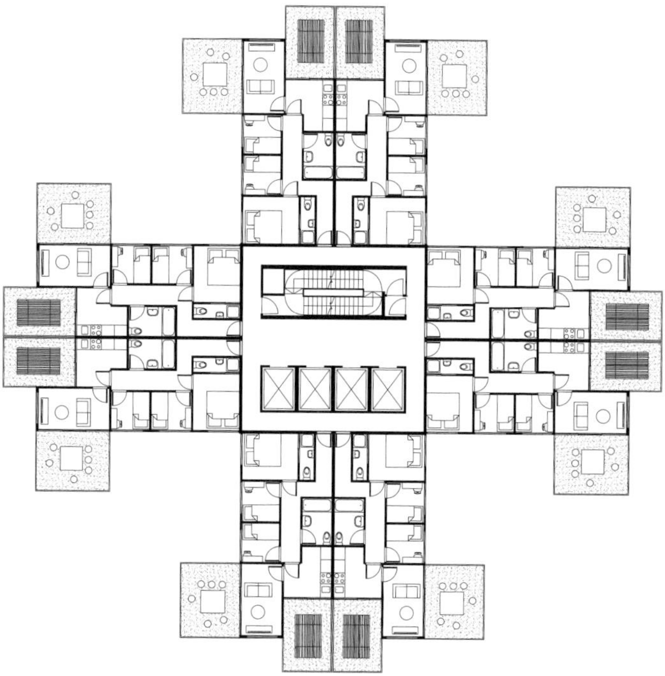

Tower floor plan, 1:400

The Cooking with Natural Breeze Tower

The apartments in this tower, which feature open kitchens with dining areas, score an average of 134 points. In this tower, natural ventilation performs at its best, while the open environment has the potential to change patterns of living. The lowest scoring apartment in this tower has 114 points, and the highest scoring apartment reaches 175 points.

139
Tower Score

114 Lowest Apartment Score | **175** Highest Apartment Score

650
Amount of Roofscape (m2)

192
Amount of Apartments

84
Tower Height (m)

9.87
Plot Ratio

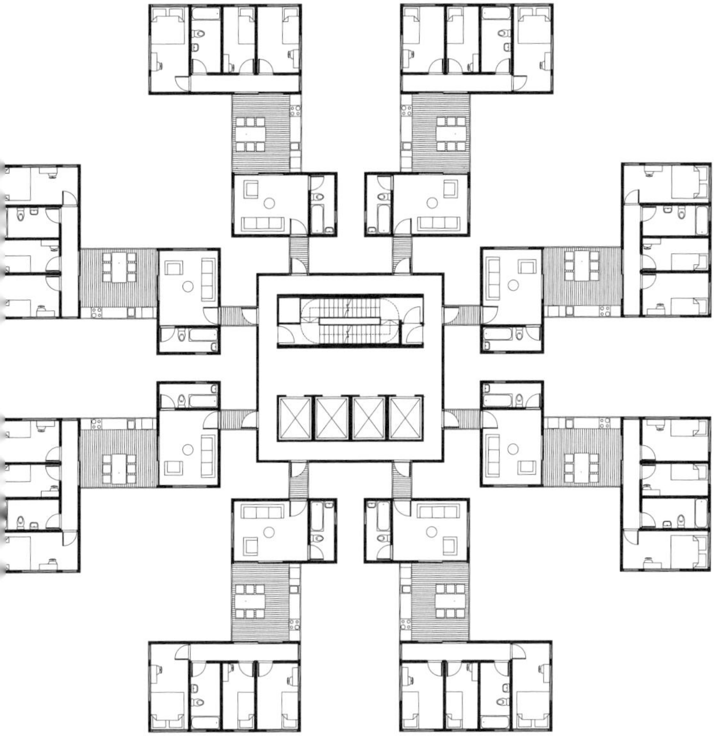

Tower floor plan, 1:400

The Enjoying Home-Grown Food Tower

This tower scores an average of 133 points, with the lowest scoring apartment totalling 130 points and the highest scoring apartment reaching 185 points. With its 'green skin', this tower not only creates valuable space for urban farming and gardening, but also provides excellent shade. Other benefits of this design lie beyond the scope of our quantitative scoring system: daily life becomes directly related to the cycles and rhythms of plants and the generation of fresh food. Different smells and colours are infused into daily life, adding a significant new aesthetic dimension to it, not only for the inhabitants of the tower but for residents in the vicinity as well. With its colourful façade, it broadcasts the appeal of a lifestyle fuelled by healthy food. This tower could offer even more growing space if the individual apartment units could gain vertical space, or if additional balcony spaces were added around the apartment.

133
Tower Score

130 **185**

470
Amount of Roofscape (m2)

192
Amount of Apartments

84
Tower Height (m)

9.87
Plot Ratio

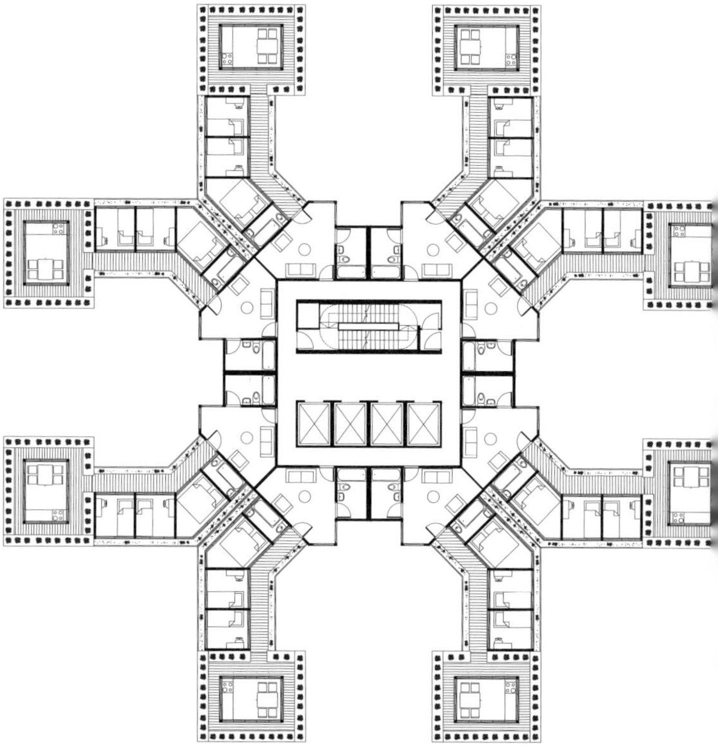

Tower floor plan, 1:400

The Observatory Tower

The apartments in the observatory tower score an average of 125 points, with the highest scoring apartment totalling 149 points and the lowest scoring apartment totalling 100 points. Views are emphasized in the design of these apartments, and the views alone bring in 64.94 points. If the apartments could be variously rotated along the vertical axis, rather than uniformly stacked, the average score of this tower would be even higher thanks to an increase of sky views with wider angles and higher levels of light.

125
Tower Score

100 Lowest Apartment Score | **149** Highest Apartment Score

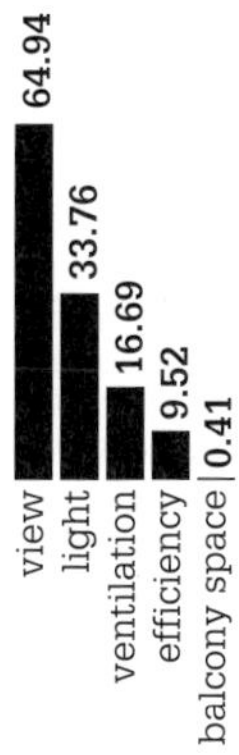

100
Amount of Roofscape (m2)

192
Amount of Apartments

84
Tower Height (m)

9.87
Plot Ratio

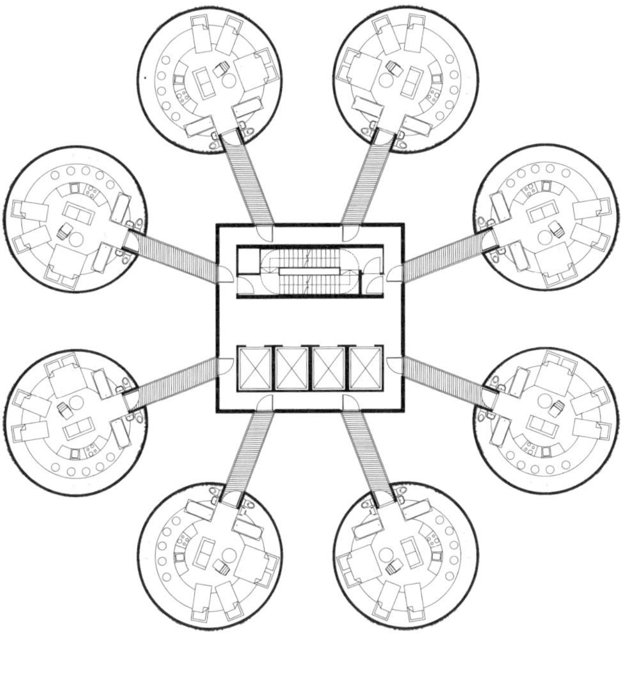

Tower floor plan, 1:400

The Separated Living Activities Tower

The separated living activities tower scores 115 points, with 98 points for the lowest scoring apartment and 146 points for the highest scoring apartment. Views alone score 54.27 in this tower. A tower consisting of these apartment units could be improved with a terraced approach to stacking, which would increase accessible outdoor space.

115
Tower Score

98
Lowest Apartment Score

146
Highest Apartment Score

715
Amount of Roofscape (m2)

192
Amount of Apartments

84
Tower Height (m)

9.87
Plot Ratio

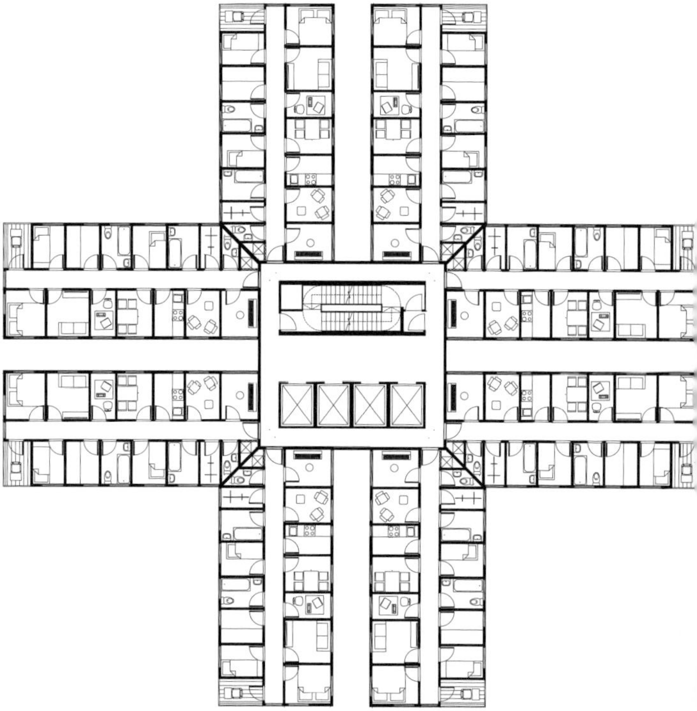

Tower floor plan, 1:400

The Maid's Own Paradise Tower

This tower has an average apartment score of 101 points. The lowest scoring apartment scores 81, and the highest scoring apartment scores 123 points. Designed to enhance the quality of life for domestic workers and the families who employ them, this apartment layout has the potential to drastically improve social dynamics while maintaining levels of light, ventilation, efficiency, and accessible outdoor space similar to those of the reference tower.

101
Tower Score

81
Lowest Apartment Score

123
Highest Apartment Score

680
Amount of Roofscape (m2)

192
Amount of Apartments

84
Tower Height (m)

9.87
Plot Ratio

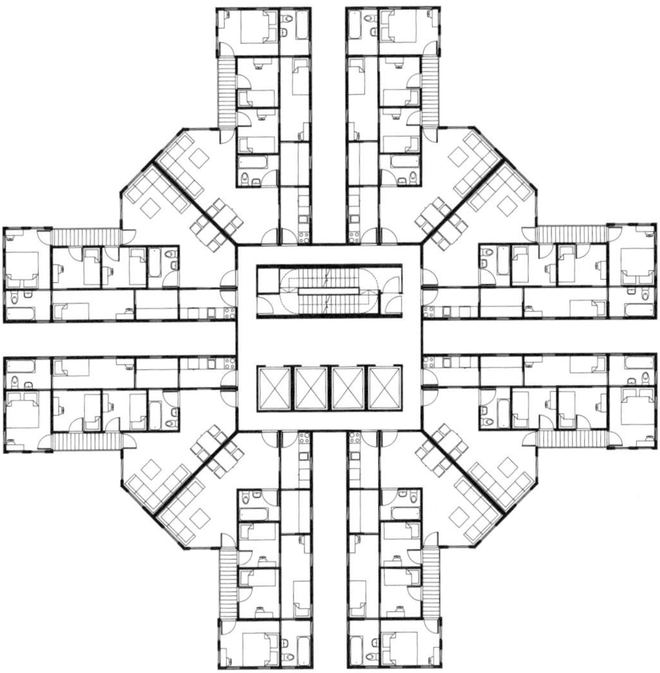

Tower floor plan, 1:400

The Meet the Maid Everywhere Tower

This tower received a score of 90, which is 10 points below the score of the reference tower. While many of the apartments in this tower achieve a score of approximately 100 points, this tower has a few low scoring apartments with only 73 points. This apartment layout scores low on qualities such as light and view, especially for the living and dining room. It would score higher if it could be supplemented with additional balcony space.

90
Tower Score

73
Lowest Apartment Score

117
Highest Apartment Score

740
Amount of Roofscape (m2)

192
Amount of Apartments

84
Tower Height (m)

9.87
Plot Ratio

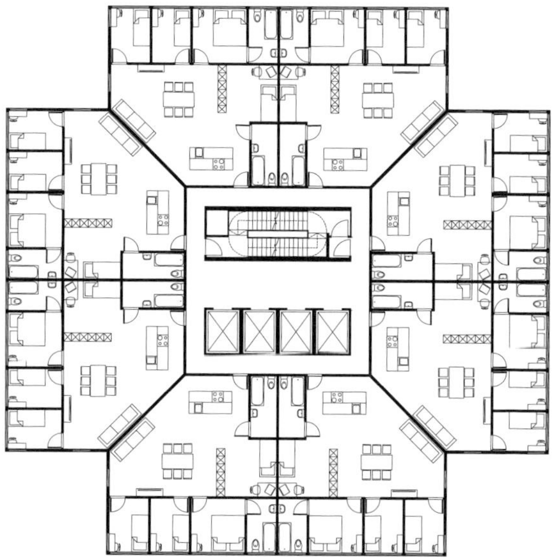

Tower floor plan, 1:400

The Central Super Storage Tower

With only 88 points, this tower is the lowest scoring tower of this lot. The lowest scoring apartment scores 65 points, and the highest scoring apartment scores 107 points. The higher scoring apartments are all located on the upper floors. The low average can largely be attributed to limited natural ventilation and the absence of balcony space. However, even if this tower is uniformly extruded, all bedrooms and living rooms have the potential to provide great views, which should be considered along with the apartment's promise to provide well organized storage space.

88
Tower Score

65
Lowest Apartment Score

107
Highest Apartment Score

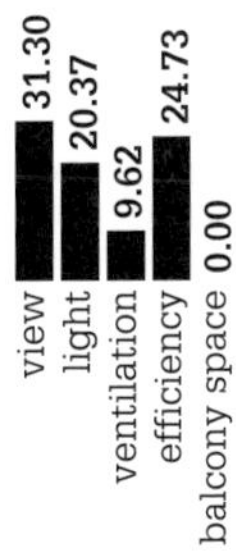

740
Amount of Roofscape (m2)

192
Amount of Apartments

84
Tower Height (m)

9.87
Plot Ratio

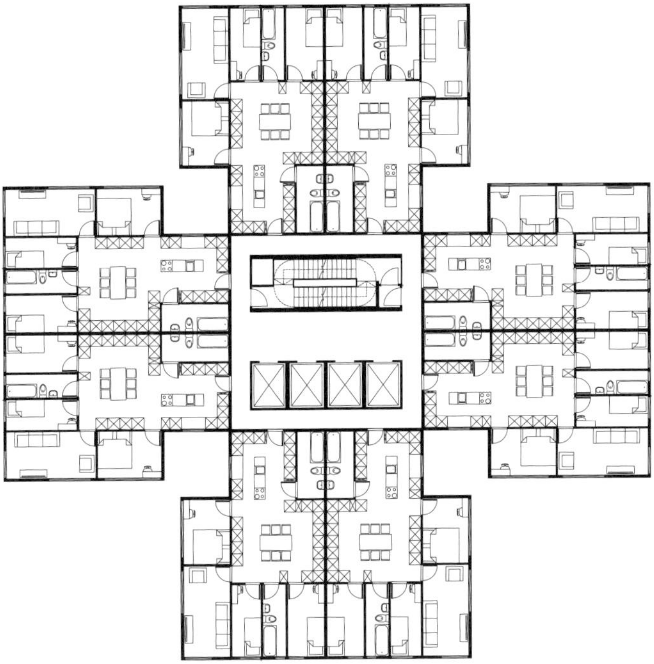

Tower floor plan, 1:400

The Hide Your Belongings in the Wall Tower

This tower with maximum storage space scores 100 points, hitting the benchmark. Although most rooms in its apartments have relatively small windows, the views receive a score of 43.83 points. Apartments with scores between 130 to 140 can be found on the uppermost floor of this tower. Most of the apartments average between 100 to 110 points. There are a few low-scoring apartments, totalling 93 points, located on the first five floors.

100
Tower Score

93
Lowest Apartment Score

140
Highest Apartment Score

740
Amount of Roofscape (m2)

192
Amount of Apartments

84
Tower Height (m)

9.87
Plot Ratio

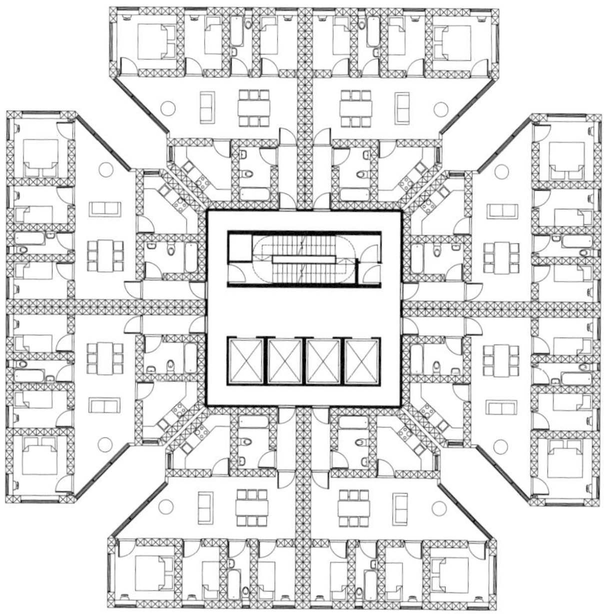

Tower floor plan, 1:400

The Books Everywhere Tower

With apartments that average 136 points, this tower has over 85 apartments that score higher than 120 points. The lowest scoring apartments, with 116 points, are mainly located on the first five floors. The apartments score an average of 50.93 points just for view, which is relatively high. The process of mirroring and flipping these apartments around a central core has a negative effect on their ability to provide privacy. If floor plans are uniformly extruded, the bedrooms and kitchens in half of the apartments will be too close to the neighbouring apartment. This could be ameliorated if the layouts of the apartments could vary. For instance, by positioning only the bathrooms, which do not necessarily need beautiful views, adjacent to neighbouring apartments, this tower could gain a considerable number of points.

136
Tower Score

116 **165**

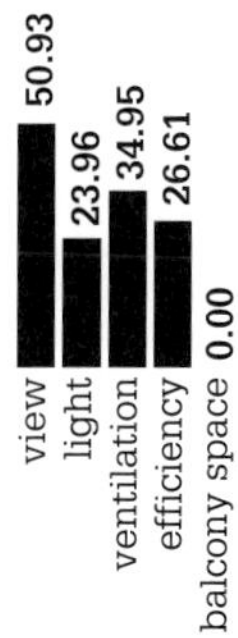

740
Amount of Roofscape (m2)

192
Amount of Apartments

84
Tower Height (m)

9.87
Plot Ratio

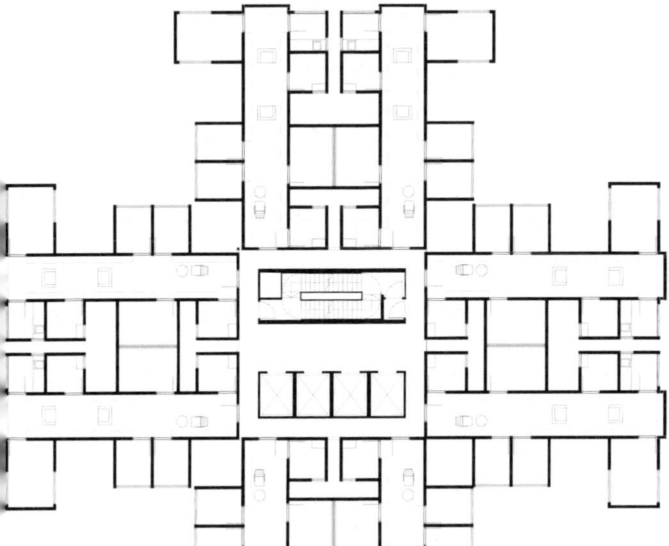

Tower floor plan, 1:400

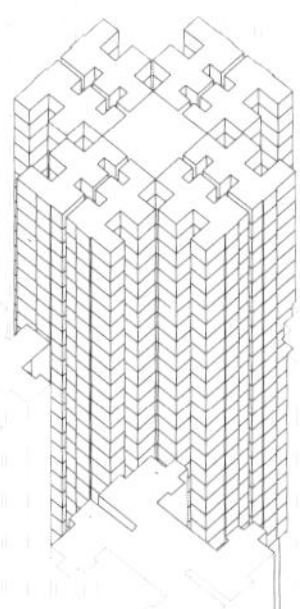

The Secluded and Quiet Study Tower

With an average score of 106 points, the secluded-study-room tower scores slightly higher than the reference tower, scoring unexpectedly low because of the merging of the kitchen with the living and dining room. By combining these rooms, qualities such as views and levels of daylight are reduced. In addition, bedroom sizes are condensed to create sufficient space for the study room. However, in most apartments, regardless of elevation, the study room scores exceptionally well in terms of providing view, natural light, and natural ventilation.

106
Tower Score

71
Lowest Apartment Score

109
Highest Apartment Score

740
Amount of Roofscape (m2)

192
Amount of Apartments

84
Tower Height (m)

9.87
Plot Ratio

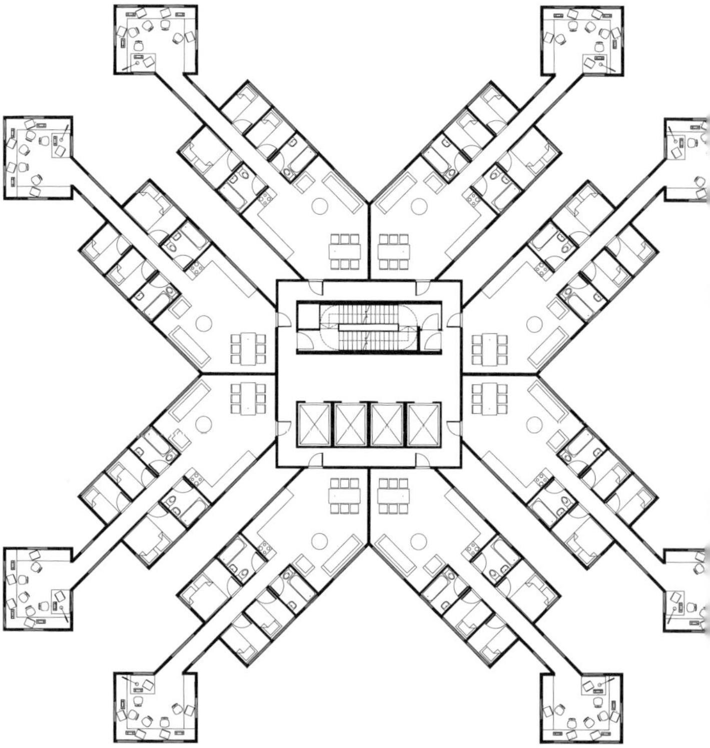

Tower floor plan, 1:400

How Do Towers with Mixed Specialized Apartments Score?

Text by Tihamér Salij

Drawings and diagrams illustrated by The Why Factory: Claudia Mainardi, Anna Dolcetta, Sylwia Franczak

Additional research by Tihamér Salij with Martine Vledder and Anna Dolcetta

Photo collage impressions illustrated by the students of The Why Factory's "Hong Kong Tower Revolution" studio at the Department of Architecture at the Hong Kong University, during Fall 2013, and by the students of The Why Factory's "Towers Beyond Extrusion" studio at the Department of Architecture at the Hong Kong University, during Fall 2014.

Hong Kong Tower Revolution, Architecture and Urban Design III (ARCH 5001), Hong Kong University.
Studio Tutors: Prof. Winy Maas and Tihamér Salij with Sander Mulders and Arend van Waart
Students: Au Wing Yi, Chak Tsz Kin, Chan Chung Man, Chan Ian Yin Yan, Chan Pui Yin, Chau Shek Lun, Cheng Ching, Ip Kai Hong, Liu Kemeng, Mok Wang Chee, Tang Ho Yin, Kong Ho Ching, Kwok Ka Ching, Lau Xin Yee, Lee Kin Wai, Li Mei Yu, Lung Man Ching, Ma Ching Yi, Suen Wing Yin, Sze Ivy, Sze Ying Ying, Yeung Cho Yui, Yeung Ho Man

Towers Beyond Extrusion, Architecture and Urban Design III (ARCH 5001), Hong Kong University
Studio Tutors: Prof. Winy Maas, Tihamér Salij, Martine Vledder with Donn Holohan
Students: Au Yeung Chun Yu JOEY, Chan Fong Tong FRED S, Cheng Pok Him BOB, Ching Ka Ho FRED, Henao Granda Jan Esteban, Ho Sheung Hay TERENCE, Hu Xiangdong HOCK, Ko Pak Kan ZETH, Li Zhixin ALLISON, Liu Chuen Yung VINCENT, Ma Yue, Qin Liting TING, Tang Tak Shing KELVIN, Wen Fan, Wu Yucong, Xie Junni, Ffion Zhang, Ho Yin SUNNY CHA, Sai Bond, Man Hei KENNIF, Han PAT

What could more freedom in the process of designing residential towers look like? There are ideas of various scales to consider, new, hybrid tower typologies to imagine, and new ways in which these typologies could add up to a cityscape that responds to the needs of a diverse urban population and reveals exciting new wishes. Practically, it is important to assess what the additional construction costs for these potential new tower configurations would be, and whether the qualities gained are worth the costs. Can developers turn a profit by selling fewer apartments with improved qualities, and by positively contributing to the built and natural environment?

The following is a showcase of specially configured towers comprised of a mix of specialized apartments. These precisely interrelated combinations have been stacked to comply with a standard tower height of 84 metres. In a variety of ways, these towers elevate the standard for residential design, whether it means adding green space, creating environments to grow food, innovating on circulation and building maintenance, or creating interesting shared spaces. Each tower follows its own unique system of vertical stacking. In many instances, their stacking generates higher porosity, assisting with natural ventilation in the apartments and ventilation at the scale of the city. Higher porosity can also enhance views and increase levels of daylight. Different approaches to stacking add up to a more diverse cityscape, breaking up the uniformity and repetition that currently characterize development in Hong Kong.

The Hanging Gardens Tower

The hanging gardens tower functions as a green lung for the city. It contains a total of 163 apartment units, most of which are the enjoying-home-grown-food apartments that support gardening. The apartments have been stacked and flipped along the core according to principles of increasing open space and maximized intake of sunlight. They are combined with four other apartment typologies: the wrap-around-balcony, the seven-private-balconies, the bathing-in-nature, and the picnicking-sky-high apartments, all of which share an emphasis on green space. With this mixture of apartment typologies, stacked to optimize conditions for green space, the hanging gardens tower generates its own microclimate. It has the potential to absorb substantial amounts of CO_2 and dust particles and release extra oxygen into the air.

Tower Configuration

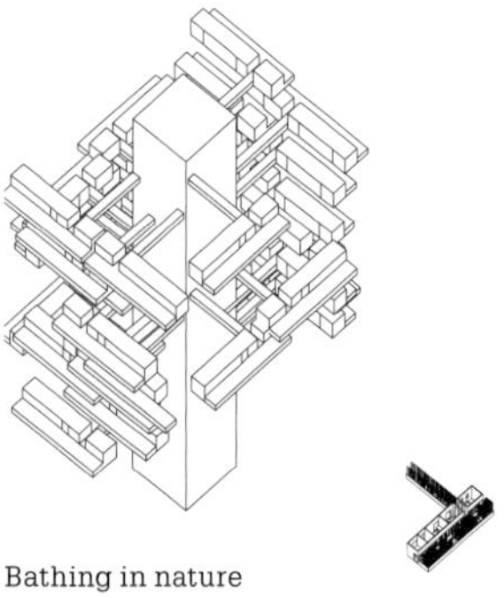

Bathing in nature

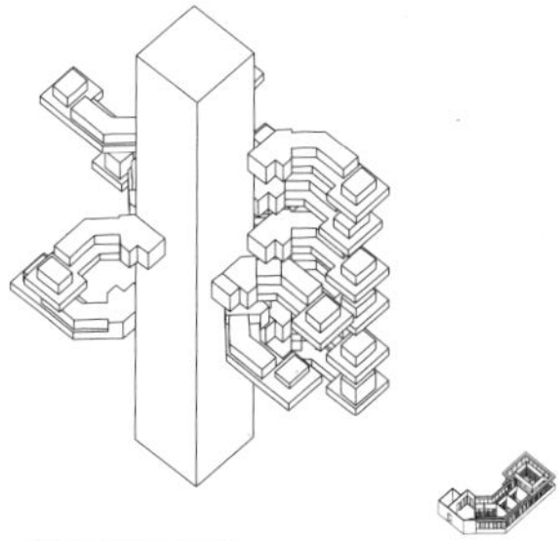

Enjoying home-grown food

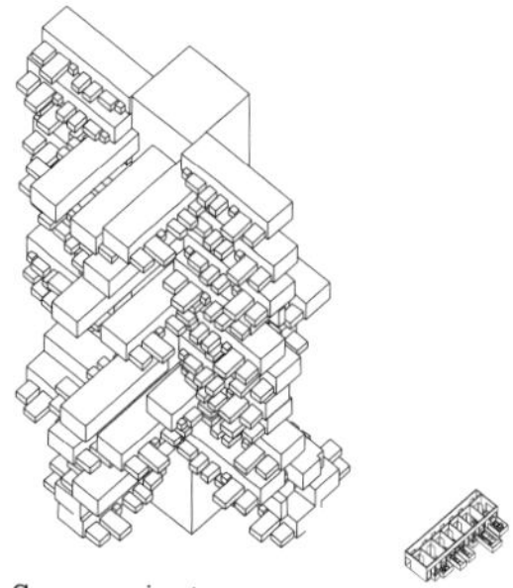

Seven private balconies

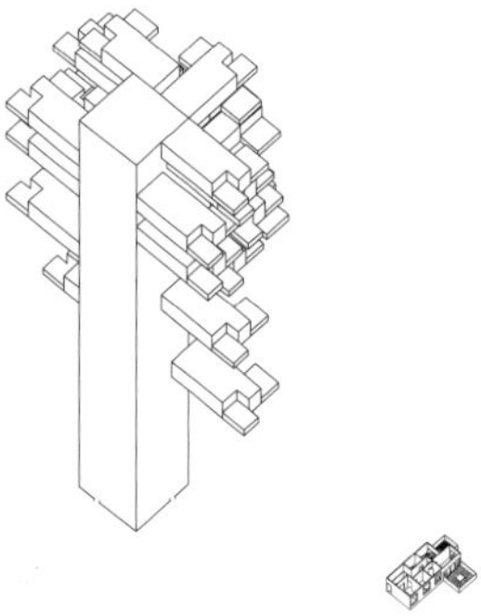

Picnicking sky-high

Wrap-around balcony

View: South-East

In terms of stacking, the wrap-around-balcony apartments are positioned at the base of the tower, while the other apartments, which need more sun, are organized and positioned at higher elevations, according to the estimated hours of sunlight needed. For example, the picnicking-sky-high apartments need the most direct sunlight to support grass growth, so they are positioned on top with a southeast and southwest orientation.

With 152 points, the tower scores relatively high. Its lowest scoring apartment has 102 points, whereas its highest scoring apartment earns an extraordinary 212 points. In addition, the tower has 5,711 m^2 of additional roof top areas, which could be used to enlarge the natural ecosystem and create more private and shared gardens. With its abundance of plants, trees and wildlife, the tower broadcasts a message of coexistence among people, plants, and animals.

Tower floor plan 1:400

Scale 1:2000, View: South-East

152
Tower Score

105

211
Highest Apartment Score

5,711
Amount of Roofscape (m2)

163
Amount of Apartments

84
Tower Height (m)

8.58

The Garden-to-Table Tower

This tower is for ideal for occupants who appreciate natural ventilation and home-grown food, especially if they are conscious of health and diet but do not want to spend too much on fresh and high-quality produce. The tower mixes apartment typologies such as the enjoying-home-grown food, cooking-with-natural-breeze, wrap-around-balcony, central-superstore, and picnicking-sky-high apartments.

Tower Configuration

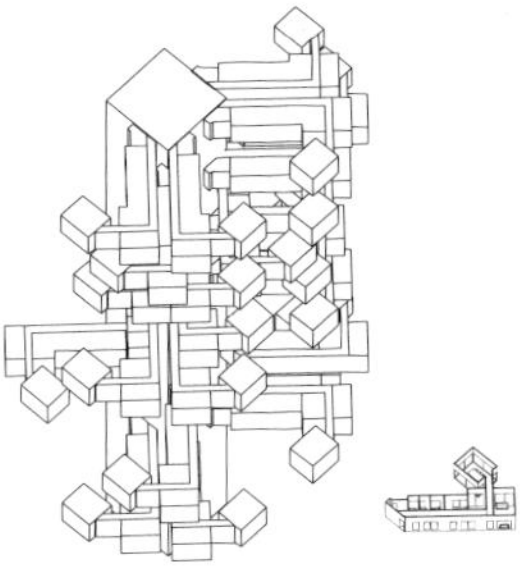

Dining with panoramic views

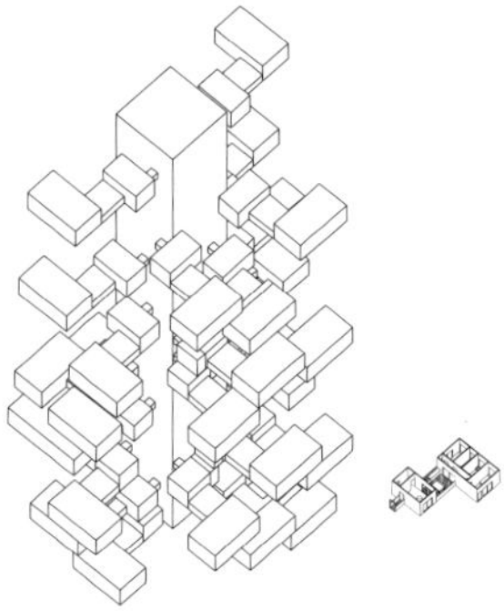

Cooking with natural breeze

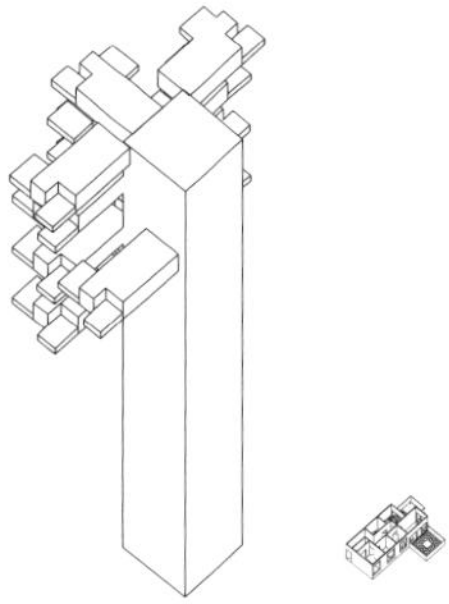

Picnicking sky-high

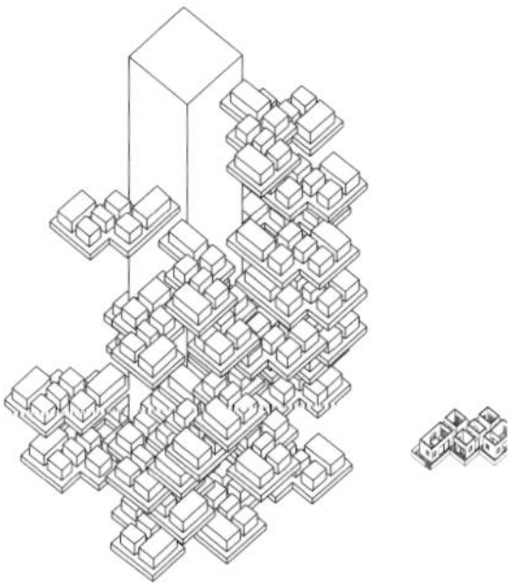

Wrap-around balcony

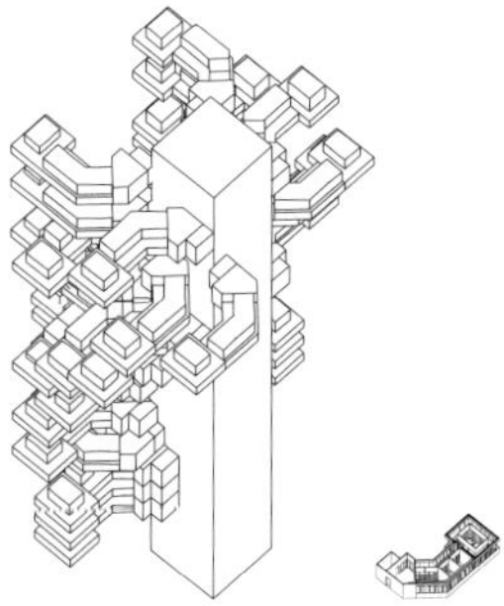

Enjoying home-grown food

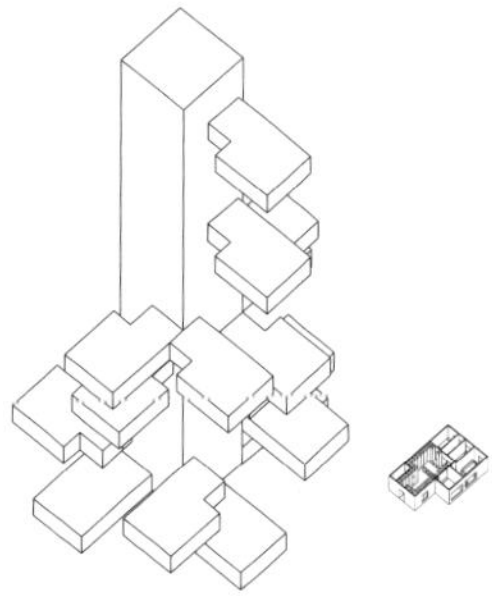

The central super store

View: South-East

When combined, these apartments have the potential to support a shared economy of farming, harvesting, and exchanging produce. Dwellers of apartments with growing space can share their harvest with neighbours in exchange for money or other items or services. The additional 5,910 m^2 of rooftop can become space for a community garden. The tower has the potential to supply a substantial amount of the food required and consumed by its inhabitants. The tower maintains a below-maximum plot ratio of 9.11.

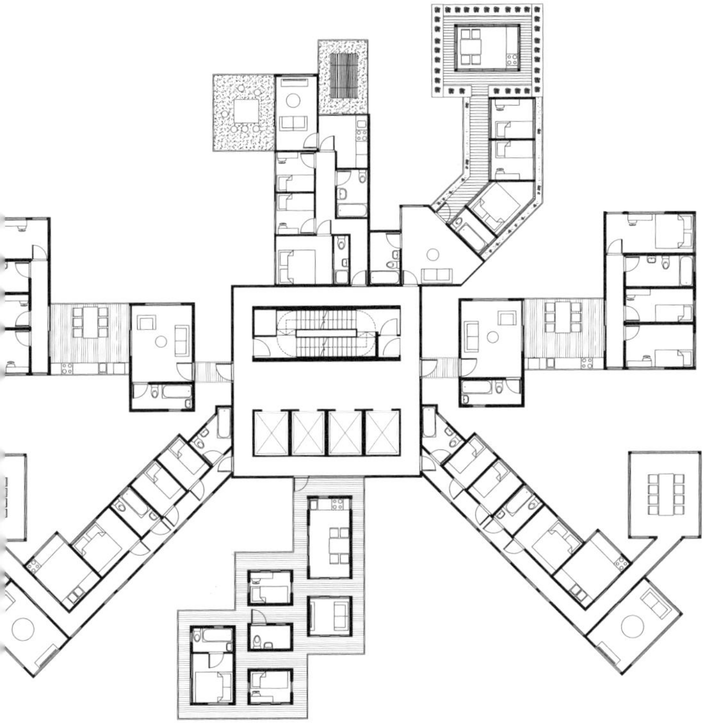

Tower floor plan 1:400

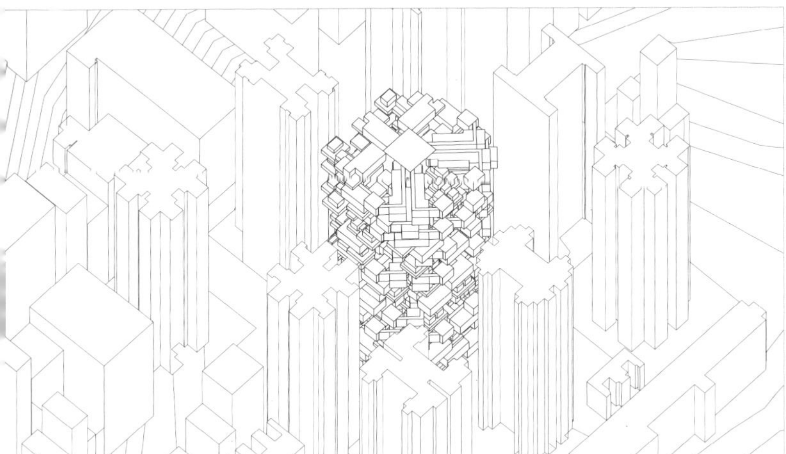

Scale 1:2000, View: South-East

156
Tower Score

70 | **206**

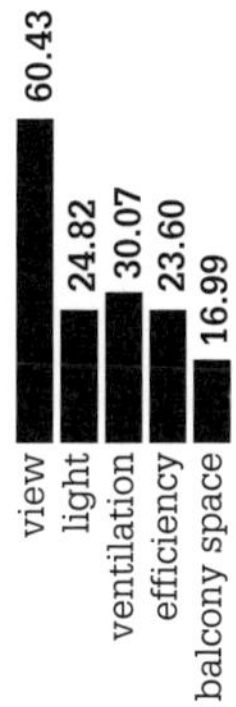

5,910
Amount of Roofscape (m2)

175
Amount of Apartments

84
Tower Height (m)

9.11

The Waterfall Tower

With its communal bathrooms and hot springs, the central core of this tower is transformed into a vital site of community, where residents can gather around shared wellness routines. This tower allows inhabitants to share pools and bathroom facilities while also enjoying private wellness areas. Each floor has a network of interconnected pools that can be separated by gates when desired. A wooden deck also serves to connect rooms and pool areas. The key to maintaining this ecosystem is the tower's water circulation system. All apartments and communal facilities are connected by a water system that filters water through a vertical water-cleansing system and recycles it to irrigate gardens and flush toilets. The tower expresses its vital circulatory system aesthetically, revealing its hydraulic complexity through features such as waterfalls and small creeks that transform the building into a dynamic landscape.

Tower Configuration

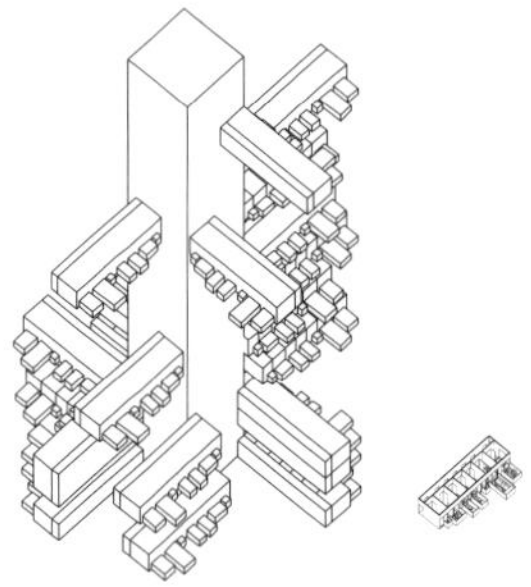

Seven private balconies

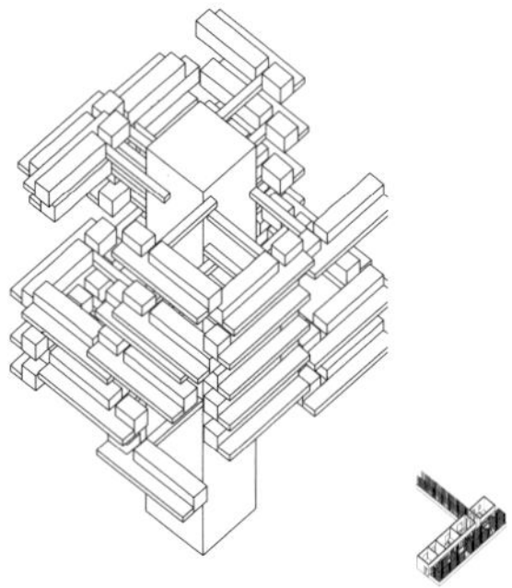

Bathing in nature

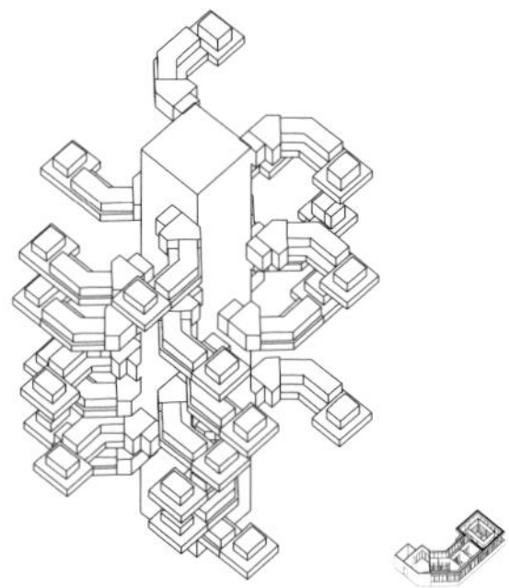

Enjoying home-grown food

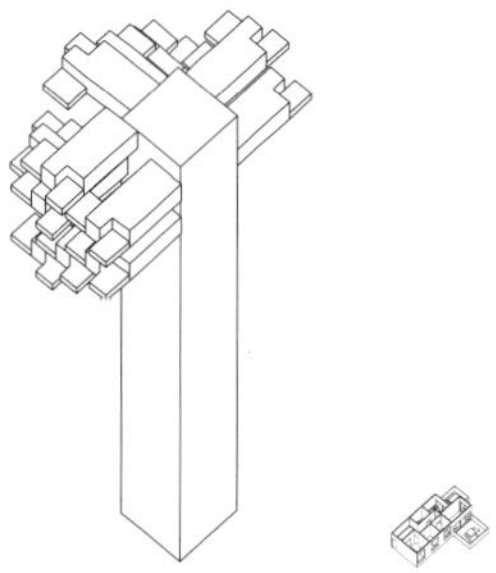

Picnicking sky-high

Swimming around the house

View: South-East

This tower is stacked to ensure that all green areas receive their necessary levels of sunlight. Rooms that receive heavy exposure to direct sunlight are cooled by the watering system. A moisture control system is also fundamental to the success of this tower, protecting against mould contamination and problems with bacteria and insects that may cause harm to respiratory health and to the building's structure and mechanical systems.

The tower scores 168 points, with its lowest scoring apartment scoring 115 points and its highest scoring apartment totalling 217 points. It contains 168 apartments and maintains a plot ratio of 8.5.

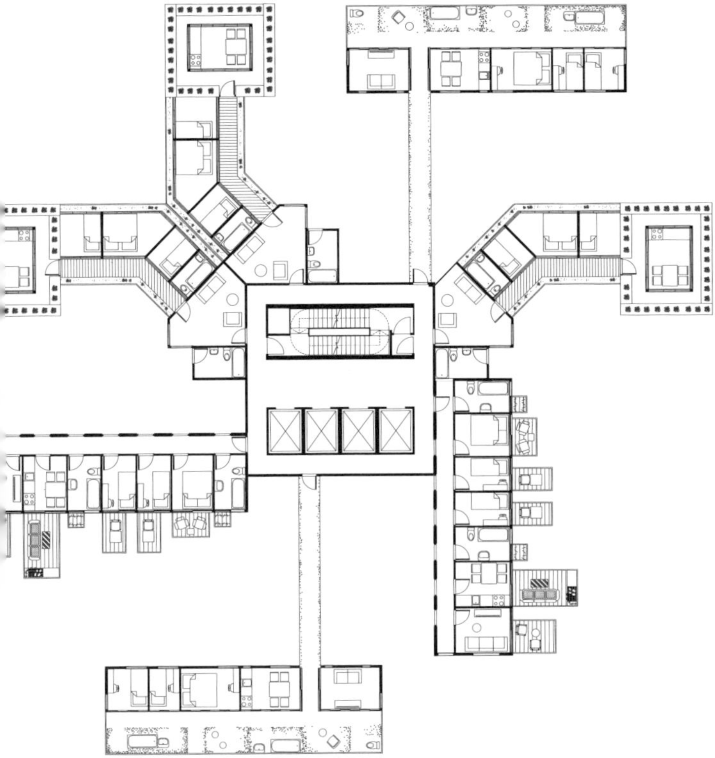

Tower floor plan 1:400

Scale 1:2000, View: South-East

162
Tower Score

115
Lowest Apartment Score

217
Highest Apartment Score

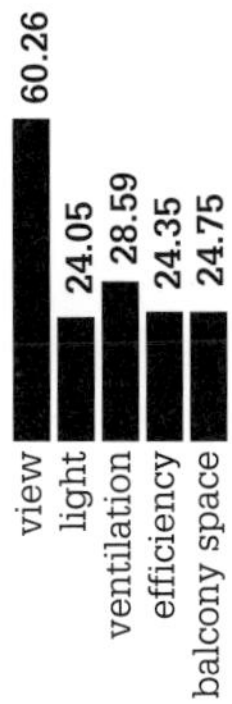

5,868
Amount of Roofscape (m2)

168
Amount of Apartments

84
Tower Height (m)

8.80
Plot Ratio

The Isolated Functions Tower

This tower consists of 175 apartments that feature layouts that support specific living activities or functions by isolating them. These include the separated-living-activities, secluded-and-quiet-studying, panoramic-dining, wrap-around-balcony, and sleeping-under-the-stars apartments. Maximum privacy became the principle for organizing and orienting the apartments. The layouts were precisely combined to preserve spaces with expansive views as well as spaces screened off for privacy.

Tower Configuration

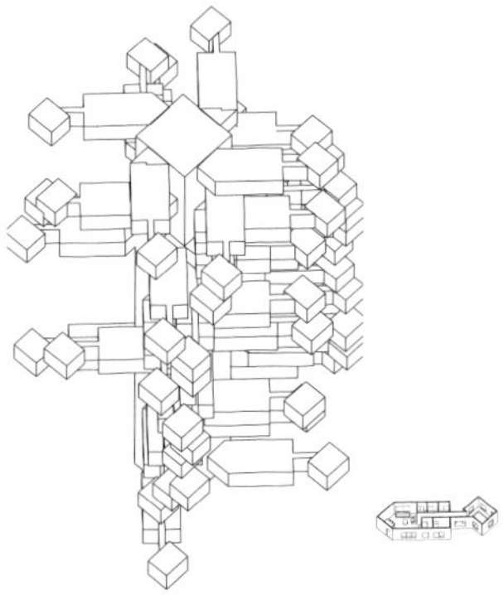

Secluded and quiet studying

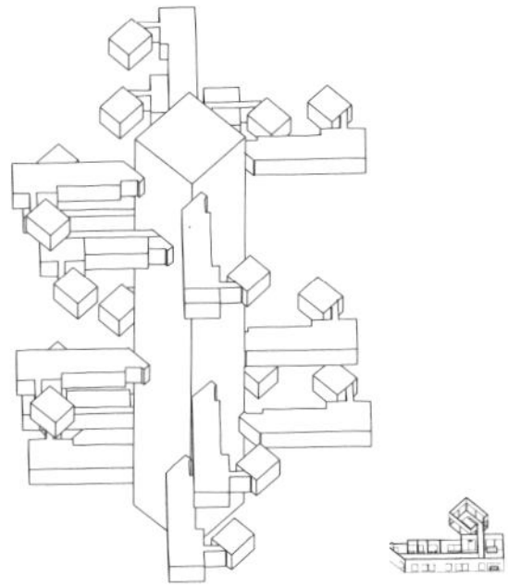

Dining with panoramic views

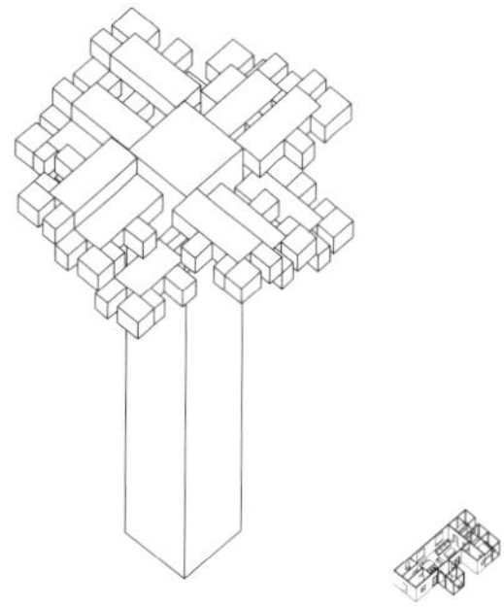

Sleeping under the stars

Wrap-around balcony

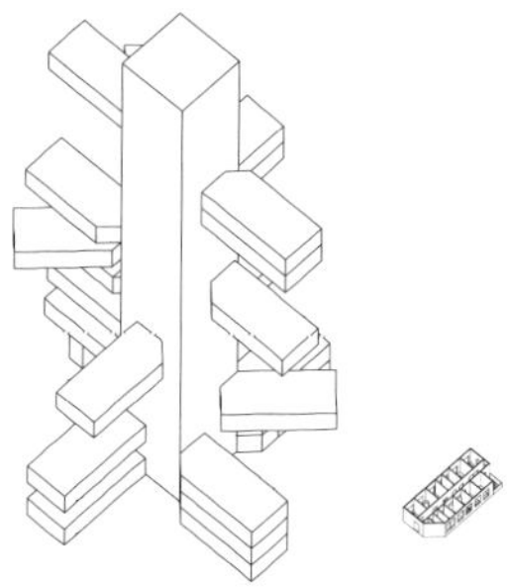

Separated living activities

Sky bridges

View: South-East

The tower scores a total of 129 points, scoring high on factors such as view and ventilation. The tower provides 6,758 square meters of additional rooftop space, giving each apartment access to a minimum of 38 square meters of private outdoor space. The tower has a plot ratio of 9.11.

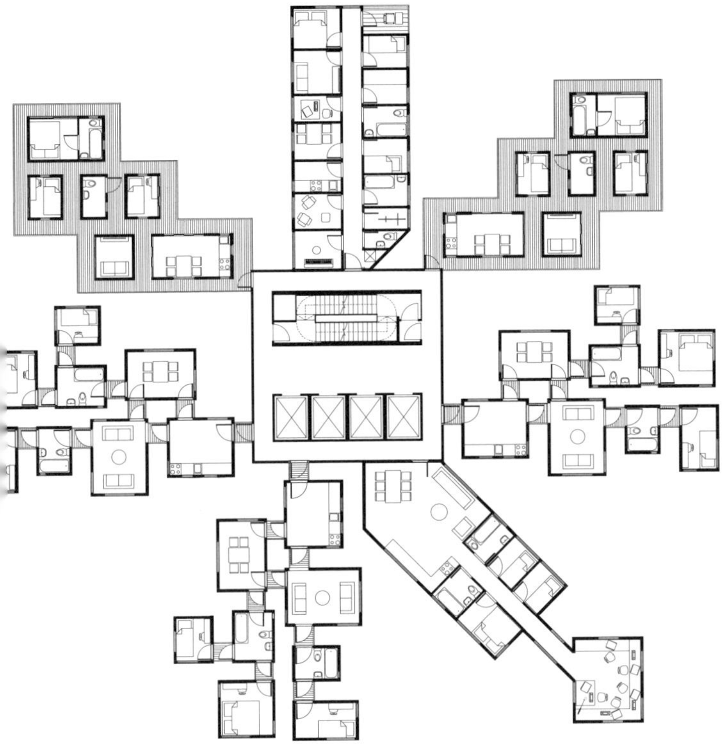

Towēr floor plan 1:400

129
Tower Score

69 | **194**

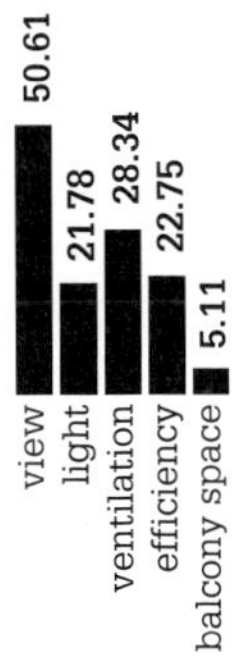

6,758
Amount of Roofscape (m2)

175
Amount of Apartments

84
Tower Height (m)

9.11
Plot Ratio

Scale 1:2000, View: South-East

The Collective Activity Tower

This tower excels in the creation of shared spaces that can be used to host collective activities, encourage social interaction, and foster community. It is composed of apartment typologies that support connectivity and mediate between private and shared spaces. For example, the swim-around-the-house apartment connects with the neighbouring apartment to enable sharing. Private balconies face each other to facilitate socializing, and they can be combined to form larger, shared balcony spaces. The design adds 5,260 m^2 of rooftop space, compared to the typical tower.

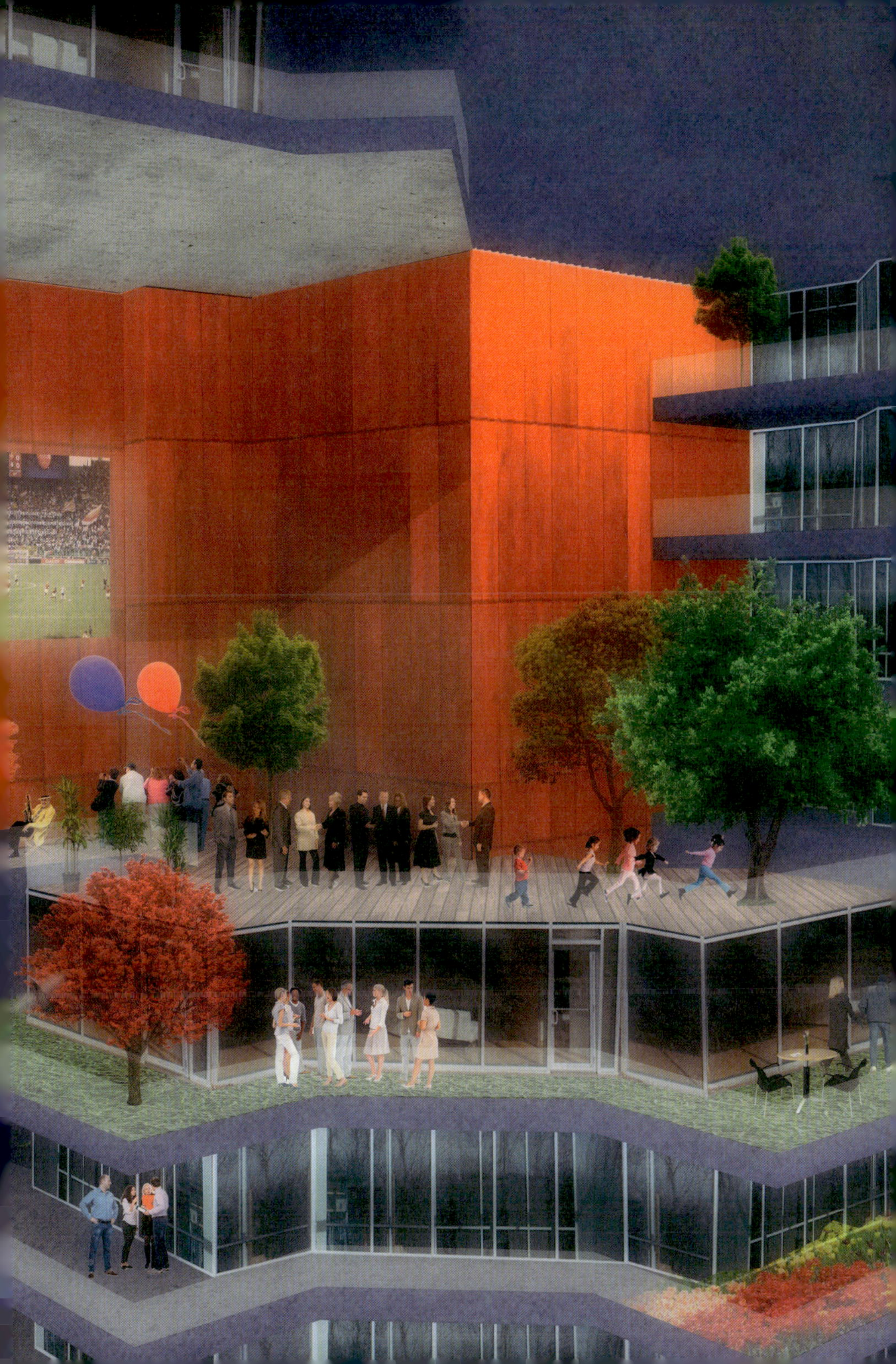

Tower Configuration

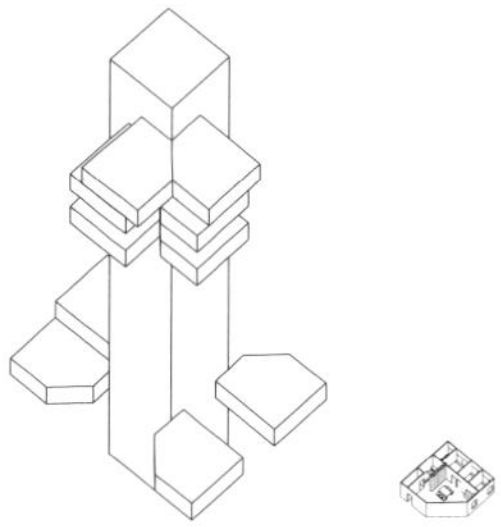

Meet the maid everywhere

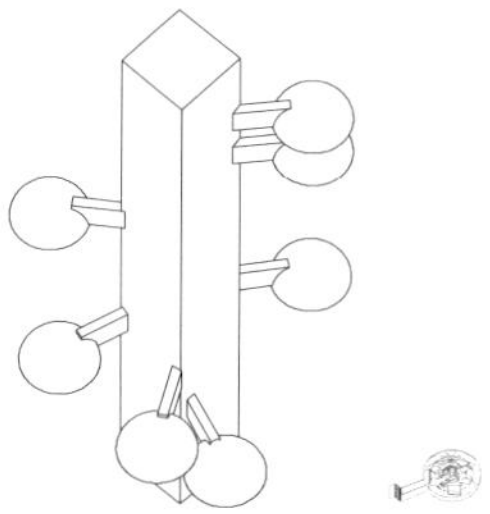

The observatory

Wrap-around balcony

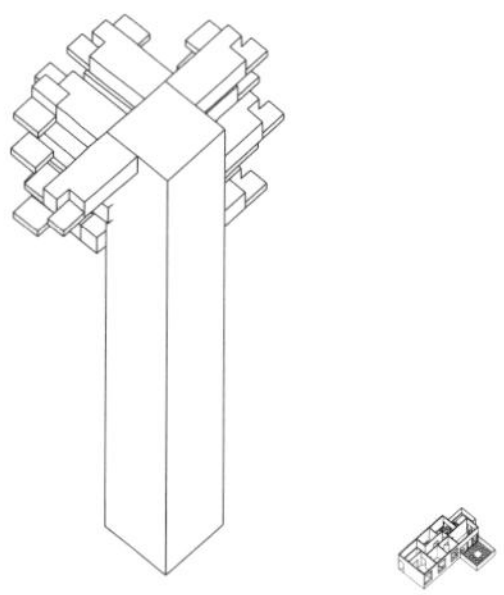

Picnicking sky-high

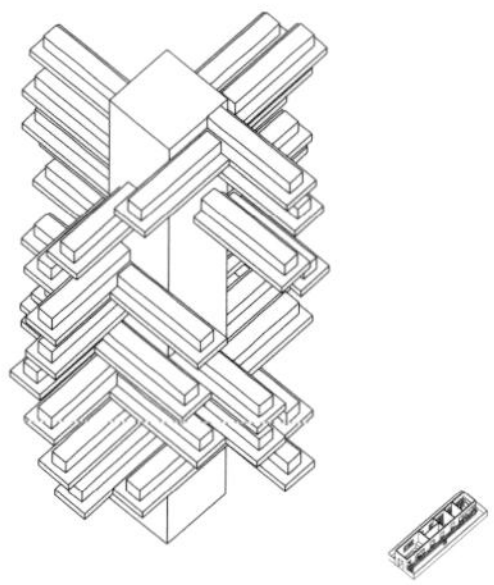

Swimming around the house

Seven private balconies

View: South-East

With larger and more abundant spaces for social interaction, this tower encourages the creation of a vertical neighbourhood enlivened by increased communal activity and communication. The tower contains 170 apartments and scores 145 points. It has a plot ratio of 8.89.

Tower floor plan 1:400

Scale 1:2000, View: South-East

145
Tower Score

65
Lowest Apartment Score

210
Highest Apartment Score

5,269
Amount of Roofscape (m2)

170
Amount of Apartments

84
Tower Height (m)

8.89
Plot Ratio

The Natural Breeze Tower

This tower stands out for its porosity. It mixes apartment typologies with the highest potential for natural ventilation. The apartments are stacked and positioned to maximize porosity and support the natural circulation of wind currents. The lower floors contain a smaller number of apartments, in order to maximize porosity, while the upper floors contain a higher density of apartments per floor, as higher elevations are subject to stronger wind currents.

Tower Configuration

Sky bridges

Wrap-around balcony

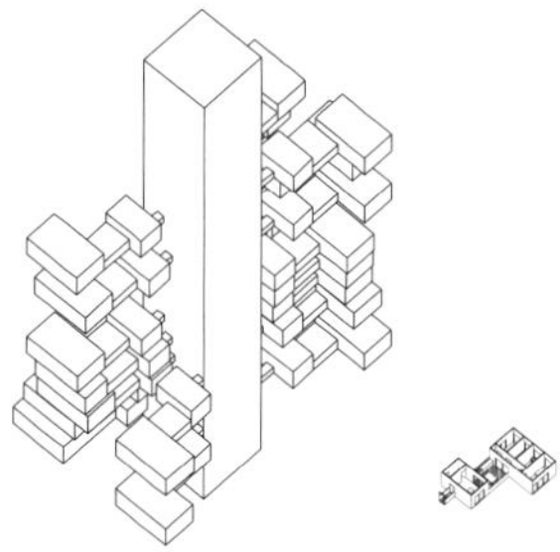

Cooking with natural breeze

Flexible space

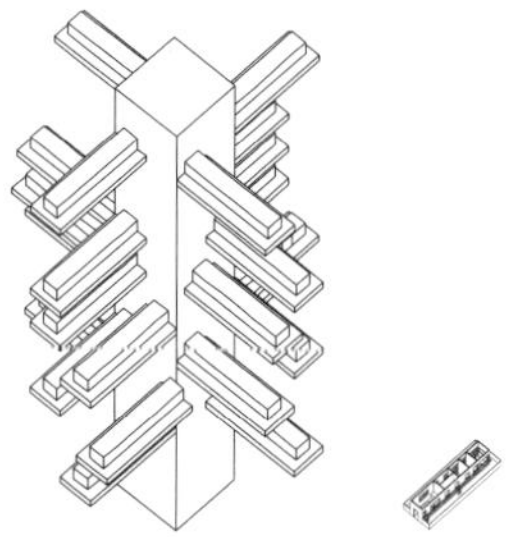

Swimming around the house

View: South-East

By letting wind currents through, this tower decreases the urban heat island effect that has become a problem in densely developed cities such as Hong Kong. It has an average score of 158 points, scoring high on factors such as natural ventilation and view.

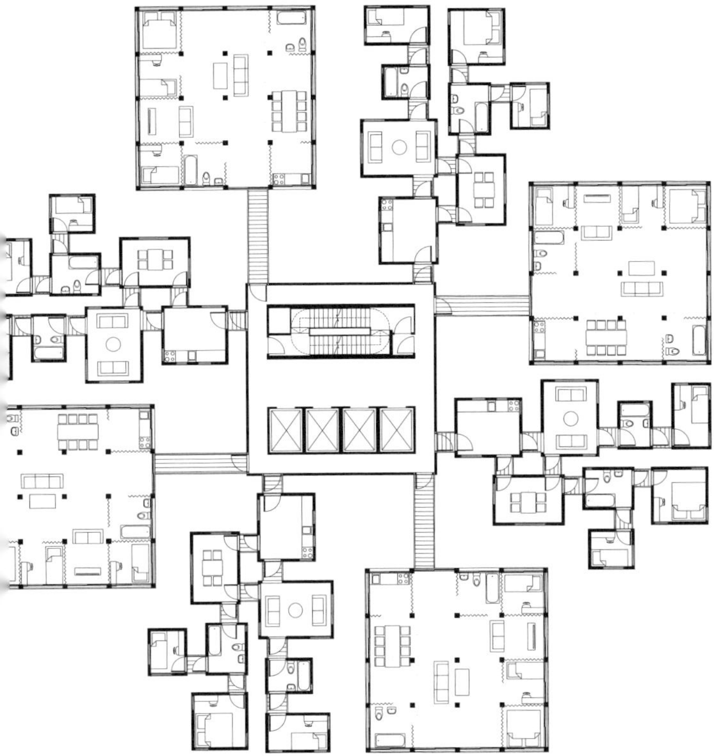

Tower floor plan 1:400

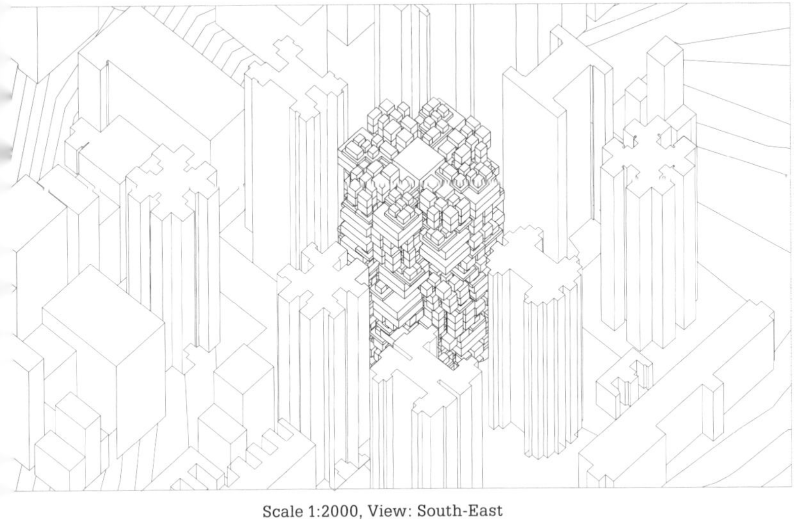

Scale 1:2000, View: South-East

158
Tower Score

93
Lowest Apartment Score

203
Highest Apartment Score

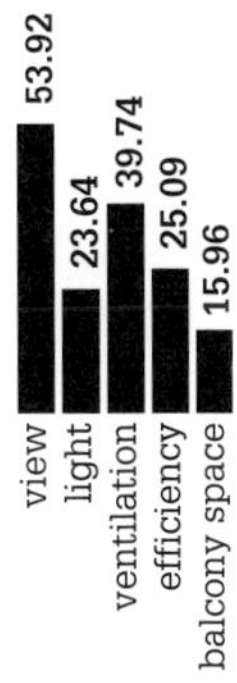

5,002
Amount of Roofscape (m2)

175
Amount of Apartments

84
Tower Height (m)

9.11
Plot Ratio

The Specialized Compact Tower

This tower was designed with the objective of stacking as many specialized apartments together as possible without adjusting initial plans. The idea was to experiment with diversifying the typical residential tower while achieving the same plot ratio. The tower fits 197 apartments—five more than the reference tower—and maintains a plot ratio of 10.09, which is only slightly above the benchmark plot ratio. The additional five apartments are fitted into the upper floors. Most apartments in this tower score 100 points or higher, and the highest scoring apartment reaches 206 points. The lowest scoring apartments, with 78 points, are located in the first four floors, where views and light are limited.

Tower Configuration

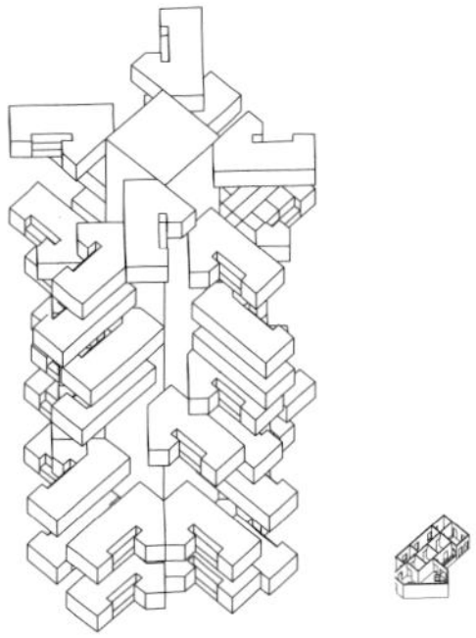

The maid's own paradise

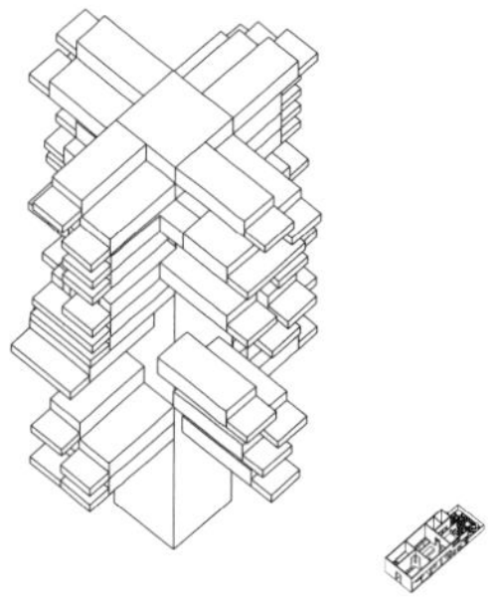

Sleeping on top of each other

Hide all your belongings in the walls

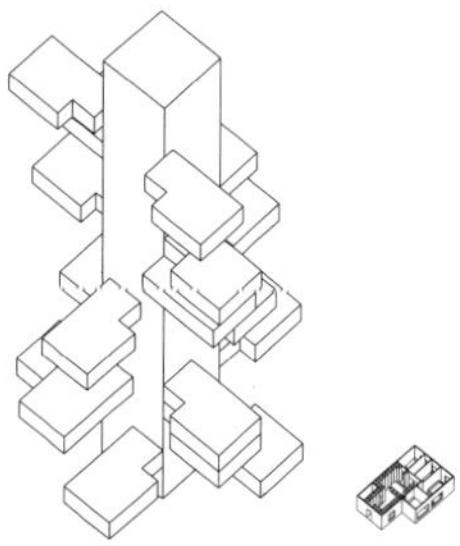

The central super store

Flexible space

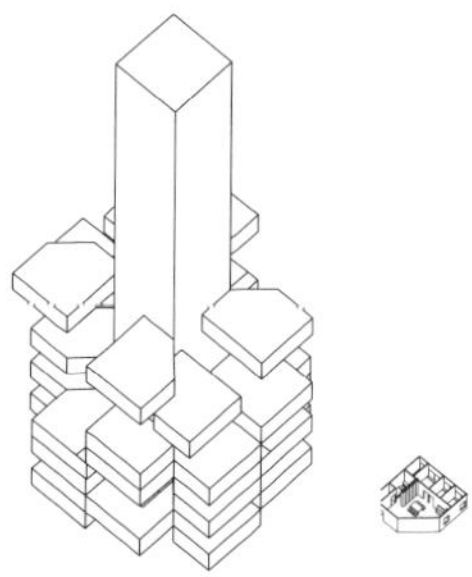

Meet the maid everywhere

View: South-East

Despite its compactness, this tower has a substantial amount of outdoor space, including 6,758 m^2 of accessible rooftop area. On average, each apartment gains 38 m^2 of additional outdoor space. If its relatively high standards for light and views are slightly lowered, the tower has the potential to be rearranged to fit over 200 apartments while maintaining its height of 84 meters.

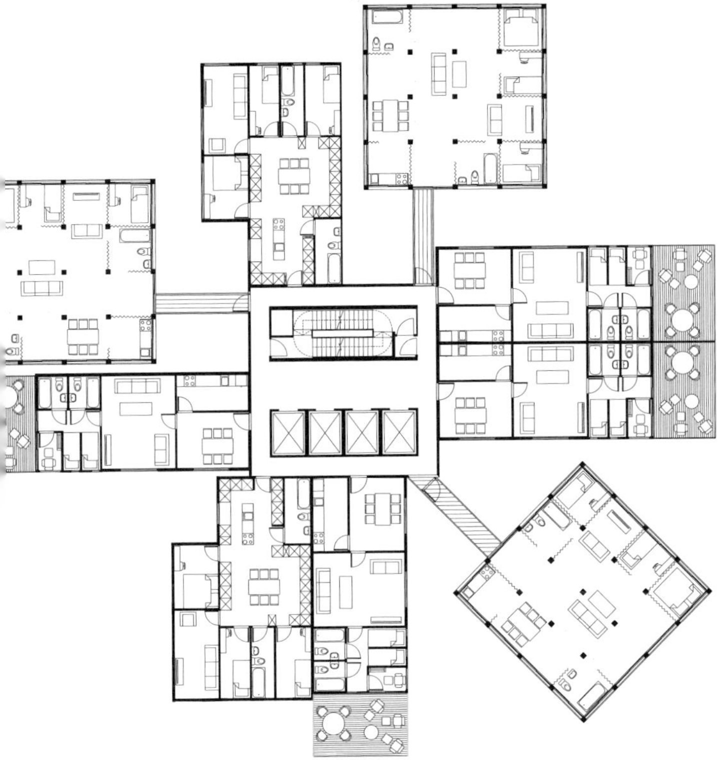

Tower floor plan 1:400

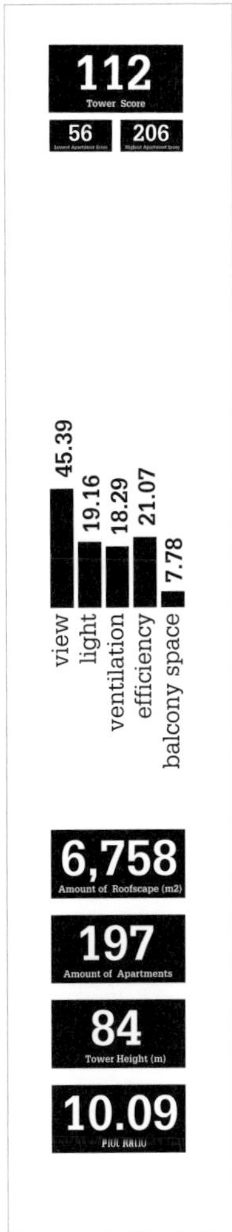

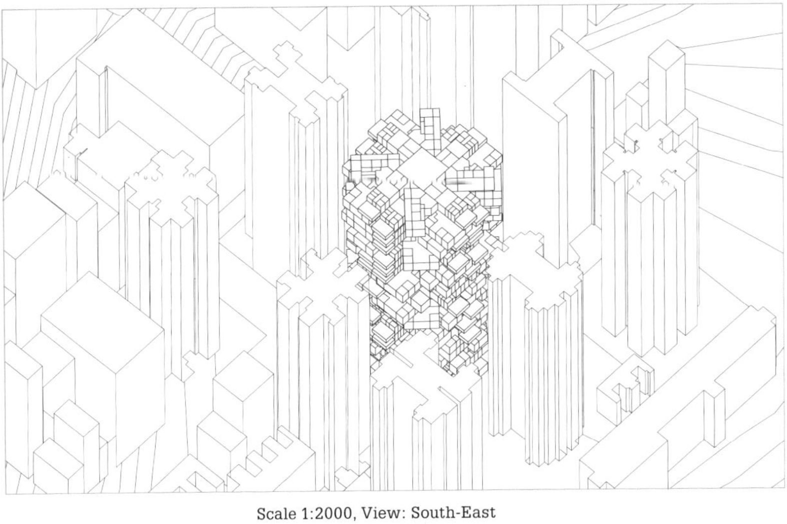

Scale 1:2000, View: South-East

The Great Outdoors Tower

What if the warmth, comfort, and security of the indoors could be instilled into an outdoor atmosphere, forming space that blurs the indoors with the outdoors? This tower combines apartment typologies that maximize this kind of hybrid space. In these apartments, the outdoor spaces are connected to the apartments in such a way that the transition from indoor to outdoor space is fluid. In total, the tower contains 171 apartments and 7,237 m^2 of outdoor space.

Tower Configuration

Wrap-around balcony

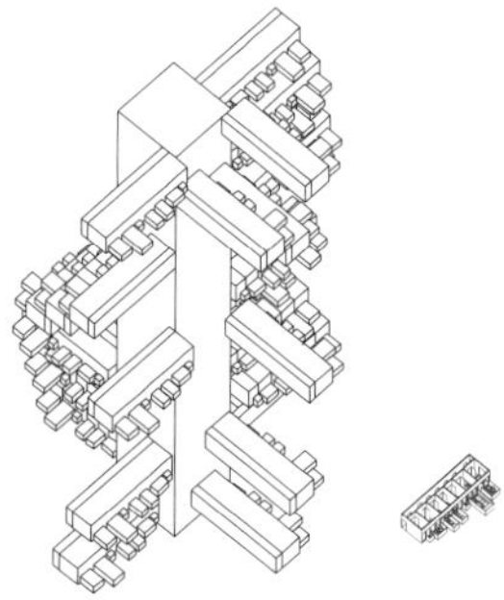

Seven private balconies

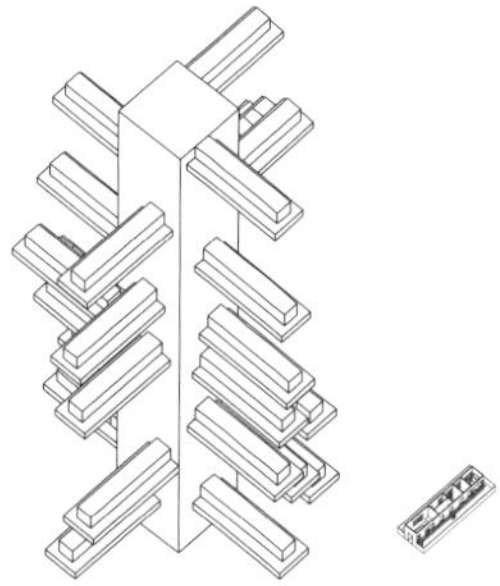

Swimming around the house

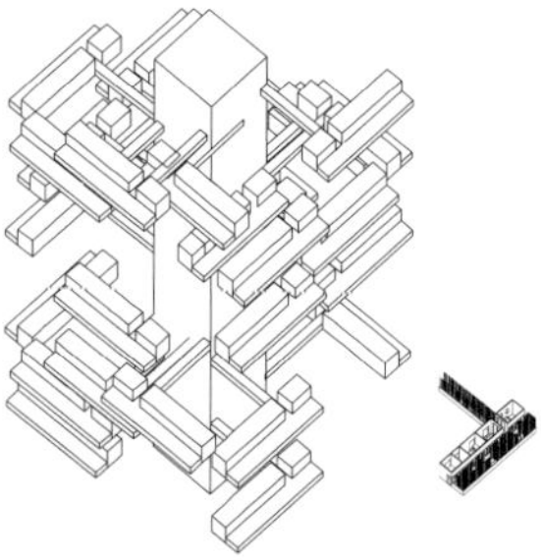

Bathing in nature

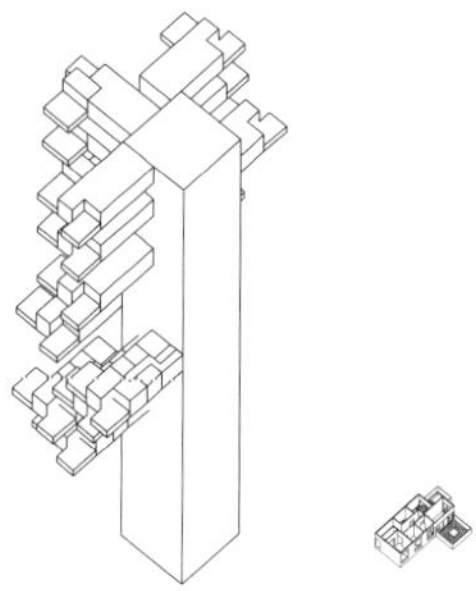

Picnicking sky-high

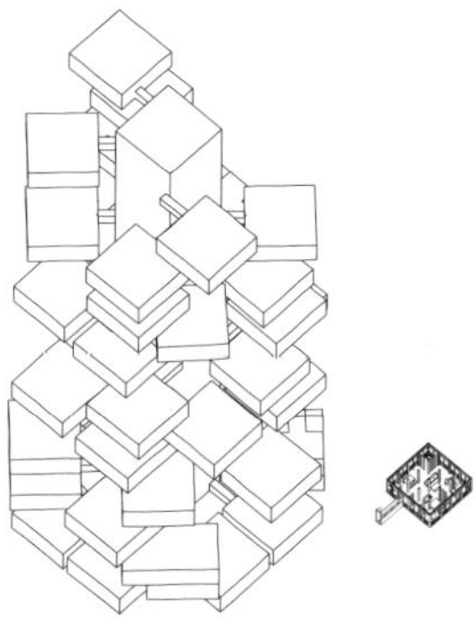

Flexible space

View: South-East

On average, each individual apartment has access to 42.30 m^2 of additional rooftop space. If the apartments are arranged following an objective of maximizing rooftop space, this tower could easily enlarge the size of the rooftop to over 8,000 m^2.

Tower floor plan 1:400

160

Tower Score

103

212

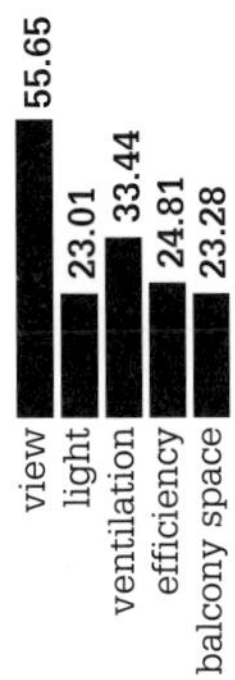

6,432

Amount of Roofscape (m2)

171

Amount of Apartments

84

Tower Height (m)

8.93

Plot Ratio

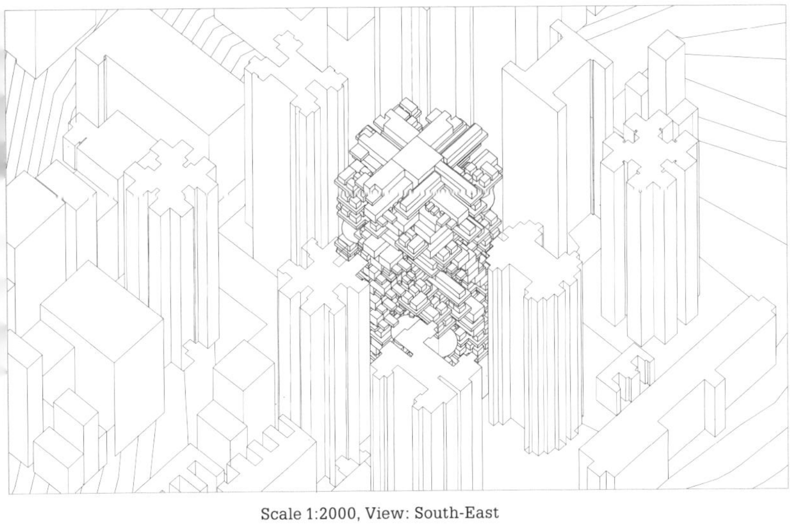

Scale 1:2000, View: South-East

The Maximum Diversity Tower

This tower is arranged according to the objective of maximizing the variety of apartments on each floor to give each floor an individual identity and a potential for unique interactions and experiences. All 20 specialized apartment typologies are included in this tower design, each appearing about 8 to 9 times but always with a different relationship to its immediate surroundings.

Tower Configuration

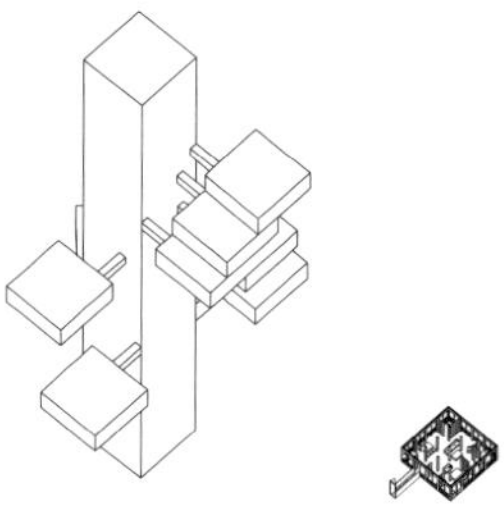

Flexible space

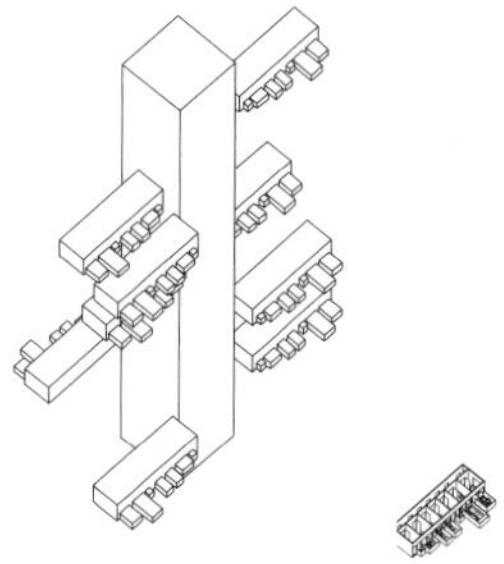

Seven private balconies

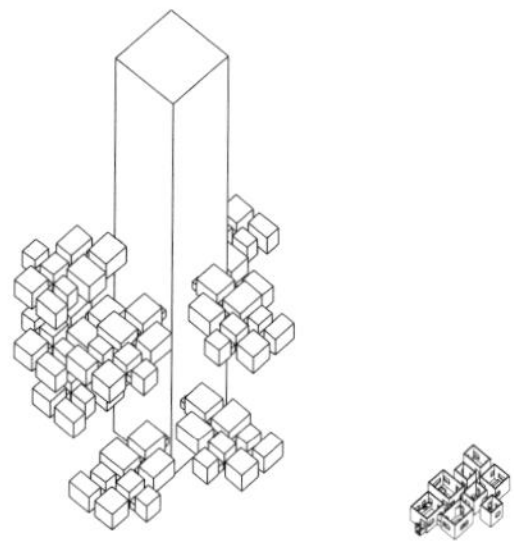

Sky bridges

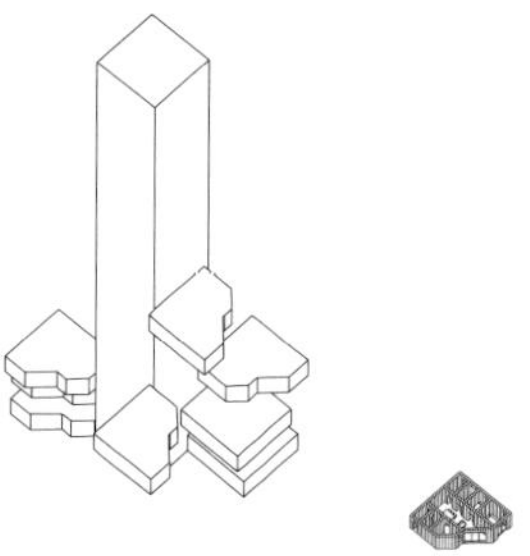

Hide all your belongings in the walls

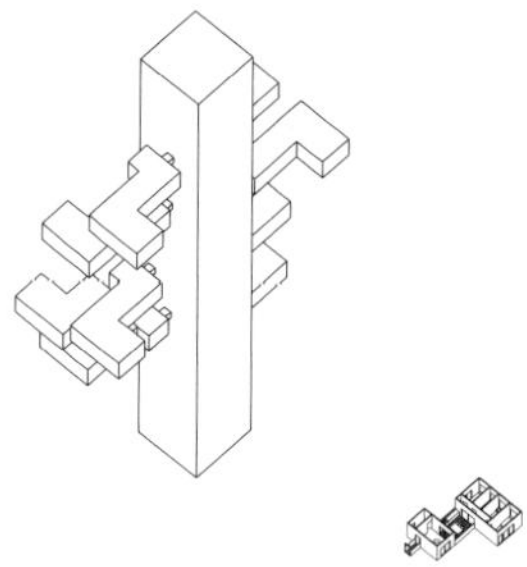

Cooking with natural breeze

Books everywhere

View: South-East

Other apartments used for this tower are: Wrap-around balcony, Bathing in nature, Swimming around the house, Sleeping under the stars, Sleeping on top of each other, Dining with panoramic views, Picnicking sky-high, Enjoying home-grown food, The observatory, Separated living activities, The maid's own paradise, Meet the maid everywhere, The central super store, Secluded and quiet studying.

The height, orientation and positioning of the apartments follow the specific needs and characteristics of each specialized layout.
The tower fits a total of 177 apartments while maintaining acceptable conditions for light and view in all apartment units. The lowest scoring apartment still scores slightly higher than the average apartment of the reference tower, with 103 points.

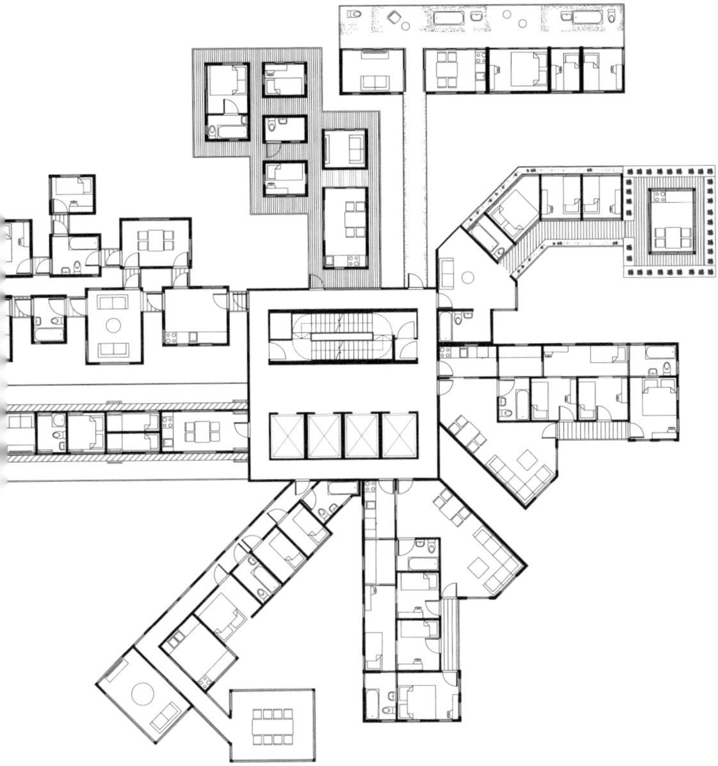

Tower floor plan 1:400

119
Tower Score

61 **211**

4,824
Amount of Roofscape (m2)

177
Amount of Apartments

84
Tower Height (m)

9.20
Plot Ratio

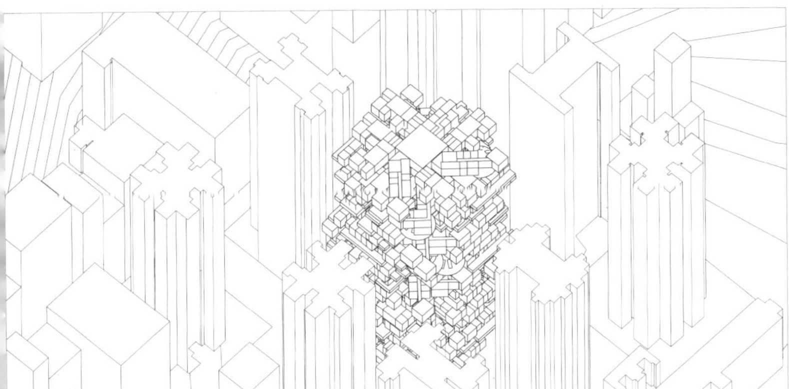

Scale 1:2000, View: South-East

Studio 1 Exhibition Models.

Text by Tihamér Salij

Modelled by the students of The Why Factory's "Hong Kong Tower Revolution" studio at the Department of Architecture (Architecture and Urban Design III, ARCH 5001) at the Hong Kong University, during Fall 2013.

Studio Tutors: Prof. Winy Maas and Tihamér Salij
with Sander Mulders and Arend van Waart
Students: Au Wing Yi, Chak Tsz Kin, Chan Chung Man, Chan Ian Yin Yan, Chan Pui Yin, Chau Shek Lun, Cheng Ching, Ip Kai Hong, Liu Kemeng, Mok Wang Chee, Tang Ho Yin, Kong Ho Ching, Kwok Ka Ching, Lau Xin Yee, Lee Kin Wai, Li Mei Yu, Lung Man Ching, Ma Ching Yi, Suen Wing Yin, Sze Ivy, Sze Ying Ying, Yeung Cho Yui, Yeung Ho Man

Students of the design studio fabricated a total of 30 model housing towers, each designed according to its own set of objectives. The model towers were arranged into three rows, representing three different motivating principles for vertical organization: the provision of shared communal spaces, the provision of private outdoor spaces, and the provision of both.

A standard housing tower, one that follows current Hong Kong regulations and demonstrates the prevailing principle of extrusion, was used as a point of reference. The model housing towers each received a score based on their performance in each value indicator.

TOWER ALFRESCO
BUFFET VILLAGE
Private Study Tower

In general, the new housing tower typologies reflected a higher degree of porosity (open space). All towers were measured against value indicators such as view, direct sunlight, indirect daylight, direct access to outdoor space, and amount of useable space.

FOOD EXPRESS
FRESHNESS CULINARY
SKYWALKER
Insular Community
Tree of Sociality

Some qualitative improvements called for higher ceilings, more window openings, more outdoor spaces, or more privacy. Others asked for different connections, better natural cooling, more sustainable measures, or better views. Each tower necessarily required a specific spatial configuration, which was studied separately on the scale of the floor plan.

The collection of proposed housing towers is meant to open up discussion and explore the possibility for more diverse forms of housing. This discussion necessarily calls existing building regulations into question and seek answers to the question of why current housing development in Hong Kong suffers from uniformity and poor living qualities.

What if we deviated from the simplex apartment standard, or from the use of a standard core? Could the podium volumes of Hong Kong's podium towers be improved, to dialogue with the living activities in the apartments they support? Could we imagine towers with a variety of different programmes, programmes that contribute to the city and correspond with the diverse wishes of their users?

The following proposed residential towers were designed with combinations of specialized simplex, duplex, and triplex apartments and joined with customized programmes that extend far beyond the generic restaurant and retail model of a conventional podium and seek to enhance the tower as a whole.

How Do Towers with Specialized Apartments and Public Programme Score?

Text by Tihamér Salij

Developed and illustrated by the students of The Why Factory's "Towers Beyond Extrusion" studio at the Department of Architecture (Architecture and Urban Design III, ARCH 5001) at the Hong Kong University, during Fall 2014.

Scoring drawings and diagrams illustrated by The Why Factory: Tihamér Salij and Claudia Mainardi with Sylwia Franczak

Studio Tutors: Prof. Winy Maas, Tihamér Salij, Martine Vledder with Donn Holohan
Students: Au Yeung Chun Yu JOEY, Chan Fong Tong FRED S, Cheng Pok Him BOB, Ching Ka Ho FRED, Henao Granda Jan Esteban, Ho Sheung Hay TERENCE, Hu Xiangdong HOCK, Ko Pak Kan ZETH, Li Zhixin ALLISON, Liu Chuen Yung VINCENT, Ma Yue, Qin Liting TING, Tang Tak Shing KELVIN, Wen Fan, Wu Yucong, Xie Junni, Ffion Zhang, Ho Yin SUNNY CHA, Sai Bond, Man Hei KENNIF, Han PAT

The Fireplace Tower

Jan Esteban Granda Henao

The concept of this tower is to provide every floor with an open fireplace and a corresponding chimney. Many of us have experienced the comfort of gathering outdoors around a warm, crackling fire under a starry night sky. Why not introduce this enjoyment into the space of everyday living? With over 400 chimneys and a total of 1,649 square meters of accessible outdoor space, this tower creates a veritable world of fireplaces. Rising 189 meters tall, the tower is comprised of 20 simplex, 100 duplex, and 72 triplex apartments, all of which score above 129 points. The highest scoring apartments, with scores of 256 points, are located in the upper floors of the tower and enjoy impressive views on all sides. The outdoor fireplaces invite inhabitants to grill and cook and host dinners against a garden backdrop. A glass-ceramic enclosure ensures safety without visually obstructing the fire.

Apartment lay outings

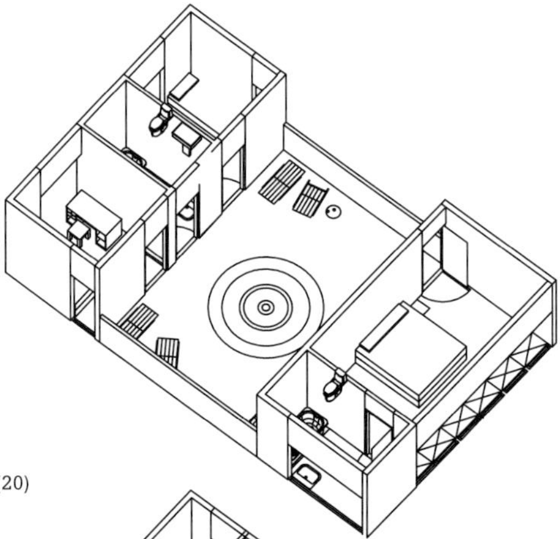

Simplex (20)

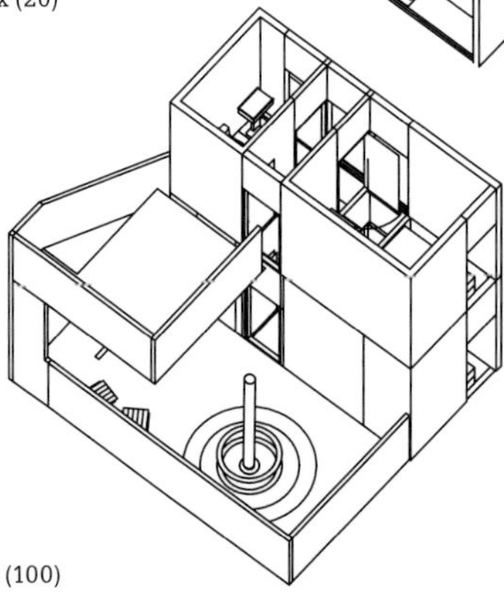

Duplex (100)

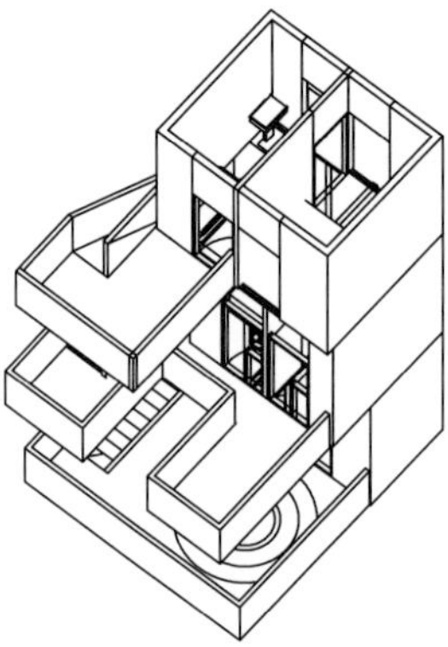

Triplex (72)

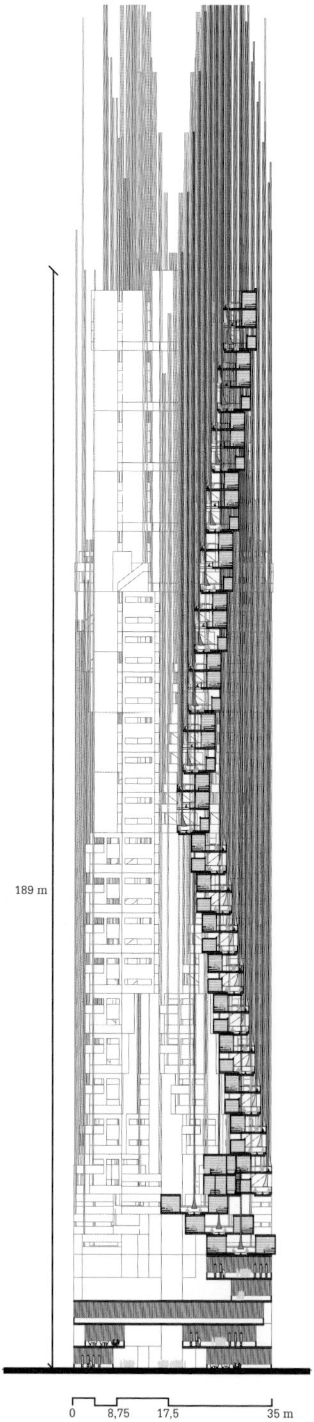

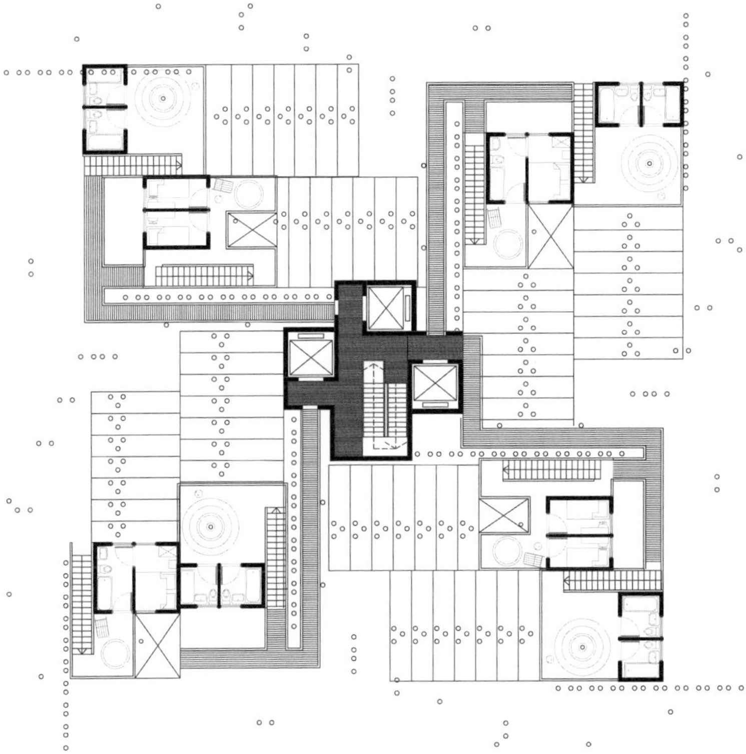

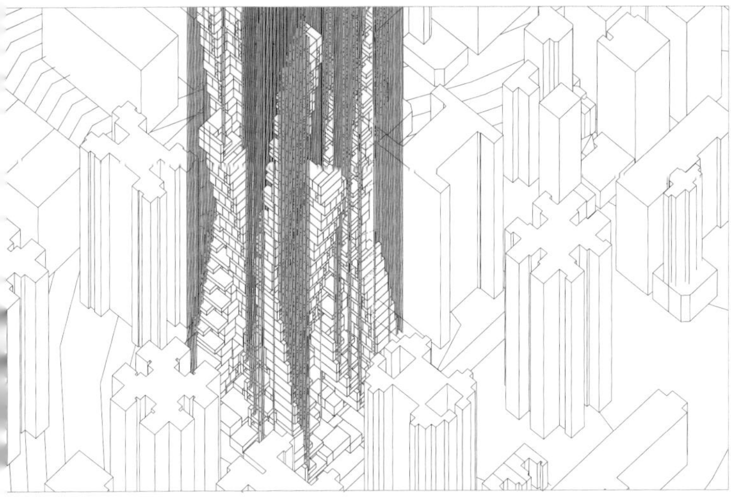

199
Tower Score

129
Lowest Apartment Score

256
Highest Apartment Score

1,649
Amount of Roofscape (m2)

192
Amount of Apartments

189
Tower Height (m)

9.87
Plot Ratio

The Labyrinth Tower

Tang Tak Shing KELVIN

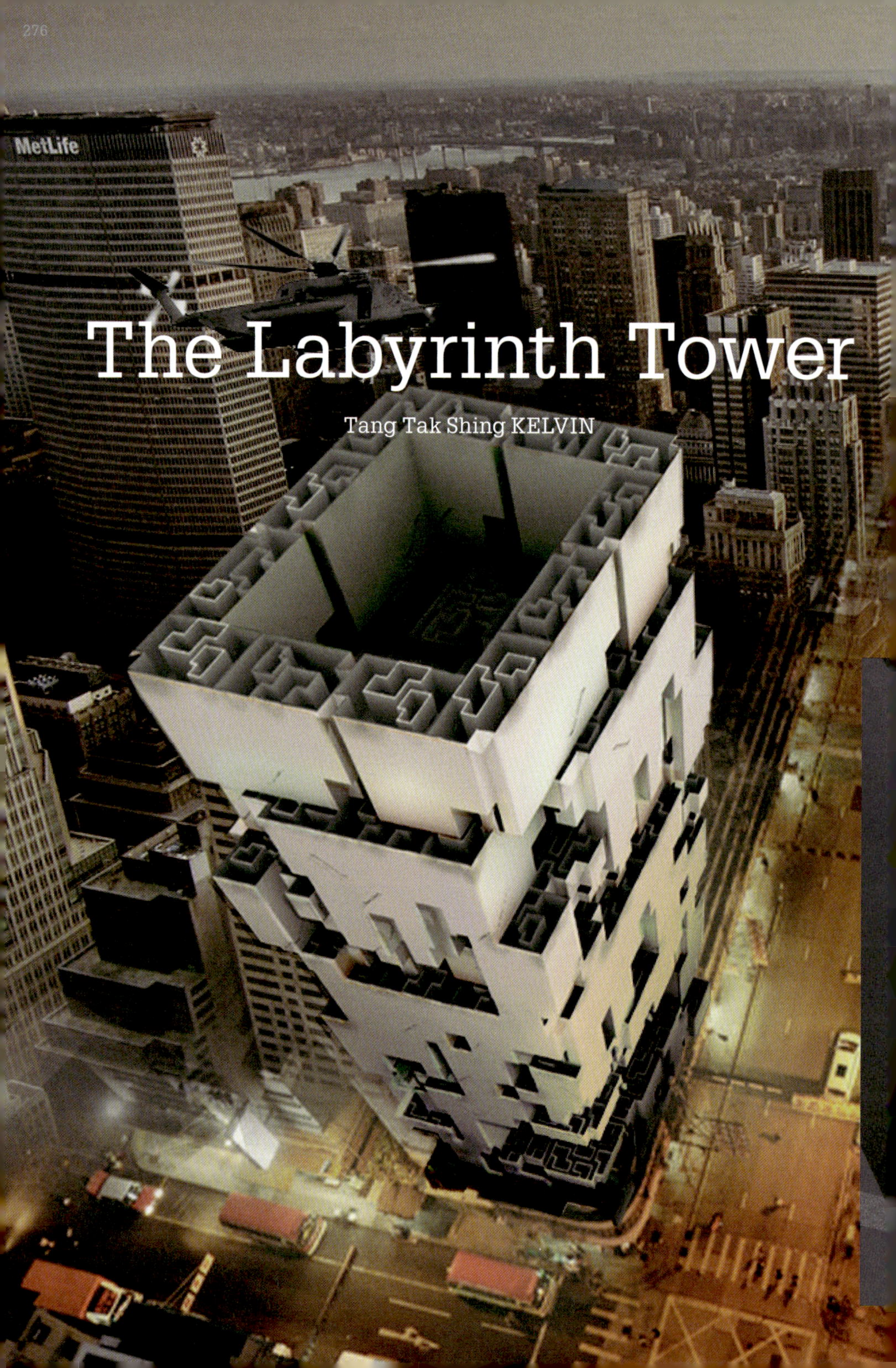

This objective of this tower is to provide extreme privacy for all inhabitants, in essence by blocking visual access to apartment units. Light and ambience are generated and controlled by glass ceilings (rooftops). A staircase system and corridors throughout the tower guarantee vertical as well as horizontal connectivity. The podium programme is used for additional light boxes, open voids that create extra needed daylight in the tower. The labyrinthine quality of the building interior generates an atmosphere of playful, hide-and-seek mystery. The 192 apartments are stacked and oriented to give each unit access to a minimum 35-degree-angle sky view through a glass ceiling. In total, the tower contains 68 simplex, 77 duplex, and 47 triplex apartments. Notably, the apartments in this tower sacrifice light and views for intensified levels of privacy. With apartments scoring between 42 and 129 points and an average score of 60 points, this tower is the lowest scoring tower in this selection.

Apartment lay outings

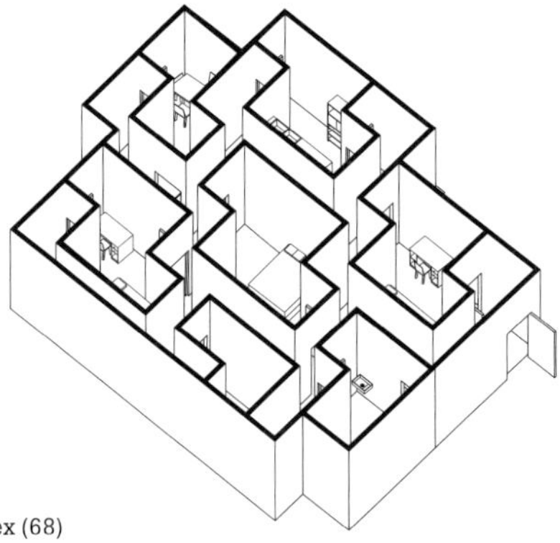

Simplex (68)

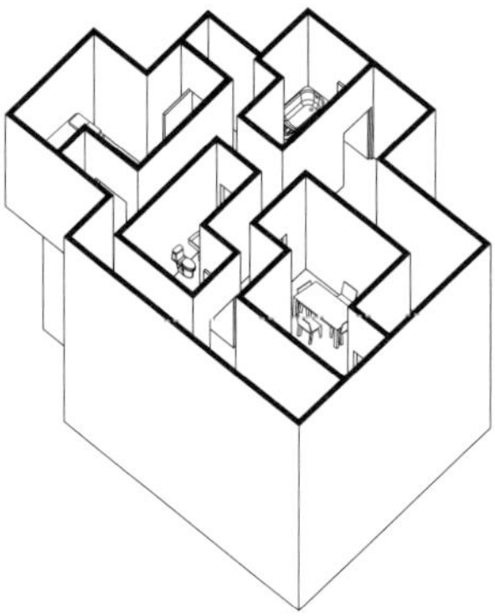

Duplex (77)

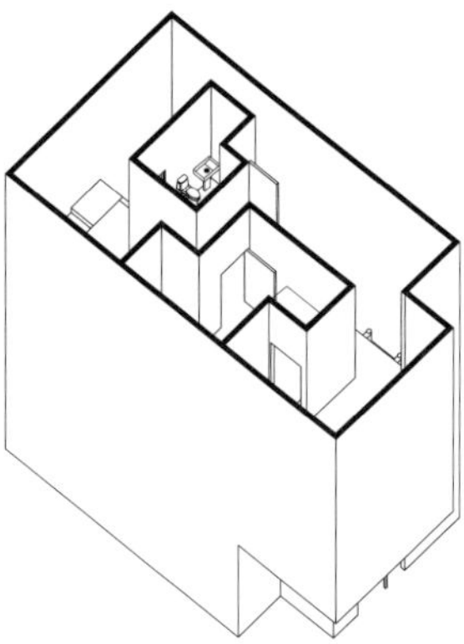

Triplex (47)

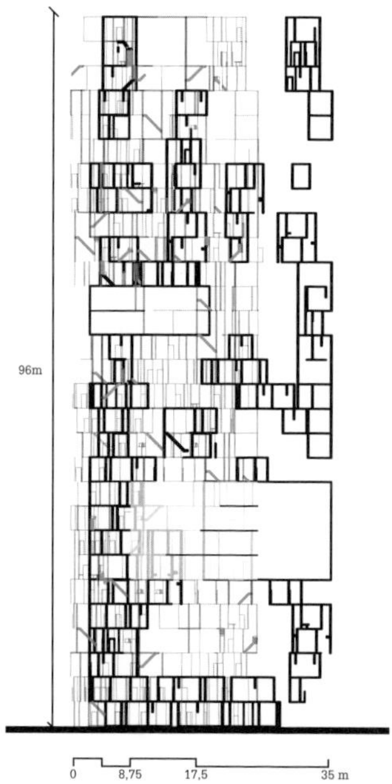

60
Tower Score

42
Lowest Apartment Score

129
Highest Apartment Score

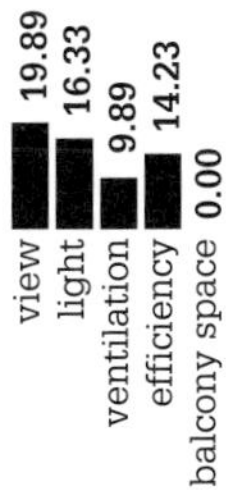

2,089
Amount of Roofscape (m2)

192
Amount of Apartments

96
Tower Height (m)

9.87
Plot Ratio

The Vertical Shopping Street

Cheng Pok Him BOB

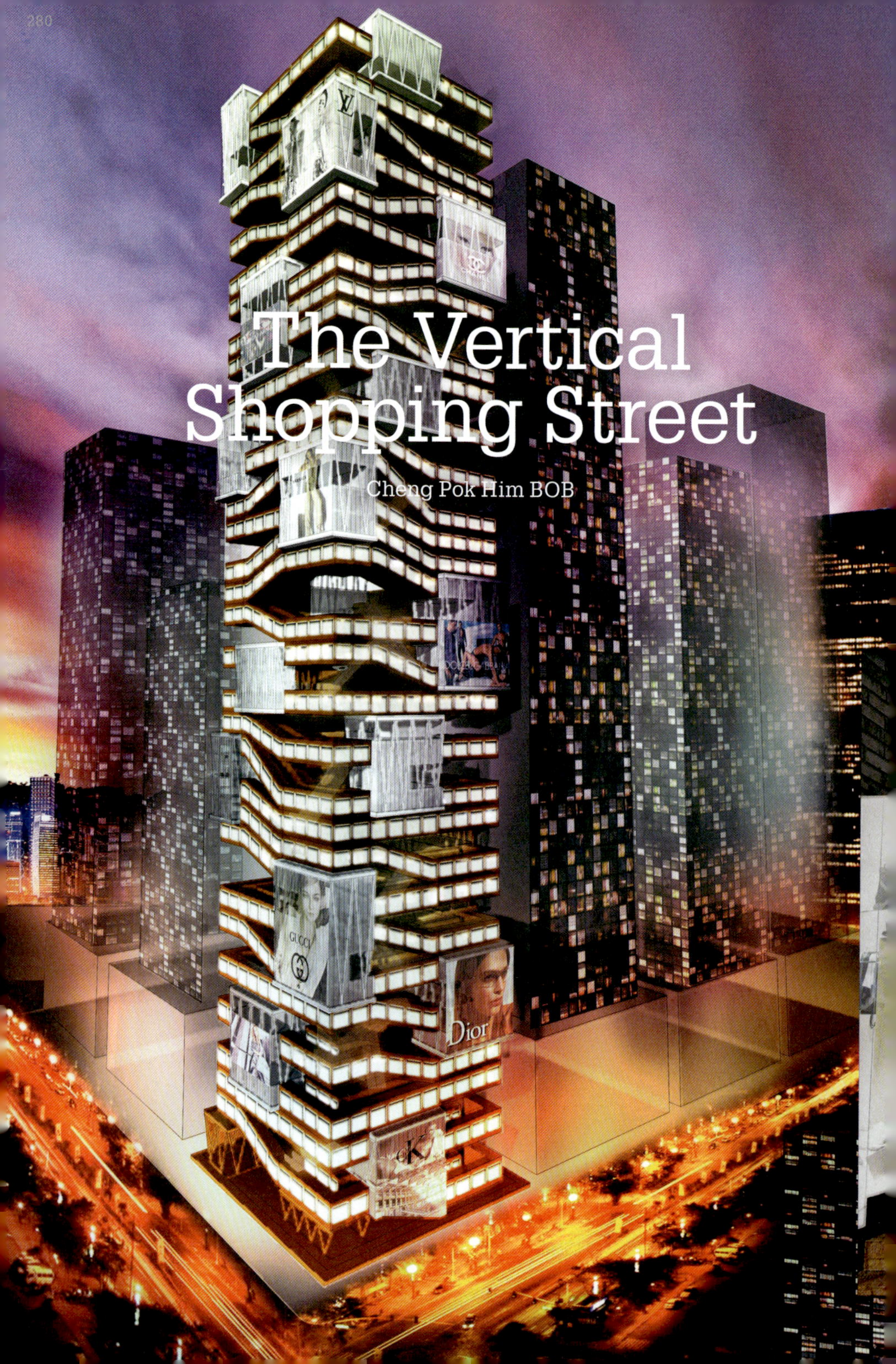

It has become almost impossible to avoid entering a mall when navigating contemporary Hong Kong. Taking this reality as a starting point, the Champs Elysees tower redefines the urban shopping experience. Rather than separating the residential tower from the retail programme typically contained in the four- to five-story podium on which it rests, the Champs Elysees tower takes a more hybrid approach. Here, dwelling and shopping are more integrated, their spaces positioned closely next to each other and folded into a vertical 'street' with an impressive backdrop of the Hong Kong skyline.

The apartments are organized linearly and divided by corridors that function as miniature streets. With their public, street-like quality, the corridors became architectural elements that create conditions for interiorized façades.

The podium is divided into shopping spaces varying in size and distributed evenly throughout the entire tower. The larger shopping spaces, that are positioned at the corners of the tower, create multiple shortcut connections between floors. Throughout the building, escalators facilitate circulation and also provide alternative routes. By stacking the apartments in a continuous strip that spirals vertically around a hollow core, this tower design generates a total of 8,234 m^2 of accessible roof top space. Apartments score between 244 and 120 points, and the tower scores a total of 186 points.

Apartment lay outings

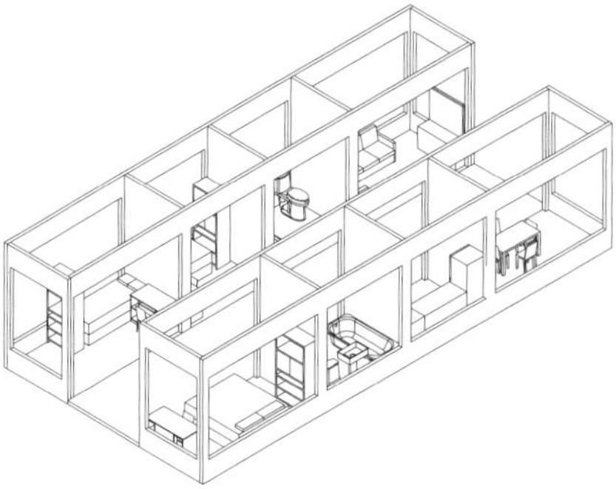

Simplex (120)

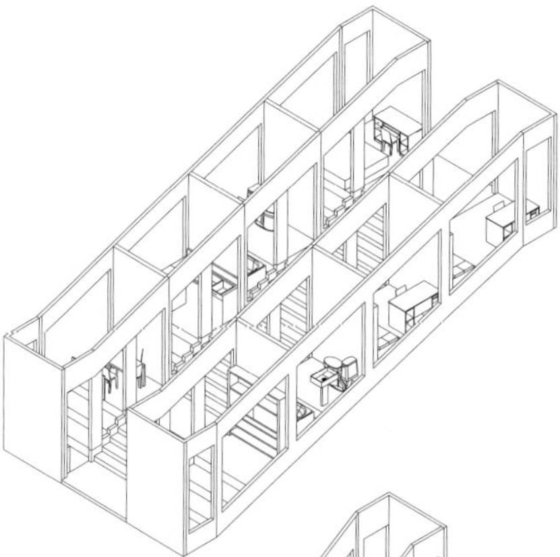

Duplex (66)

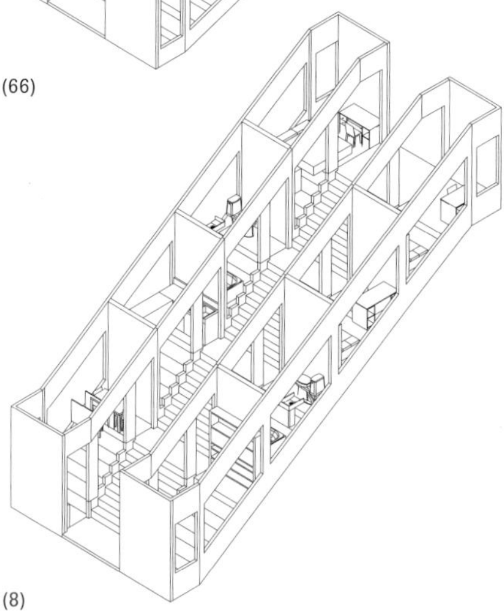

Triplex (8)

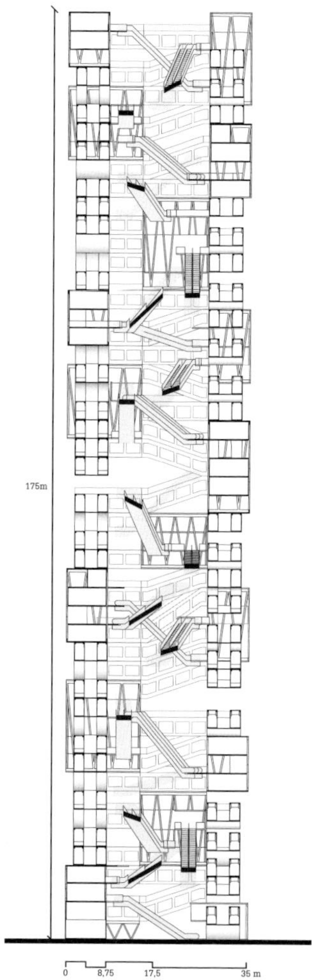

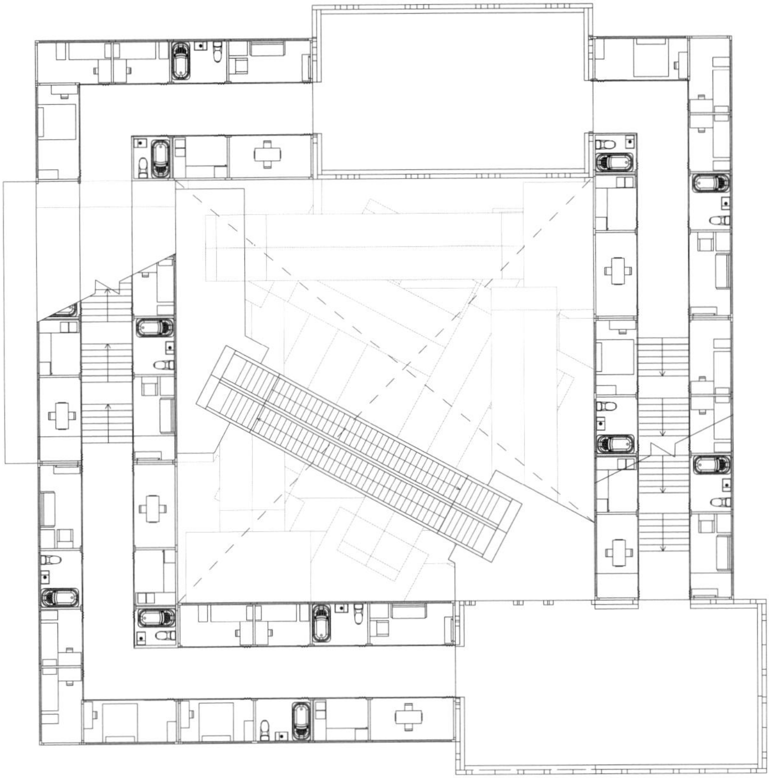

186
Tower Score

120
Lowest Apartment Score

244
Highest Apartment Score

8,144
Amount of Roofscape (m2)

192
Amount of Apartments

175
Tower Height (m)

9.87
Plot Ratio

The 24/7 Cinema Tower

Wen Fan

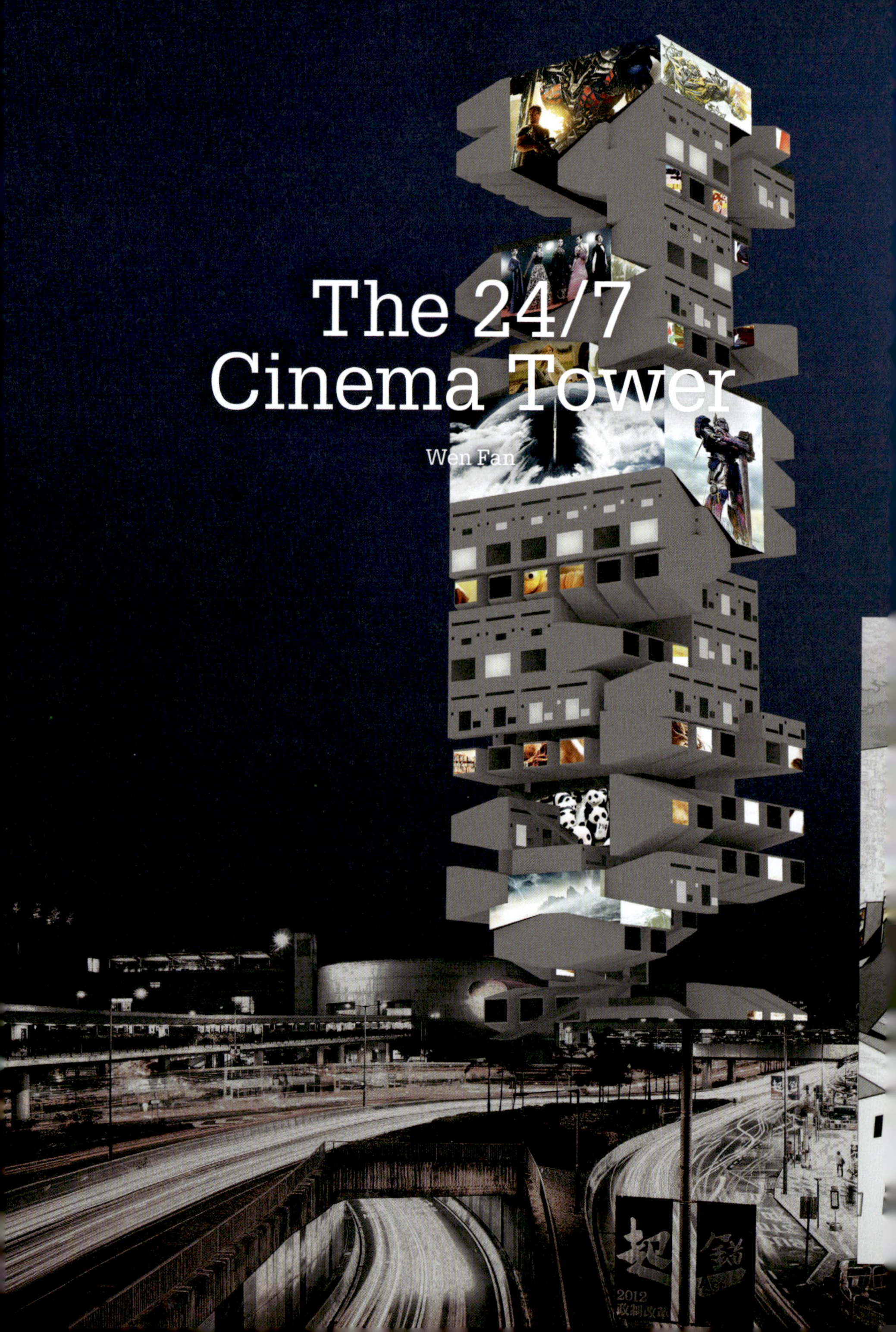

This tower was designed on the premise of integrating entertainment and multimedia experiences with everyday living. Each apartment features a home theatre with a large screen that can be seen from any corner of the apartment. Additional cinemas, screening rooms, and lounges, as well as a film academy and multimedia lab are featured in the building.
The apartments of the cinema tower are stacked in such a way that they join together to form the I-MAX theatre and smaller cinemas. Inhabitants of this tower are constantly surrounded by multimedia projections—a unique, playful environment that mixes the real with the virtual.
The 24/7 cinema tower is comprised of 19 simplex, 56 duplex, and 117 triplex apartments and has a height of 146 metres. It has 1,004 m^2 of outdoor rooftop space. The tower achieves a score of 139 points, with its lowest scoring apartments, with 101 points, situated on the lower floors, and its highest scoring apartments, with 202 points, situated on the highest floors. Qualitative indicators such as light, view and ventilation score relatively high in comparison to the reference tower. This tower could become a media icon and cultural magnet for the city.

Apartment lay outings

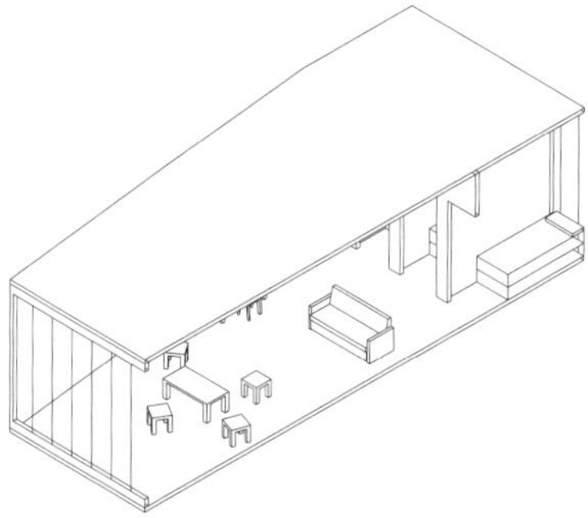

Simplex (19)

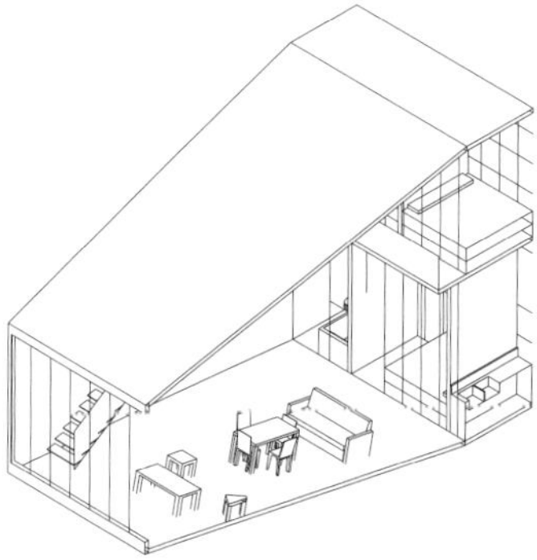

Duplex (56)

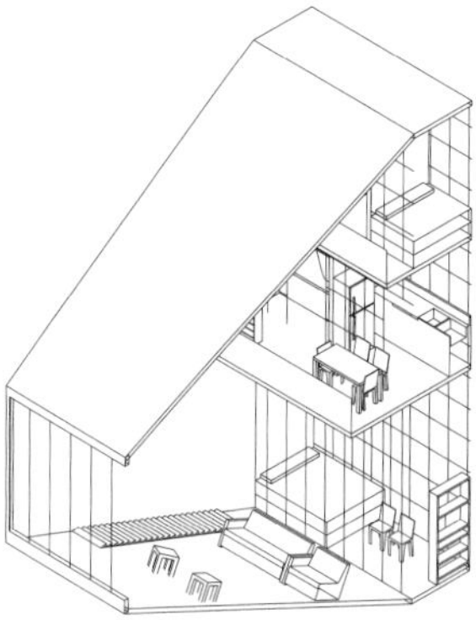

Triplex (117)

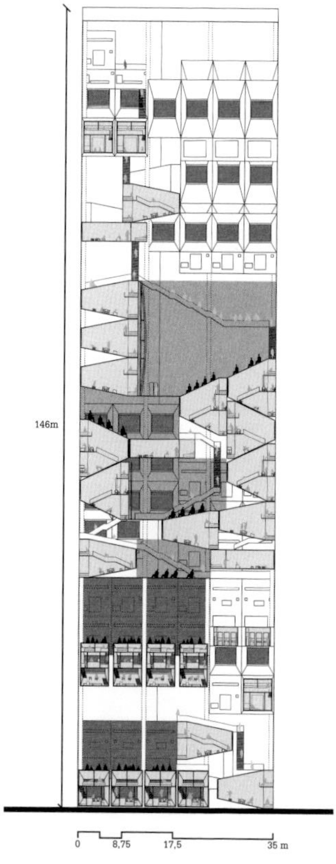

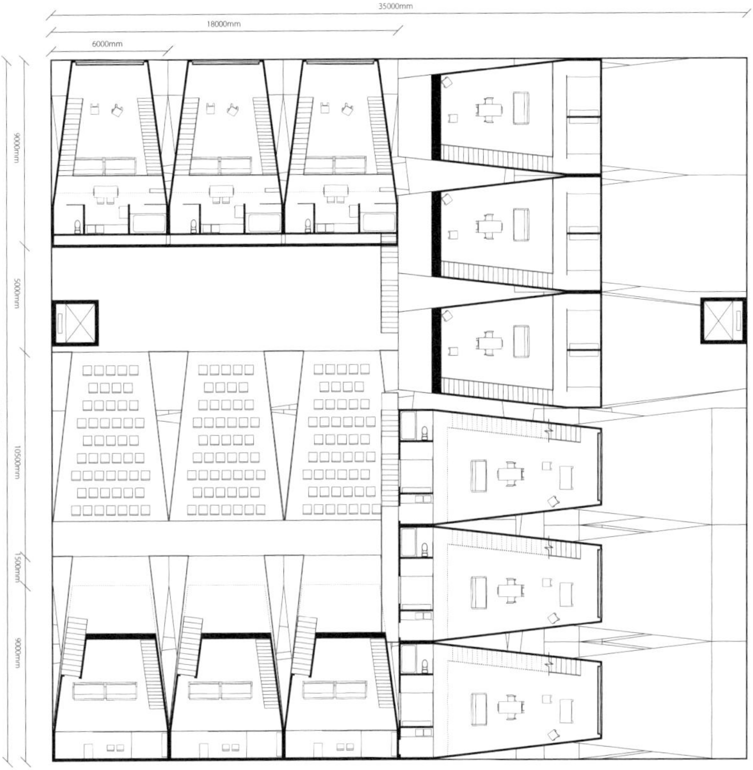

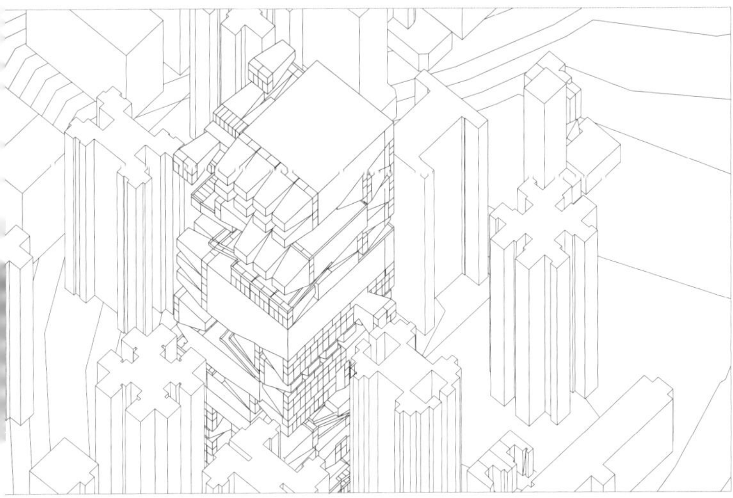

139
Tower Score

101
Lowest Apartment Score

202
Highest Apartment Score

1,004
Amount of Roofscape (m2)

192
Amount of Apartments

146
Tower Height (m)

9.87
Plot Ratio

The Sea Life Tower

Li Zhixin ALLISON

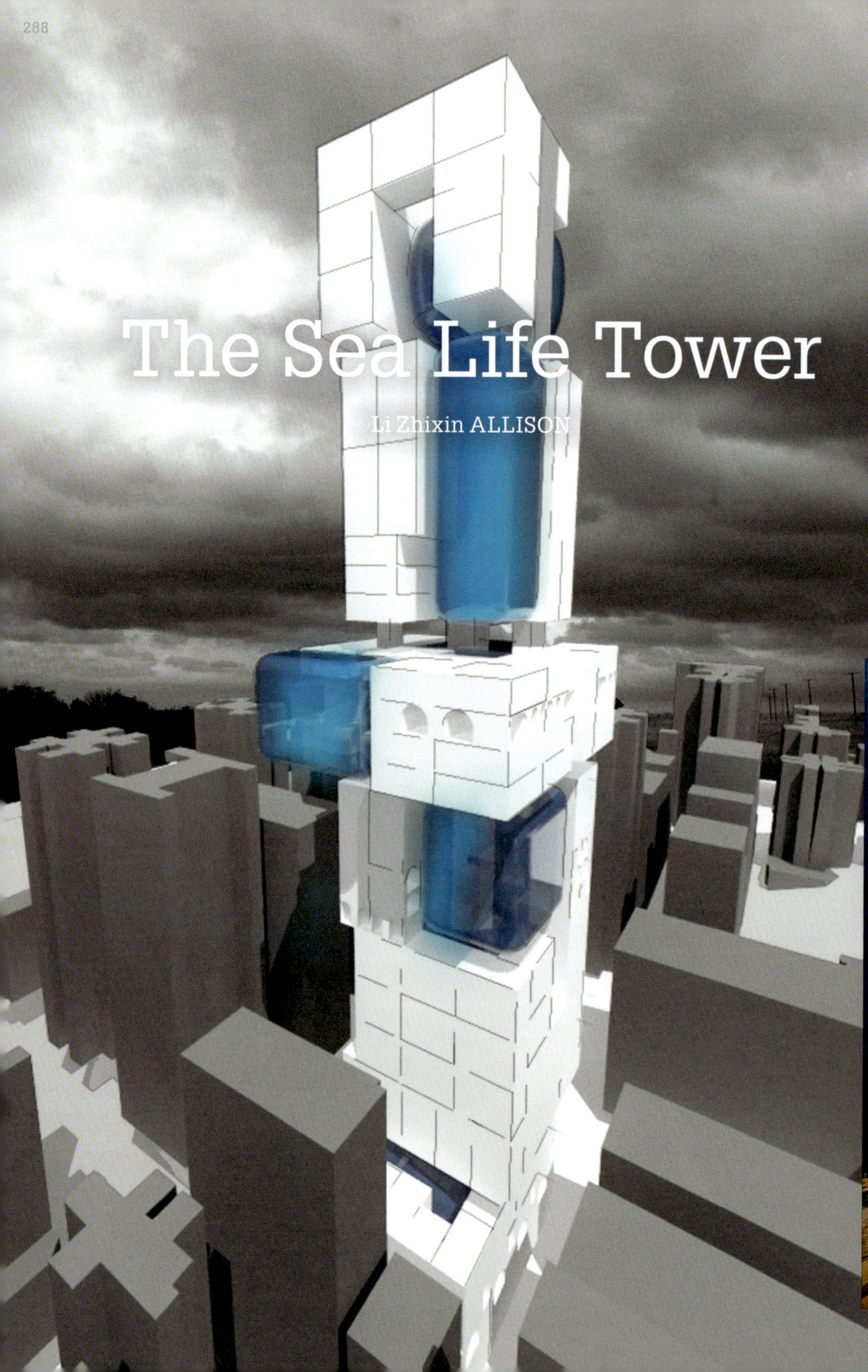

This tower explores the concept of integrating a spectacular aquatic ecosystem with urban life. Each of the 192 apartments has visual access to one of seven giant aquariums installed in the tower. The podium programme is adapted to house six additional aquariums that are provided for public enjoyment. Sharks, tortoises, sea lions, stingrays, and various species of tropical fish will animate the exterior of the tower and generate a sense of wonder. In the interior, inhabitants and visitors will find fish restaurants and fish farms breeding prized species of fish such as the popularly consumed but endangered Napoleon wrasse and coral grouper. The tower aims to raise public awareness about over-fishing and water pollution by providing a site for educational programmes. A diving school will also be located on site. The aquarium tower contains 42 simplex, 84 duplex, and 66 triplex apartments. It rises 158 metres high and provides 2,920 m^2 of accessible outdoor rooftop space. The highest scoring apartments are located near the larger water tanks, with apartments scoring highest on the upper floors. The lowest scoring apartments score between 56 and 70 points and are located on the first five floors. If visual access to the aquariums had been included i n the evaluation of views, the tower would have scored much higher. Nonetheless, all apartments are connected to the façade, ensuring sufficient levels of daylight, natural ventilation, and view. The tower scores a total of 113 points.

Apartment lay outings

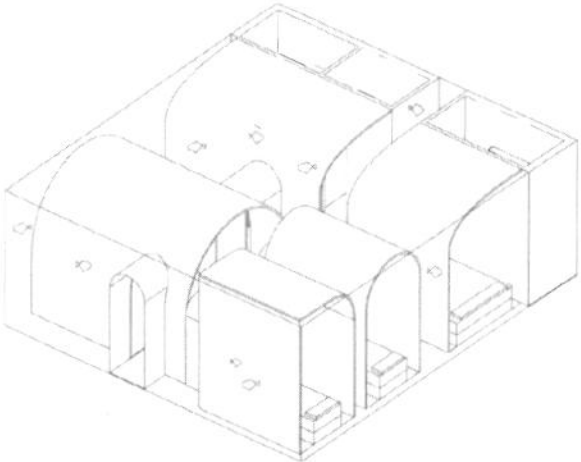

simplex (52)

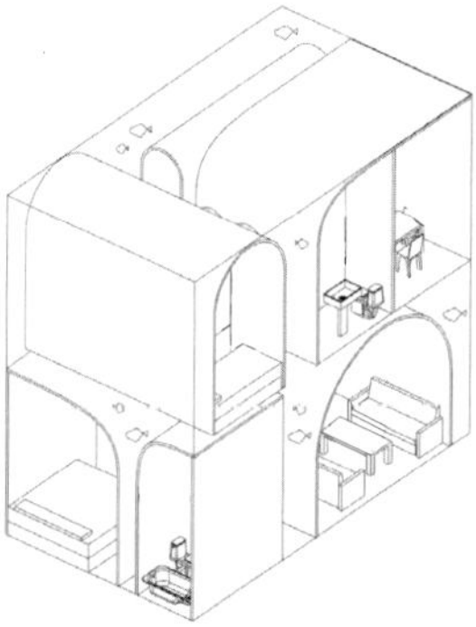

Duplex (84)

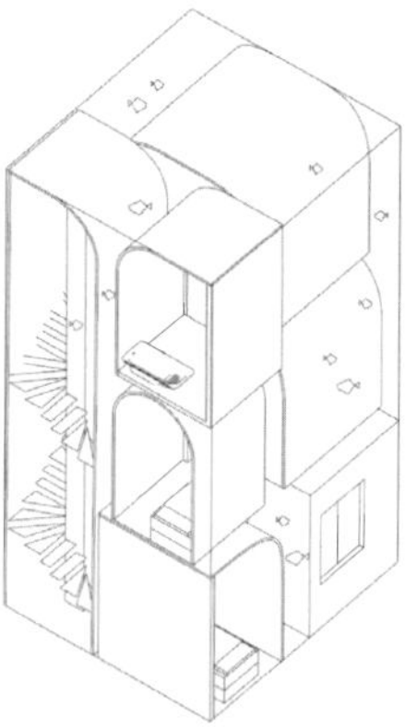

Triplex (66)

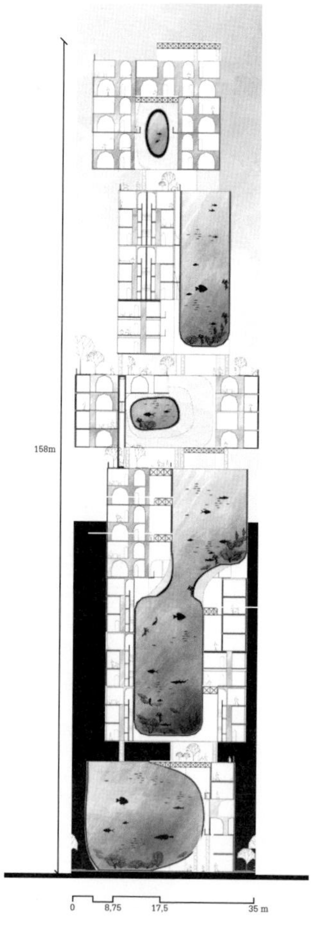

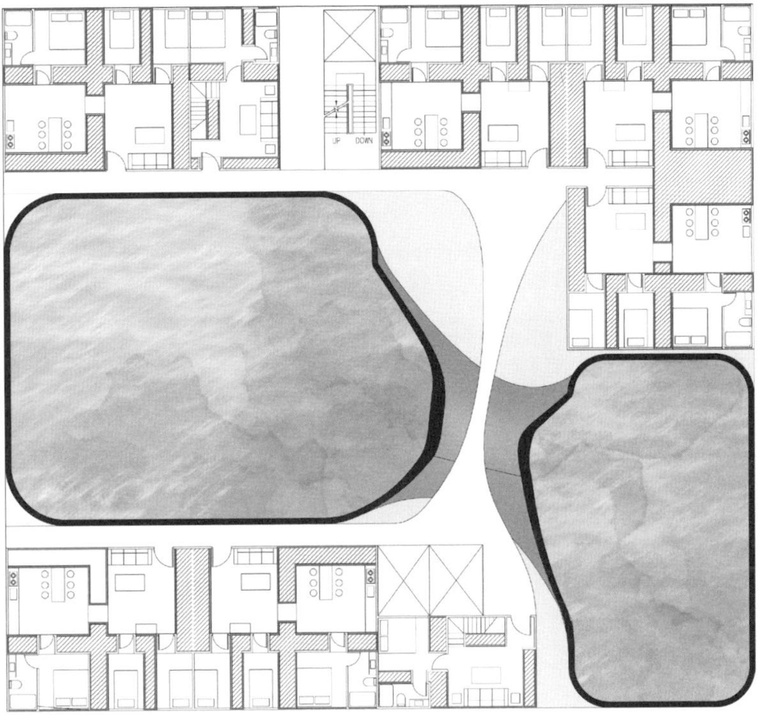

113
Tower Score

57
Lowest Apartment Score

179
Highest Apartment Score

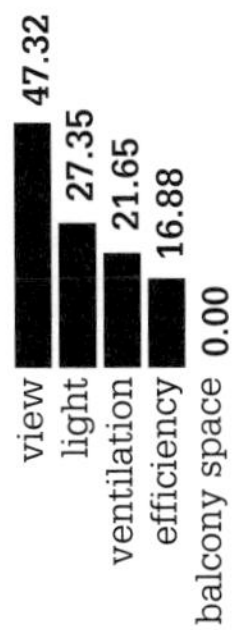

2,920
Amount of Roofscape (m2)

192
Amount of Apartments

158
Tower Height (m)

9.87
Plot Ratio

The Playground Tower

Au Yeung Chun Yu JOEY

This tower creates a unique, vertical playground featuring trampolines, rope swings, slides, hammocks, net climbers, seesaws, swings, and sky gardens. Not only does this tower provide beautiful views of the city, but it gives a strikingly colourful image back to its surrounding. The individual apartments are equipped with hammocks, slides, and swings that turn the home into a landscape of excitement and joy. Each apartment has a view onto a large playground in the core of the tower. The units are also connected to a giant central slide that spirals downwards inside the hollow core of the tower, connecting all apartments and playgrounds to the ground floor in a fun and direct way. The tower's numerous open platforms and rooftops add up to a total of 3,245 m^2 of accessible outdoor space. The playground tower measures a height of 162 metres and has a score of 176 points, with its lowest scoring apartment totalling 144 points and its highest scoring apartment reaching as high as 264 points.

Apartment lay outings

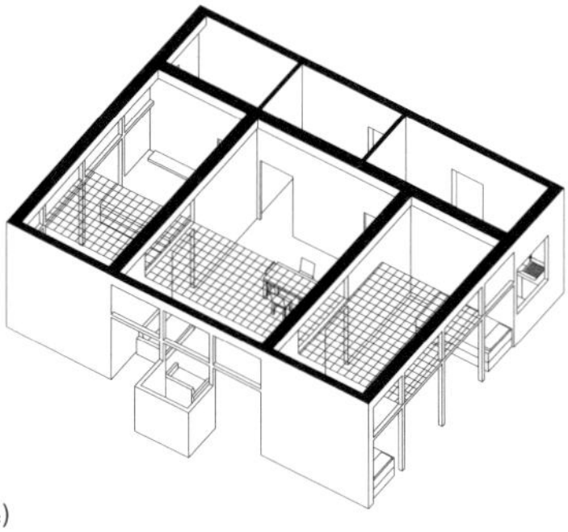

Simplex (64)

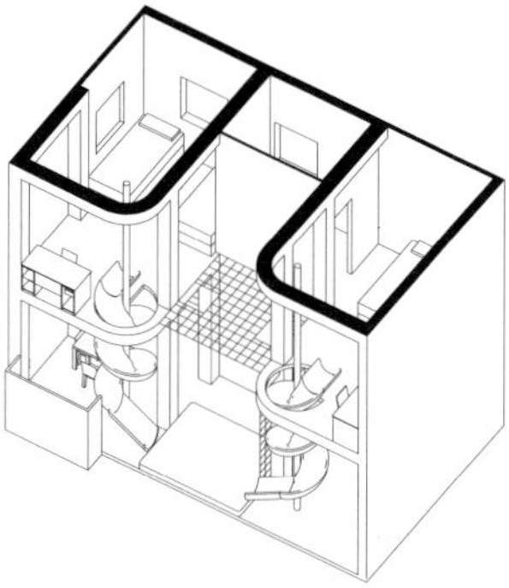

Triplex (64)

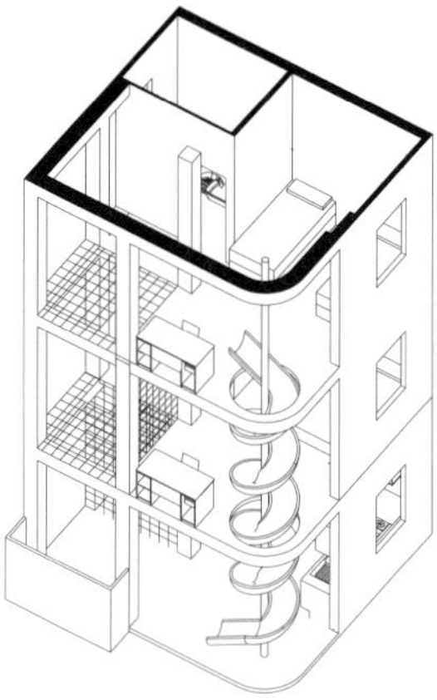

Duplex (64)

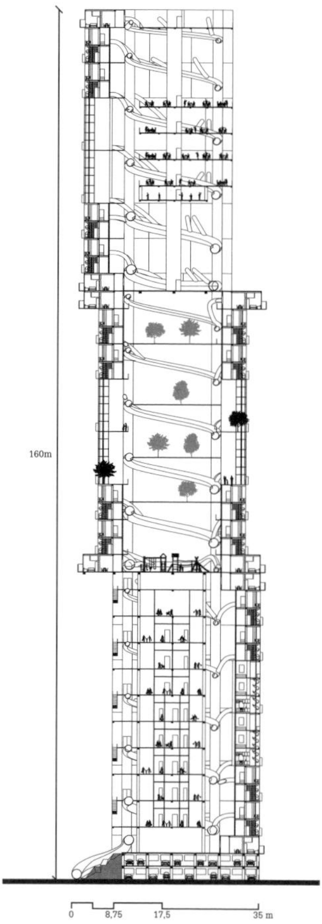

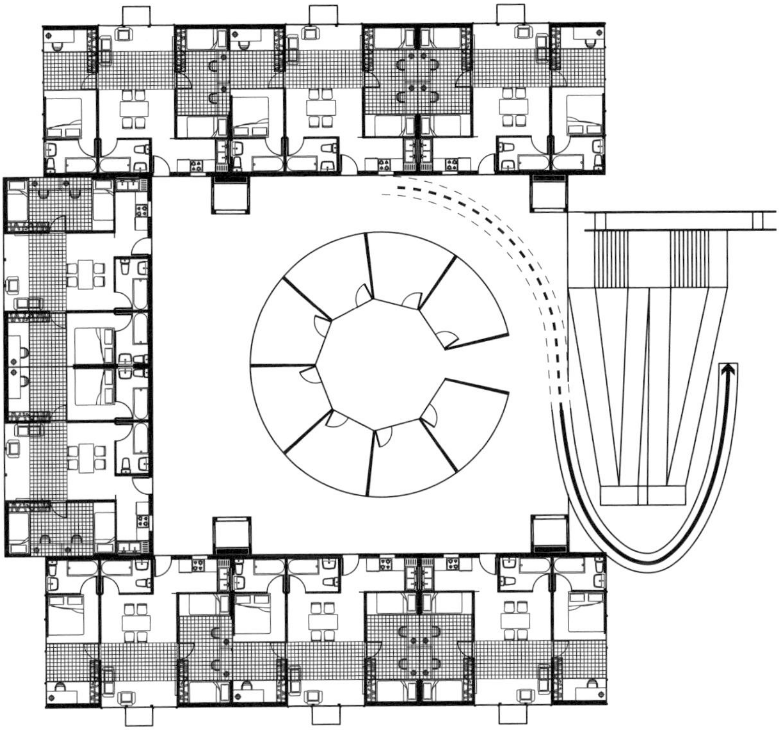

176
Tower Score

144
Lowest Apartment Score

264
Highest Apartment Score

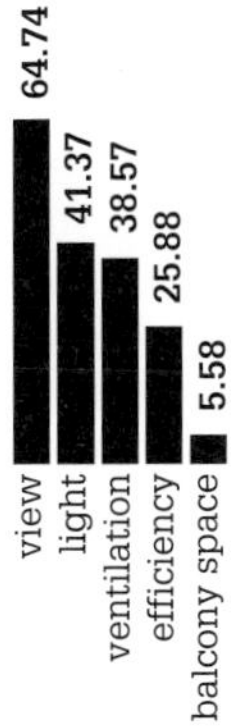

3,245
Amount of Roofscape (m2)

192
Amount of Apartments

162
Tower Height (m)

9.87
Plot Ratio

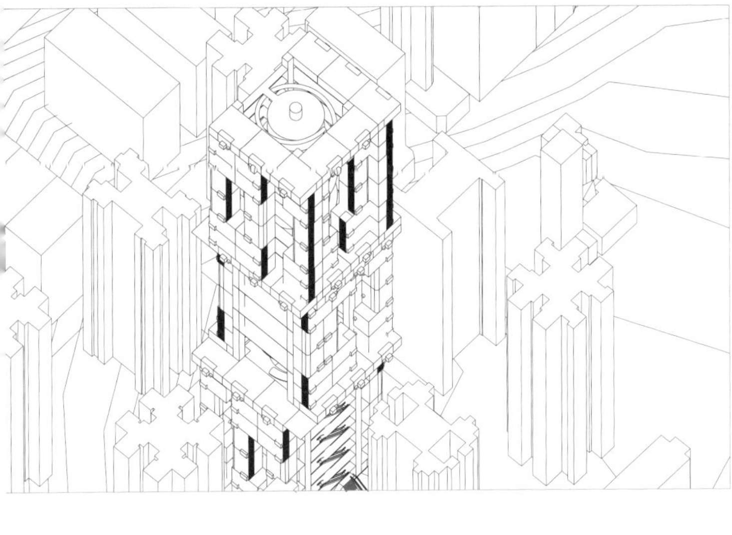

The Climbing Tower

Xie Junni

The climbing tower introduces climbable architecture to Hong Kong, encouraging users to develop their sense of balance, precision, and courage. Climbing is supported on both the interior and exterior of the building. The hollowed core of this 168-metre tower is turned into one of the largest climbing walls in the world. The apartments are stacked in such a way that they form a giant cave with multiple climbing routes. Each route leads to the top of the tower, with several resting platforms on the way. The tower gives the public an exciting new object for recreation, while adventurous residents can make climbing a daily activity and reach their homes through different vertical routes leading to windows that function as entryways. The tower also offers sports facilities and amenities such as a gym, a swimming pool, a sports academy, several fitness areas, and a wellness area and spa, making the tower a real magnet for sport lovers. The rooftops of the 192 apartments provide a total of 4,180 m^2 of accessible outdoor space. The tower scores 178 points, with its highest scoring apartment located on the upper floor with extensive north-facing sea views.

Apartment lay outings

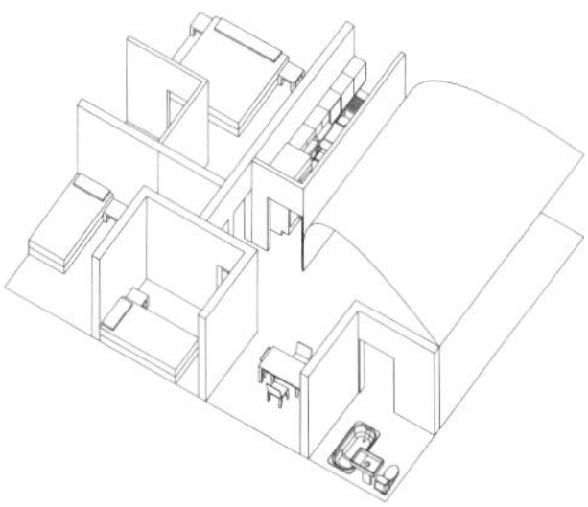

Simplex (64)

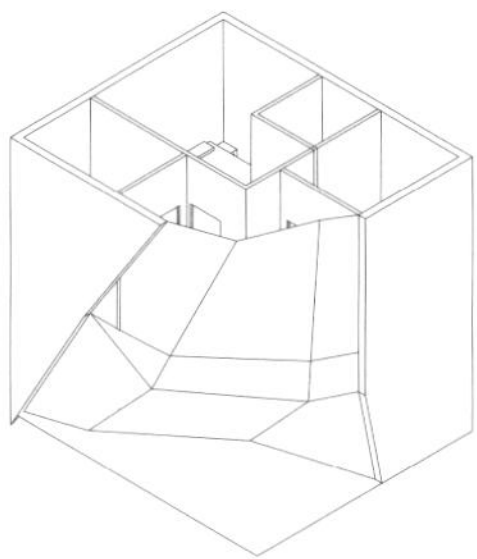

Duplex (64)

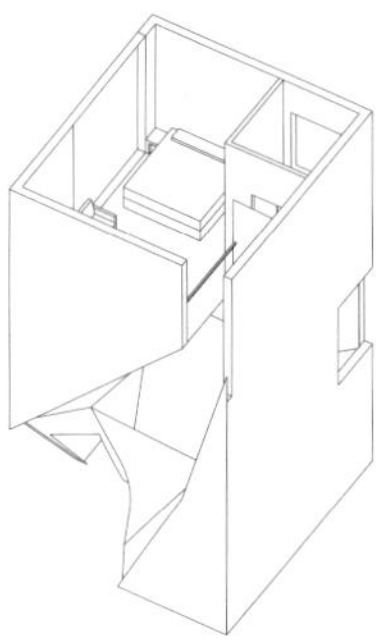

Triplex (64)

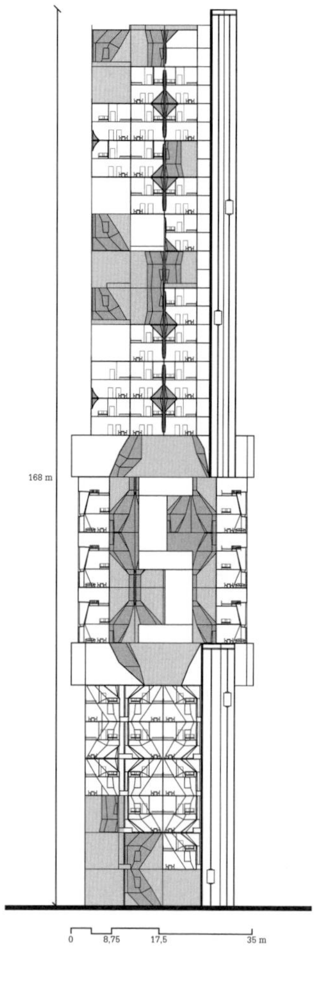

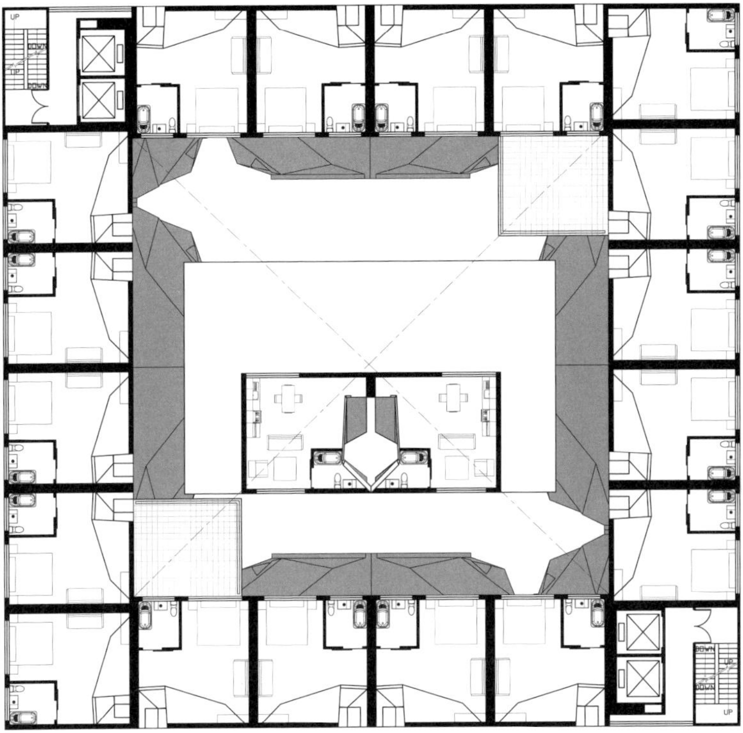

65m plan 1:150

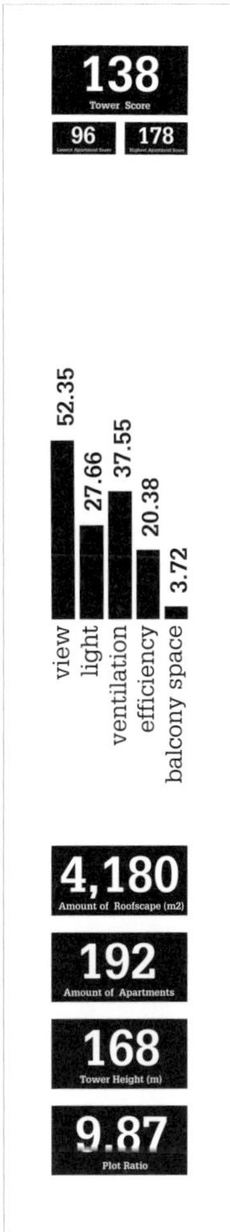

The Family Business Tower

Qin Liting TING

Each of the 192 apartments in this tower supports a small family business. The apartment layouts are designed to allocate at least half of the total floor area to office space. The podium volume of the tower is subdivided into three parts, featuring a showroom, a storage space, and a production space. The showroom hovers proudly in a glazed box on top of the tower, offering amazing views from the inside while attracting attention from the street by exhibiting products designed and manufactured locally by the residents who run their businesses in the tower. Visitors can come for the view and get a survey of the activities and talents of the local economy. The tower aims to support and facilitate the important, small-scale family-based economy that has been there for generations and to cultivate awareness and appreciation of local and traditional crafts as part of Hong Kong's cultural heritage. The tower provides 5,009 m^2 of accessible outdoor space. It achieves an average score of 168 points, with 111 points for lowest scoring apartments and 199 points for highest scoring apartment.

Apartment lay outings

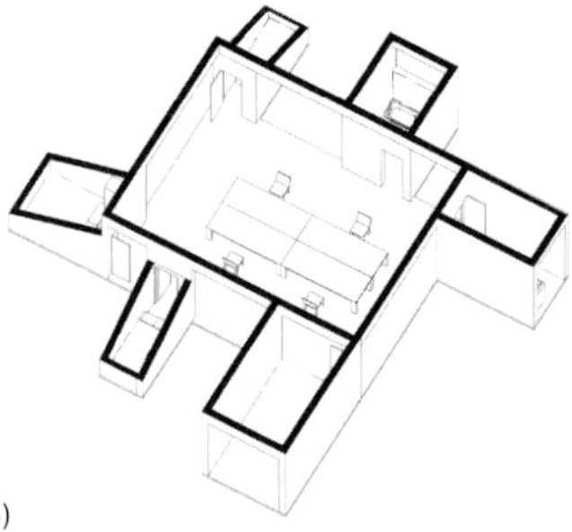

Simplex (65)

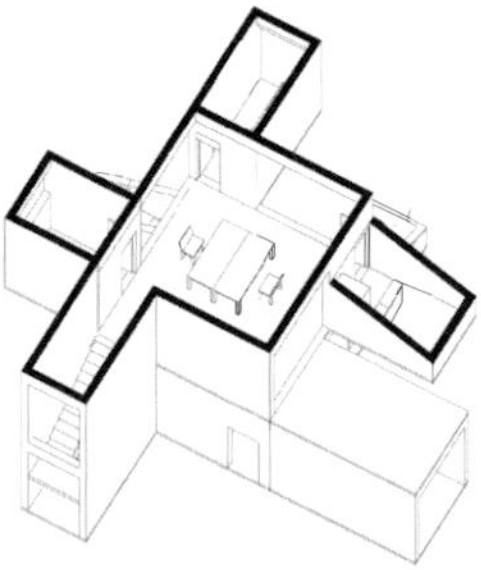

Duplex (40)

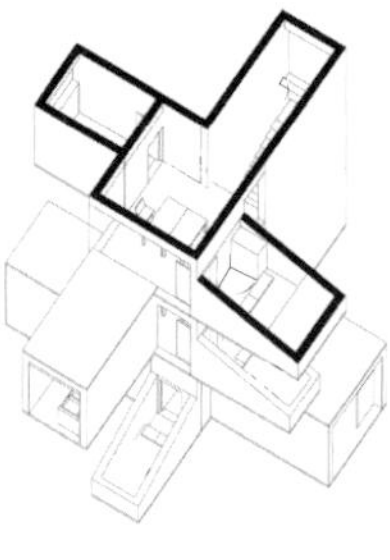

Triplex (87)

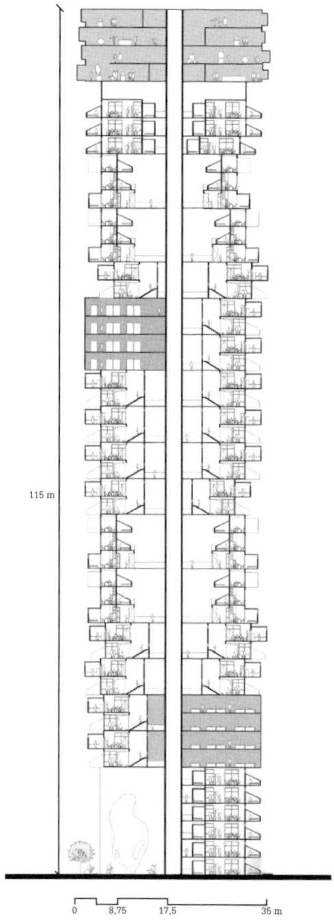

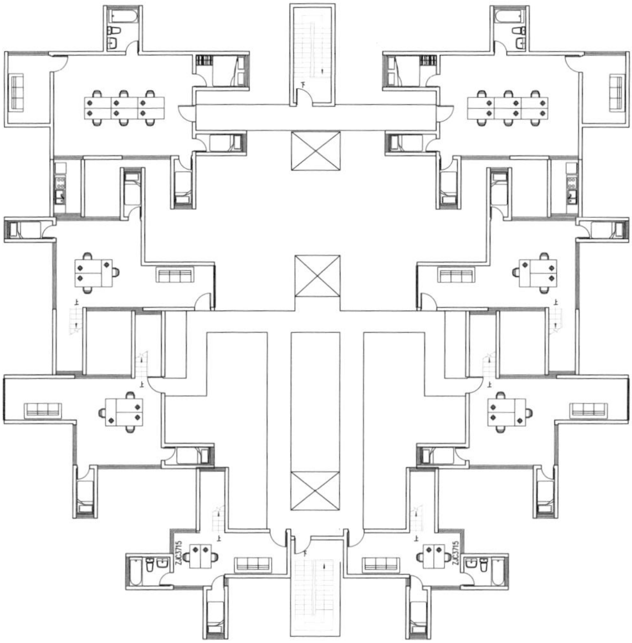

168
Tower Score

111
Lowest Apartment Score

199
Highest Apartment Score

5,009
Amount of Roofscape (m2)

192
Amount of Apartments

115
Tower Height (m)

9.87
Plot Ratio

Studio 2 Exhibition Models.

Developed and modelled by the students of The Why Factory's "Towers Beyond Extrusion" studio at the Department of Architecture (Architecture and Urban Design III, ARCH 5001) at the Hong Kong University, during Fall 2014.

Studio Tutors: Prof. Winy Maas, Tihamér Salij, Martine Vledder with Donn Holohan
Students: Au Yeung Chun Yu JOEY, Chan Fong Tong FRED S, Cheng Pok Him BOB, Ching Ka Ho FRED, Henao Granda Jan Esteban, Ho Sheung Hay TERENCE, Hu Xiangdong HOCK, Ko Pak Kan ZETH, Li Zhixin ALLISON, Liu Chuen Yung VINCENT, Ma Yue, Qin Liting TING, Tang Tak Shing KELVIN, Wen Fan, Wu Yucong, Xie Junni, Ffion Zhang, Ho Yin SUNNY CHA, Sai Bond, Man Hei KENNIF, Han PAT

Forest Tower,
Wu Yucong
Elevator Tower, Ma Yue
The Climbing Tower,
Xie Junni
Cooking Tower, Han PAT
Jaret
Tang
KELV

tical street
wer, Ho
eung Hay
RENCE

The Playground Tower,
Au Yeung Chun Yu
JOEY

Fire Place Tower,
Henao Granda
Jan Esteban

he Sea Life Tower,
Zhixin ALLISON
Forest Tower,
Wu Yucong
Vertical Shopping
Street Tower
(Champs Elyssees),
Cheng Pok Him BOB
Cooking Tower, Han PAT
The Climbing Tower,
Xie Junni

Jareth's Castle,
Tang Tak Shing
KELVIN

Fire Place Tower,
Henao Granda
Jan Esteban

The Playground Tower,
Au Yeung Chun Yu
JOEY

24/7 Cinema Tower,
Wen Fan
PicnicTower,
Liu Chuen Yung
VINCENT

The Climbing Tower, Xie Junni
Cooking Tower, Han PAT
Vertical shopping street tower, Cheng Pok
The Aquarium Tower, Li Zhixin ALLISON
Sky View Tower, Tang Tak Shing KELVIN
The Playground Tower, Au Yeung Chun Yu JOEY

Fire Place Tower,
Henao Granda Jan Esteban
The Climbing Tower,
Xie Junni
The Picknic Tower,
Liu Chuen Yung VINCENT
The 24/7 Cinema Tower,
Wen Fan

The Sea Life Tower,
Li Zhixin ALLISON
Forest Tower,
Wu Yucong
Jareth's Castle, Tang Tak
Shing KELVIN
ground Tower,
g Chun Yu JOEY

EPIL

OGUE

On 23 June 2015, a group of thinkers and stakeholders in the development of Hong Kong came together for a round-table discussion. The primary aim was to reveal the forces driving the current model of real estate development, specifically in the housing market. The current model has been linked with the overwhelming uniformity found in the Hong Kong cityscape: towering screens of monotonous residential high-rises are designed and built through simple extrusions of the most basic and profitable floor plans. In other words, Hong Kong's current housing stock critically lacks diversity.

Flexible Regulations May Lead to More Choice

Text by Martine Vledder
based on a conversation hosted by prof. Winy Maas and prof. Weijen Wang
with Karen Chang (Partner, Globe Creative), Donald Choi (Managing Director, Nan Fung), Ivan Fu (Director, LWK &Partners), Iris Hwang (Sustainability Consultant, ARUP Hong Kong), Kar-kan (KK) Ling (Director of Planning, Planning Department HK SAR), Kelvin Tang (Student, University of Hong Kong), Rocco Yim (Founder, Rocco Design)
Moderation by Alexandra Seno (Freelance writer and Managing Partner, AXS Asia Partners)
Debate Program and Organization by Tihamér Salij with Martine Vledder and Tris Kee.

The debate was held on 23 June 2015 at PMQ, Hong Kong.
With special thanks to PMQ and their team for their great support in giving us such a great venue to gather for the roundtable discussion.

During the conversation, three characteristic trends in housing development came to the surface: overly prescriptive and out-dated regulations, an unmanageable demand for affordable housing, and an overpriced private housing market. By better understanding the system of forces that produce and perpetuate the current condition, we stand a better chance at effectively re-appropriating these forces. What follows are excerpts from this conversation—quotes that were deemed the most illuminating for the research conducted at The Why Factory in collaboration with the University of Hong Kong—as well as a series of annotations that elaborate on the main themes of the discussion.

Introducing the stakeholders

Hosts
Winy Maas, Founder MVRDV and Professor, The Why Factory, Delft University of Technology
Weijen Wang, architect, Professor and Head of Architecture Department, University of Hong Kong

Organization and Programming
Tihamér Salij
With special thanks to PMQ and their team for their support in giving us a great venue to gather for the round-table discussion.

Participants
Karen Chang, Partner, Globe Creative
Donald Choi, Managing Director, Nan Fung
Ivan Fu, Director, LWK &Partners
Iris Hwang, sustainability consultant, ARUP Hong Kong
KK Ling, Director of Planning, Planning Department HK SAR
Kelvin Tang, student, University of Hong Kong
Rocco Yim, Founder, Rocco Design

Moderator
Alexandra Seno, freelance writer and Managing Partner, AXS Asia Partners

Invited stakeholders included the two academic initiators of this research, Prof. Winy Maas and Prof. Weijen Wang; government representative, KK Ling; one of Hong Kong's largest private real estate developers, Donald Choi; two well-known Hong Kong architects, Ivan Fu and Rocco Yim; a specialist in the activation of public and private spaces, Karen Chang; an architect and urban planner specialized in sustainability, Iris Hwang; and Hong Kong resident and student, Kelvin Tang. The meeting was moderated by Alexandra Seno.

First, it is interesting to note that the invited stakeholders have a certain duality to their roles. While the participants have their specific—sometimes opposing—goals and responsibilities relating to their professional discipline, they are also inhabitants of Hong Kong, each calling the city their home.

Winy Maas: ***The main goal of this research is to consider the possibilities of a more diverse city, a city with a housing stock that enables and facilitates choice and perhaps thereby even encourages diversity amongst the city's residents.***

Besides improving quality of life, increased diversity, in theory, contributes to long-term sustainability; diversity, if truly manifested, allows for a preferred result for everyone. To that end, the focus of this research is to reimagine the current environment of monotonous residential towers. The effort works along two scales. First, it is imperative to consider the individual apartment unit, so that even if the current model of mono-extrusion and mechanically reproduced floor plans continues to dominate, there can still be improvements to the quality of the individual apartments. Secondly, the towers themselves can be re-envisioned and designed with the goal of enhancing the quality of life in residential high-rises in Hong Kong.

Hong Kong's Regulations Are Overly Prescriptive

Alexandra Seno: ***Are there opportunities to change the development model, given the current situation of regulations and economic conditions? Or is the current tower layout the only way?***

KK Ling: ***I would like to quote a statement articulated in the publication dummy. Winy Maas wrote, 'Hong Kong's housing tower design is strongly controlled by the Hong Kong Planning and Buildings Ordinance, and it therefore lacks diversity.' Tell me, which densely populated city is not strongly governed by building and planning regulations?***

Donald Choi: ***As a Hong Kong developer, I do experience regulations that are far too prescriptive in comparison to those in other places. Of course, every city needs regulations. The question is: are they flexible enough for quality solutions to emerge?***

Winy Maas: ***A question addressed to the two local architects at the table: do the current regulations allow for more than designing, say, the position of the windows?***

Ivan Fu: ***Yes. As an architect, I feel constrained by regulations when trying to deliver more diversified designs. But the strict regulations are the logical product of the current urban development model of a high-density city like Hong Kong. Besides that, I don't feel architects are in the position to truly change the system.***

Rocco Yim: ***The current design for most residential towers is really just an extruded block, very much in the Hong Kong spirit. It is both practical and efficient. From my point of view, the extruded tower is a monotonous spatial experience for everyone. As architects, we should be looking for new spatial typologies.***

Do current building regulations compromise diversity and stifle the potential to improve the quality of residential towers and their apartment units? Hong Kong's remarkable density is a virtue that has the potential to enhance the environmental sustainability of the city. In addition to facilitating a high level of efficiency and productivity, density provides the critical mass for high-quality public infrastructure, such as public transportation. Indeed, 90 percent of Hong Kong's population commutes by public transport, which significantly reduces the amount of energy per capita. [11] Theoretically, density also functions as a starting point for cultivating diversity—diversity in the needs, desires, and habits of residents, which should be reflected in the built environment. And yet, in the past decades, Hong Kong's housing stock has become far less diverse.

Paradoxically, it seems that regulations that were originally established to improve poor living conditions and establish a minimum quality of life for all inhabitants are currently impeding improvements to that same quality of life. Beginning in the 1940s, several Buildings Ordinances did in fact improve living conditions for many Hong Kong inhabitants. However, as widely acknowledged, legislation has lagged behind reality, and the Ordinances no longer seem to serve their intended function.

Has limiting creative solutions to those that effectively raised the quality of life in Hong Kong decades ago rendered the city's current regulations too strict? Is the architectural profession restricted to solely assembling puzzle pieces predefined by these regulations—or worse, to endlessly copying the most commercially compelling typology? Do developers have any other choice than to construct these walls of monotonous housing towers? Or are these prescriptive regulations still crucial to the responsible development of a densely populated city like Hong Kong? Some discussion participants suggest that Hong Kong couldn't have developed as it did without the benefit of its strict regulations.

Iris Hwang: ***Although regulations shouldn't specifically hinder architects' creativity, what Hong Kong has done as a city, in housing its people, is incredible. If we didn't have these strict regulations, quality of life would have been much worse.***

Donald Choi: ***You seem to be saying that regulations are merely in place to secure a minimal standard of living and provide enough housing to cover the high demand. Yet I feel that quantity and quality can and should enhance each other.***

KK Ling: ***The most challenging job for Hong Kong is determining how to sustain and enhance the flexibility in order to provide for more quality of life within the high-density context.***

Weijen Wang: ***The problem comes from the building codes.***

Considering the historical development of the city and its housing, it seems likely that strict regulations were necessary in times of enormous need. However, it seems that these laws—established to provide better living conditions for everybody—have been co-opted into a framework oriented towards commercial profit, so that Hong Kong is fast becoming a city that is unaffordable to all but a few. Let's look more closely at specific regulations.

Winy Maas: ***If we want to avoid monotony, which, from an economic point of view, is a very vulnerable position, then planners have to help***

encourage variety. In my professional experience, in cities across the world—including, Hong Kong, Paris, Vancouver, and Amsterdam—the law is used to enforce a mix of commercial and non-commercial programmes and set a percentage of public and private housing within the residential programme.

Diversity is often considered a virtue of bustling Asian cities. Developers and relevant government representatives both agree that Hong Kong's building regulations prohibit the development of a diverse mix of housing tower typologies. Why, over the years, has Hong Kong's government enacted regulations that discourage diversity?

Donald Choi: ***I am not able to provide more desirable, usable outdoor space for my clients. But if there is a willingness to pay for something extra, such as bigger balconies, the government has a role to change the regulations to make that possible.***

Any regulations on accountable gross floor area (GFA), also known as saleable area, have a direct impact on the design of the apartment unit and the residential tower as a whole. Let us take the balcony for example. Under current regulations, if a balcony is open on three sides, it is considered a 'green feature', and therefore its floor area is exempt from the total GFA and site coverage. This incentivizes developers to include balconies in apartment designs. However, following the rigid division of indoor and outdoor space in current regulations, balconies are limited to occupying 2.5 percent of the usable floor area of an apartment. If developers choose to include balconies that exceed this maximum allowance, the balcony area can again be considered saleable area, making apartments with this feature unaffordable to most consumers. Therefore, most balconies are entirely counted as GFA, to the deficit of the consumer.

One easy solution to encourage developers to build more apartments with balconies would be to make balconies account for 30 or 50 percent of the floor area, rather than 100 percent. This amendment to the existing regulation would minimize the impact of larger balconies on the price per square meter. Of course, significantly larger balconies will lead to higher prices. Another potential solution, which has been implemented in Singapore, is to totally exempt the balcony area from the GFA, on the condition that more than two floors of uninterrupted space is kept open above the balcony.

Weijen Wang: ***Is it possible to have different housing typologies if the market pays for the potentially higher cost? Or would any regulation stop you from doing so?***

Donald Choi: ***Yes. Site coverage regulations really limit plans. They significantly discourage cantilevered structures, among other things. Because the open space below is also calculated as GFA, you inevitably end up exceeding the allowed maximum.***

Site coverage is another area of regulation that could be modified to great effect. Current regulations allow for 100-percent site coverage for non-residential programmes. This prompts developers to maximize non-residential programs in their development in order to generate higher revenues, which often results in ungainly, blind plinths with excessive amenities, such as indoor shopping malls or floors devoted exclusively to parking. These features negatively affect the quality of public space, as pedestrians walking down the street are totally surrounded by blind plinths and aboveground parking garages.

With current regulations, there are no incentives to design more creative and well-integrated non-residential programmes that have high commercial potential and also provide more open and green space for the public to encourage social interaction., The 100-percent site coverage maximum encourages developers to incorporate a non-residential programme on the ground floor, which is efficient, because the ground floor is typically less suitable for residential programmes. However, the regulations do not ensure that the transition from the publicly accessible street and the commercial podium is well designed. Many podiums that support residential towers are poorly designed, with abrupt, insensitive transitions from the public space of the street to the private space of the podium. Improved regulations should more explicitly curtail the development of private, commercial programmes that deny their relationship with public space.

Rocco Yim: ***Flexibility in applying site coverage restrictions would help to create more diversity in building form and bring about a more meaningful urban dialogue.***

Following the financial crisis of 2008, Europe has witnessed a trend of experimentation with free plot ratio. Governments are determining only the ground price of land that is up for bid, leaving the programme and density flexible for developers to determine in their proposals. Proposals are then judged exclusively by qualitative parameters. This radical de-emphasis on plot ratio stimulates developers, encouraging them to spend their time and resources on developing higher quality plans and prompting genuine collaboration with architects and urban designers, beginning early in the development process. The resulting plans are more flexible, and therefore more responsive to changing conditions and often much more sustainable.

Winy Maas: ***Why can't we open up the building envelopes? Why not make towers taller in compensation for potential added quality?***

Donald Choi: ***As a developer, I am not allowed to build ceilings higher than four metres; the required three-metre ceiling is the norm.***

Another overly prescriptive regulation related to plot ratio is the rigid definition of minimum and maximum building height. Why does the government restrict ceiling height, when higher ceilings can potentially generate more light and increase 'unobstructed internal air per adult', which were two objectives of the first Public Health and Building Ordinance of 1903? Assuming that other variables—including the total floor area of the apartments and the number of apartments per floor—stay the same, increased ceiling heights will inevitably result in taller towers.

Are taller towers problematic for Hong Kong? Why are increased floor heights difficult to sell, politically? In certain areas, the economic importance of the Hong Kong Airport plays a role in restricting building heights, as high-rises are not allowed to obstruct flight paths. That said, there are still ample areas where building heights could be increased without affecting air travel. Towers with commercial programmes, such as offices and shopping malls, are allowed to have bigger footprints, which would be a technical requirement for higher towers, due to light regulations. It is of course possible that certain design solutions can address these problems concerning light—for instance, by increasing the porosity of a tower.

The problem of 'urban heat islands' is often cited in the debate over increased building heights. Large cities or metropolitan areas are known to be significantly warmer than surrounding rural areas, in part because of concentrated human activity. Cities are often built with hard or non-porous materials that store rather than conduct the 'waste heat' given off by human activities. Taller towers would imply more hard surfaces; in addition, waste heat accumulated during the day lingers between high-rise buildings.

Currently, developers are financially motivated to acquire large plots of land to develop into long, continuous apartment 'slabs', which has intensified the phenomenon of urban heat islands. These types of developments maximize the number of apartments with valuable views, but they have the aesthetic effect of erecting massive walls throughout the city. Current regulations allow for a maximum 60 metres of uninterrupted building frontage. Developers often ignore the need for open spaces between the continuous apartment slabs to facilitate natural ventilation and cool down the city. In response, the government has installed ad hoc regulations to counteract this destructive trend in development. For example, a new regulation restricts the length of a building's façade when it reaches a certain height.

When considering improvements to the design of residential towers, there is a consensus that more green space—such as rooftop parks—will benefit the public. Not only would green spaces facilitate social interaction, but they would also bring more 'soft' surfaces, composed of more permeable materials, into the city. This would improve ventilation as well as the absorption of waste heat, thereby mitigating the urban heat island effect.

Another argument against increasing tower height is the theory that increased verticality will 'detach' daily life from the lively ground level. Arguably, the way a tower connects with the liveliness of the city's streets is of comparable significance to the measured proximity of a living space to the ground level. A more sensitively designed connection between the tower and the street level could potentially address concerns about the proper grounding of daily life.

In addition, Hong Kong stands out for its appreciation of the three-dimensionality of its urban fabric. Multiple levels of public space already function with relative success in Hong Kong. This is just a start. If urban density continues to increase, so will the need for truly three-dimensional city. Zoning could operate vertically, rather than just horizontally, to focus the development of Hong Kong's three-dimensional potential and create more diverse high-rise environments connected by networks that exist on more than just two or three levels. When envisioning these new architectural typologies, height should be liberated from the constraints of regulation and outmoded financial limits.

If the objective is to stimulate the development of apartments with taller ceilings, one approach would be to apply a more three-dimensional conception of space to the design of the individual apartment unit. Cubic metres, rather than square metres, of space could become the new metric. This would involve a rigorous new perspective on the design and use of apartments. Architects would have an abundance of new questions to consider. For instance, who needs a 3.5-metre-high ceiling in their toilet? Could unoccupied cubic space be used to create more storage, a bigger kitchen, or more outdoor space? Beyond the creation of sleeping pods, there are ways to organize available space into much more efficient compositions of three-dimensional volume.

Considering the regulations analyzed during the round-table discussion, it seems that Hong Kong's regulations are indeed suffocating and, moreover, not representative of reality.

Winy Maas: ***In Paris, for example, the mayor has launched a marvellous initiative to encourage innovation in real estate development.*** [12] ***The government is providing many leftover sites, without strict regulations. The most innovative development proposals win the bids.***

KK Ling: ***The example you mentioned of greater flexibility in Paris also leads to more uncertainty, particularly in relation to the neighbours. I have had bitter experiences with school principals who believe residential towers and school buildings are not compatible. We need to find a balance between more flexibility and providing enough certainty.***

Winy Maas: ***Of course, cities are full of contradictions, but with proper communication these contradictions can be used, even to overcome lethargy.***

Weijen Wang: ***Have the governmental housing departments done sufficient studies to support their building regulations? I don't think so.***

In most large cities across the world, governments—in conjunction with architects, urban planners, and their related institutions—initiate design research. The Hong Kong Housing Department could potentially effect change by conducting more design research, both internally and in collaboration with actual stakeholders. The government could encourage more experimentation within current regulations. It could create zones for testing free height and free plot ratio development, or initiate a rigorous study of the building envelope. Relaxing regulations in high-density urban areas always carries risks, for both the professional parties involved in real estate development and the consumers. Yet a better balance between flexibility and calculable certainty is worth searching for. Communication among all relevant stakeholders is essential.

The Urgent Demand for Affordable Housing

KK Ling: ***There is a high demand for affordable housing, and this is one of the reasons for the monotonous development of housing in Hong Kong. And because land is so scarce, politicians are always challenged to assure that we have maximized a site's development potential.***

Many solutions for providing higher quality housing to Hong Kong residents—such as creating higher floor heights—will potentially limit the number of apartment units per residential development. Hong Kong's current Chief Executive, Carrie Lam, is facing difficulties in fulfilling the promise of building 290,000 affordable apartments over the next decade. To build less housing is, at present, a politically unpopular decision. The government is already being criticized for allowing low plot ratios.

Ivan Fu: ***Housing, housing, housing. Housing is a pressing need for the general public.***

Karen Chang: ***Quality of life is being sacrificed for quantity.***

Donald Choi: ***There is no shortage. There is a vast mismatch in the housing market. The consumer doesn't have any choice. The government doesn't allow the market mechanism to fully function.***

Karen Chang: ***Indeed. Consumers should be asked about their needs, rather than having the market assume those needs.***

More than one stakeholder at the table is critical of the government's current focus on the development of housing. Is there truly an acute demand for housing in Hong Kong? Or is the root problem the underlying financial system that perpetuates such a demand to its own ends?

It could be argued that this perceived mismatch between supply and demand is not caused by private developers misunderstanding the housing market, but rather by Hong Kong's government prescribing the types and sizes of the homes to be built. When it comes to the housing market, the average consumer is often unaware of what could be available to them, due to a lack of consumer education and exposure to what is possible in dense urban conditions. Western consumers have become more and more influential, but this trend has not taken off in Asia yet.

Some statistical analysis suggests that the fundamental problem is not an urgent demand for more housing stock but an urgent demand for greater access to affordable housing. Nearly half of the population in Hong Kong lives in housing subsidized and primarily built by the Hong Kong Housing Authority and the Hong Kong Housing Society. However, with a set income level of no more than HK$46,000 per month, 80 percent of households qualify for public housing. Currently some Hong Kong residents wait more than two years for an affordable home. The wealthy do not experience this kind of delay.

Let's also look at some general statistics. Since 2000, Hong Kong has experienced its slowest period of growth in more than 70 years. Between 2001 and 2011, Hong Kong added only 5.4 percent to its population, a decline of more than two-thirds from its rate of growth in 1991–2001. And, like many other developed parts of the world, Hong Kong is home to an aging population. Due to low birth rates, it is estimated that in 2033, 26.8 percent of the population will be 65 or older, compared to 12.1 percent in 2005. There were 12.6 live births per 1,000 people in 2010, and only 8.6 in 2014. [13]

The rate of migration to Hong Kong should also be considered. When looking at national comparisons of net migration rates conducted by the CIA, Hong Kong has one of the lowest migration rates in the region. In comparison to neighbouring Singapore, which is ranked 8th, and Macau, which is ranked 33rd, Hong Kong ranks 52nd on a list of 222 countries. One reason for this low net migration rate seems to be the growing prosperity of Mainland China, a phenomenon that has made Hong Kong less attractive for migrants. Historically, Hong Kong's population growth was driven by its better standard of living in relation to the Mainland.

Another global trend affecting the demand for housing is the fact that the number of households is increasing, as the number of people per household is decreasing.
Generally speaking, the total demand for housing has not been growing drastically. But if we focus specifically on affordable housing, the demand is pressing.

Ivan Fu: ***Consumers don't have an abundant choice in affordable housing. Property is a luxury for many.***

Karen Chang: ***Those who can afford it have very good choices. But if you are not earning that much, you are really in a very tight spot. Where do you go?***

How might we solve this pressing demand for affordable housing?
The answer is simple. Create more affordable housing! But who will pay the price?

Within the current financial model, private real estate developers claim that they are unable to provide affordable housing. The Hong Kong government has to take on the responsibility of providing housing for all income levels. The government can intervene by redistributing a higher percentage of the total housing stock to lower-income residents, which would result in a higher overall percentage of public housing. This approach seems to work in places such as Singapore, where an extraordinary 80 percent of the total housing stock is allocated for public housing. Hong Kong and Singapore have a healthy, competitive relationship, perhaps in part because they have many similarities: both are characterized by a scarcity of land, dense urban areas, and high land values; both have tax systems that make them attractive to large numbers of global companies; and both host extensive expatriate communities, which also indirectly raises real estate prices.

The government should monitor and adjust the percentage of total housing stock available for public housing based on the changing economic climate and come to consider housing as a public asset. There are advantages to having a certain stock of public housing. In the Netherlands, for example, the government has sold parts of its public housing stock in times of high economic conjecture, generating savings.

Iris Hwang: ***There is a great divide between the public and private housing markets. People want to get into public housing, and they don't want to get out. Households that qualify for public housing sometimes earn HK$2,000 while others need to pay HK$20,000 for a decent place.***

The high demand for affordable housing is generated, in part, by the currently insurmountable gap between public and private housing. Young Hong Kong residents who wish to buy a home typically cannot afford private housing, so they apply for public housing. Once a family manages to acquire subsidized housing, they have little incentive to enter the private housing market. One response to this pattern would be to introduce a more incremental system for distributing housing rather than one based on set income levels.

Besides increasing the percentage of housing marketed as affordable public housing, another obvious, though complex, solution to meeting high demand is to free up more land and generate more space to build residential towers. Only 30 percent of the Hong Kong area is urbanized. Approximately 70 percent is used for the preservation of natural green space, including a small percentage of space used for agriculture (6.1 percent). 38 percent of total available land in Hong is designated as parkland. Government-proposed plans to rezone these parks have met with considerable resistance. While some political voices have been advocating for the government to sell more land on the market, some public voices have opposed initiatives to urbanize and reclaim more land. It is unclear who is behind this voice of dissent—genuinely concerned environmental activists or wealthy people living on the peak? Global issues of resource and food shortage have made potentially arable land a valuable asset, but at the same time, if Hong Kong residents are living on an average residential floor space of 15 m^2 per person—with the average person in Hong Kong having about a quarter of the living space of the average Australian or American—there are obvious reasons to explore how freeing up more land for development could temper land prices. [14]

Does the government want to free up more land for development? Some would argue that there is no way the government could increase supply significantly enough to affect the situation—or that the government has no real intention to do so. Scarcity of land is an ongoing issue, but the pace of turning undeveloped land into developable land also needs to be seriously considered. Land transformation processes can easily take up to 15 years or longer. Improvements to the process of making land developable could make this solution more practicable and politically appealing.

A City of Exorbitantly High Land Values

In late 2014, it was forecasted that in 2015 property prices in Hong Kong would drop due to property market cooling measures implemented by the government. [15] This prediction couldn't be further from the truth; land value continues to rise. In May 2015, residential property prices in Hong Kong reached a record high, increasing more than 20 percent compared to prices recorded in the same month the previous year. Hong Kong has become the world's most expensive place to own a home. [16] As stated in an annual study by the consultancy Demographia, Hong Kong has the least affordable housing of 378 metropolitan areas in nine countries. The median home price is 17 times the average household income.

Donald Choi: ***The Hong Kong government owns all the land! The cause of the current development model is the high price of land. We need to build the maximum allowed site coverage to achieve the GFA.***

Weijen Wang: ***But the monotony in the current development model also has to do with the developers. There aren't enough developers willing to take risks.***

It is believed that exceptionally high land values have forced developers to build monotonous high-rises in order to make a profit. While there is room for contention in that statement, what is true is that the high land prices demanded by the government discourage real estate developers from providing more quality or freedom of choice for their customers.

Is high demand the only cause of inflated land prices? Of course, with the undersupply of real estate in the last five to seven years, prices naturally went up. Yet other mechanisms besides high demand can drive up prices. Excessive speculation is one such mechanism. Over the past decades, a higher number of Mainland Chinese have been buying significant amounts of property in Hong Kong for speculative reasons, driving up real estate prices. Not only are apartments priced further out of reach for most Hong Kong residents, but they are also left uninhabited. Due to the high demand for housing, however, most owners have sought to rent out their apartments for moderate, short-term profits, which is not the case in Mainland China's 'ghost cities'.

Could certain financial actions be taken to limit excessive speculation? This has proven to be a complicated matter, because the government, and perhaps even developers, reap the rewards of speculation by wealthy Mainland Chinese buyers. But in the long term, the dangers involved in speculation are not to be overcome. To temper the influx of foreign investment in Hong Kong real estate, the government has installed a 'Buyer's Stamp Duty', which requires non-citizens who purchase real estate to pay the government an additional 15 percent on top of the total purchase. After a few years of implementation, this penalty is slowly showing its effect, demonstrating that negative incentives can be effective. Increased real estate taxes could result in higher revenues for the government, which could be invested into subsidized housing.

Another, more governance-based issue is important to consider when examining the factors contributing to high land prices. Over the past few decades, the number of developers has been reduced from over a thousand to approximately ten significant players, resulting in a very competitive market. This monopoly on real estate development could be partly responsible for the sky-high prices. It is easy to imagine a model in which developers and government representatives both drive up land prices and sell property to wealthy consumers and investors who can pay. In Hong Kong's capitalist system, this type of market mechanism is rampant. Is this wrong? In the case of the government, aren't profits reinvested for the public good?

In any case this model is unsustainable. If only a few, wealthy real estate tycoons keep on making more and more money and keep paying for more and more land sold by the government, the necessary and intrinsically competitive character of the market mechanism will be lost. Whether it is by lowering or increasing prices, it is clear that this monopoly held by a few big real estate companies—and, interestingly, as also mentioned at the table, a few big architects—is ultimately unhealthy for Hong Kong's real estate market.

Weijen Wang: ***Is it fair to assume that Hong Kong developers make a much bigger profit than those in other places, and that they rarely take any risks?***

Winy Maas: ***In the United Kingdom and in the Netherlands, the government sets a range of acceptable profit margins for developers.***

Ivan Fu: ***People are losing confidence in the property market at this moment, when prices are still out of a sensible range.***

Do real estate developers in Hong Kong make astronomically high profits compared to those working in other cities with relatively high land values? Or is there significant weight to developers' complaints of almost being unable to make a reasonable profit? If we compare real estate profit margins of Hong Kong's real estate developers to those of developers in London, for example, a quick glance at media coverage shows that developers active in London 'wouldn't bother when profit margins drop below 20%' as quoted from a 2014 article in *The Guardian*. [17] An article from Moody's titled 'Chinese property developer margins under pressure' predicted that average gross margins would stay around 30 percent, compared to 33 percent in 2012.10 Hong Kong profit margins vary between 30 to 35 percent. [18]

While the real numbers regarding profit margins have yet to be publicly disclosed and discussed, it would appear that Hong Kong developers are not making significantly more profit than developers in other cities with high land values. This doesn't imply that there is no possibility of lowering these profit margins, but the current imbalance between supply and demand has naturally raised both prices and profits.

More transparency would ameliorate the distrustful dynamic between developers and the government. There is currently not enough incentive for any stakeholder other than the consumer to change the current model. Someone needs to make a move to initiate change.

Iris Hwang: ***I'm playing the devil's advocate here, but it seems that there is no immediate pressure to actually respond to market demands and start to innovate. There is this model that has worked over the last 50 years. Why bother changing it?***

Donald Choi: ***Why is the government not stepping up its effort to provide more public housing?***

Ivan Fu: ***Government should correct the current unbalanced situation. They have to redistribute the interests.***

The obvious conclusion is that there is a delicate balance between private and public return on investments. If we acknowledge that governments have a fundamental responsibility to look after the public good—which, in this case, means controlling the housing market—Hong Kong's government should take an active role in correcting the financial real estate system.

Historically, Hong Kong's government has actively intervened in the real estate market, but only under the circumstances of a true crisis. After the 1997 Asian financial crises, the prices of the private residential market plunged as much as 70 percent. During that period, the government enacted a programme to support the private residential market. If no stakeholders make a move to initiate change, perhaps what it will take is another financial crash like that of the 1990s. An economic depression might be forceful enough to significantly reduce real estate speculation from wealthy Mainland Chinese.

Of course, we hope that there are creative rather than destructive ways, ways that draw from the ideas of the design community, that might keep Hong Kong a lively and affordable city. The participants in our round-table meeting came with radically different professional perspectives, but they also came as individuals invested in the well-being of Hong Kong. As we navigate the terrain of messy, interrelated technical and bureaucratic issues, this shared perspective has to be kept in mind.

Towers of Choices is the product of two Master track studios given by The Why Factory at the Faculty of Architecture at the Hong Kong University, during the fall semesters of 2013 and 2014. Numerous students, teachers, and researchers were part of the project and each of these contributors informed the results presented in this book.

Credits

The Why Factory is a global thinktank and research institute, run by MVRDV and Delft University of Technology and led by professor Winy Maas. The Why Factory's Future Cities research programme explores possibilities for the development of our cities by focusing on the production of models and visualizations for cities of the future. The results of this research programme are presented in a series of books—the Future Cities series—published in association with nai010 publishers in Rotterdam and designed by Bastiaan de Wolff of Thonik / BENG in Amsterdam.
***Towers of Choices* is the twelfth publication in this series, following *The Why Factor(y)*, *Visionary Cities*, *Green Dream*, *Vertical Village*, *Hong Kong Fantasies*, *City Shocks*, *We Want World Wonders*, *Barba*, *Absolute Leisure*, *Copy Paste*, and *PoroCity*.**

For more information see:
www.thewhyfactory.com

Authors

Winy Maas

Prof. Ir. Ing FRIBA HAIA, architect and urban planner, is one the founding principals of MVRDV, an interdisciplinary studio that works at the intersection of architecture and urbanism. The award-winning Dutch practice was set up over two decades ago and has established an international identity with a wide variety of building typologies and scales that are self-generated, innovative, experimental and theoretical.
Winy advocates denser, greener, more attractive and liveable cities, with an approach to design that, regardless of typology or scale, reflects a user-defined, innovative, and sustainable consideration for the built environment. In 2008, Winy founded The Why Factory at the TU Delft, a research institute on future cities, which he leads as director. He has been a Visiting Professor at GSAPP Columbia and IIT Chicago and has also held teaching positions at the ETH Zurich, the University of Louvain, the University of Hong Kong, the Berlage Institute, the Architectural Association (AA) in London, the Massachusetts Institute of Technology (MIT), Yale University (Eero Saarinen Chair), Ohio State University and the Rotterdam Building Academy. Winy sits on numerous international boards and juries. He was recently named Supervisor of Almere Floriade 2022 and Eindhoven City, and has been Supervisor of Barcode Urban Development in Oslo. Previously, he sat on the boards of the Economic Development Board of Rotterdam, the Spatial Quality Boards of both Rotterdam and Barcelona, the Netherlands National Planning Office and the Netherlands National Design Group.

Tihamér Salij

Tihamér Salij, researcher, spatial designer and artist, is founder of Space Intelligence Agency, an explorative and cross-disciplinary research and design office based in Rotterdam. It aims to set an international agenda for research, design, and innovation about what society is and in particular what the city, its products, architectures, landscapes, infrastructures and networks could be. Space Intelligence Agency develops and offers speculative research and design education programmes that focus on a unique research-through-design methodology with a strong cross-disciplinary approach, which is crucial for the preparation of the next generation of designers.
Tihamér worked at the architectural firm MVRDV on several projects, including The Region Maker, 3DCity, RhineRuhrCity, and Pig City. He co-curated the exhibition RhineRuhrCity in Düsseldorf and co-edited the publication *KM3 – Excursions on Capacity*. Tihamér has been lecturer at the Creative College in Amersfoort where he has been Team Coordinator and leading the implementation of a new educational learning system. As Research Programme Leader of the Future Cities Program and Coordinator of the Future Cities Publication series, Tihamér has been affiliated with the think-tank The Why Factory from its establishment in September 2007 till March 2015. He has been coordinator of the international education programme of the DutchDesignFashionArchitecture Programme (DDFA) funded by the Ministries of Education, Culture & Science, Economic & Foreign Affairs and has been initiator of the multi-disciplinary, cross-cultural research & design programme 'Next City - Next Education'. Tihamér has been teaching at various universities worldwide, including the Hong Kong University, Hong Kong Design Institute, the China Academy of Fine Arts (Beijing), ENSAV (Paris), the Berlage and Willem de Kooning Academy (Rotterdam). He has written numerous articles and published books about a wide range of topics with particular focus on conceptions of utopia, the ideal city, and generating city models.
Tihamér currently holds the position of Head of Fine Art at the AKI Academy of Art & Design - ArtEZ University of the Arts in Enschede, Netherlands. He became a member of the management team, to stabilize and refine the existing education.

Content Credits

Concept and content:
The Why Factory:
Winy Maas and Tihamér Salij
with Martine Vledder, Arend van Waart, Sander Mulders, Claudia Mainardi, Anna Dolcetta and Sylwia Franczak
Editors: Winy Maas and Tihamér Salij
Guest contributions by: Weijen Wang, Tris Kee and Wah Sang Wong
Text Editors: Kelly Chan and Rachel Julia Engler
Cover image: Ip Kai Hong and Mok Wang Chee

Based on work from The Why Factory's 'Hong Kong Tower Revolution' studio at the Department of Architecture at the Hong Kong University, during Fall 2013, and of The Why Factory's 'Towers Beyond Extrusion' studio at the Department of Architecture at the Hong Kong University, during Fall 2014.

Hong Kong Tower Revolution, Architecture and Urban Design III (ARCH 5001), Hong Kong University.
Studio tutors: Prof. Winy Maas and Tihamér Salij with Sander Mulders and Arend van Waart
Students: Au Wing Yi, Chak Tsz Kin, Chan Chung Man, Chan Ian Yin Yan, Chan Pui Yin, Chau Shek Lun, Cheng Ching, Ip Kai Hong, Liu Kemeng, Mok Wang Chee, Tang Ho Yin, Kong Ho Ching, Kwok Ka Ching, Lau Xin Yee, Lee Kin Wai, Li Mei Yu, Lung Man Ching, Ma Ching Yi, Suen Wing Yin, Sze Ivy, Sze Ying Ying, Yeung Cho Yui, Yeung Ho Man

Towers Beyond Extrusion, Architecture and Urban Design III (ARCH 5001), Hong Kong University
Studio Tutors: Prof. Winy Maas, Tihamér Salij, Martine Vledder with Donn Holohan
Students: Au Yeung Chun Yu JOEY, Chan Fong Tong FRED S, Cheng Pok Him BOB, Ching Ka Ho FRED, Henao Granda Jan Esteban, Ho Sheung Hay TERENCE, Hu Xiangdong HOCK, Ko Pak Kan ZETH, Li Zhixin ALLISON, Liu Chuen Yung VINCENT, Ma Yue, Qin Liting TING, Tang Tak Shing KELVIN, Wen Fan, Wu Yucong, Xie Junni, Ffion Zhang, Ho Yin SUNNY CHA, Sai Bond, Man Hei KENNIF, Han PAT

PREFACE

Rethinking Hong Kong Housing Typologies
Text by Weijen Wang

Make Your Tower!
Text by Winy Maas

OBSERVATIONS

State of Housing in Hong Kong
Text by Tihamér Salij

This text is adopted and modified from an original article by Tihamér Salij: 'A Call for Housing Beyond Uniformity', in *OCCUPY HOUSING*, *HKIA Journal*, Issue 72, 2016.

What Do the Media Say?
Text by Tihamér Salij

This text is adopted and modified from a conceptual text by the students.

Collection of newspaper articles compiled by the students of The Why Factory's 'Hong Kong Tower Revolution' studio at the Department of Architecture (Architecture and Urban Design III, ARCH 5001) at the Hong Kong University, during Fall 2013, and students of The Why Factory's 'Towers Beyond Extrusion' studio at the Department of Architecture at the Hong Kong University, during Fall 2014.

Hong Kong Tower Revolution, Architecture and Urban Design III (ARCH 5001), Hong Kong University.
Studio tutors: Prof. Winy Maas and Tihamér Salij with Sander Mulders and Arend van Waart
Students: Au Wing Yi, Chak Tsz Kin, Chan Chung Man, Chan Ian Yin Yan, Chan Pui Yin, Chau Shek Lun, Cheng Ching, Ip Kai Hong, Liu Kemeng, Mok Wang Chee, Tang Ho Yin, Kong Ho Ching, Kwok Ka Ching, Lau Xin Yee, Lee Kin Wai, Li Mei Yu, Lung Man Ching, Ma Ching Yi, Suen Wing Yin, Sze Ivy, Sze Ying Ying, Yeung Cho Yui, Yeung Ho Man

Towers Beyond Extrusion, Architecture and Urban Design III (ARCH 5001), Hong Kong University
Studio Tutors: Prof. Winy Maas, Tihamér Salij, Martine Vledder with Donn Holohan
Students: Au Yeung Chun Yu JOEY, Chan Fong Tong FRED S, Cheng Pok Him BOB, Ching Ka Ho FRED, Henao Granda Jan Esteban, Ho Sheung Hay TERENCE, Hu Xiangdong HOCK, Ko Pak Kan ZETH, Li Zhixin ALLISON, Liu Chuen Yung VINCENT, Ma Yue, Qin Liting TING, Tang Tak Shing KELVIN, Wen Fan, Wu Yucong, Xie Junni, Ffion Zhang, Ho Yin SUNNY CHA, Sai Bond, Man Hei KENNIF, Han PAT

A Brief History of the Buildings Ordinance and Tower Typologies in Hong Kong
Text by Tris Kee

Drawings by Jan Henao and Claudia Mainardi

Mega-housing Form in New Towns of Hong Kong
Text by Weijen Wang and Ryo Fuyimori

Drawings by Ryo Fuyimori

Design Constraints on Residential Space, and a Possible Breakthrough
Text by Wah Sang Wong

EXPERIMENTATIONS

Diversifying Housing in Hong Kong
Text by Tihamér Salij

The Typical Hong Kong Apartment
Text by Tihamér Salij

Drawings by Cheng Pok Him BOB, Claudia Mainardi and Sylwia Franczak

Apartment typology is based on work from The Why Factory's 'Towers Beyond Extrusion' studio at the Department of Architecture (Architecture and Urban Design III, ARCH 5001) at the Hong Kong University, during Fall 2014.

Studio Tutors: Prof. Winy Maas, Tihamér Salij, Martine Vledder with Donn Holohan
Students: Au Yeung Chun Yu JOEY, Chan Fong Tong FRED S, Cheng Pok Him BOB, Ching Ka Ho FRED, Henao Granda Jan Esteban, Ho Sheung Hay TERENCE, Hu Xiangdong HOCK, Ko Pak Kan ZETH, Li Zhixin ALLISON, Liu Chuen Yung VINCENT, Ma Yue, Qin Liting TING, Tang Tak Shing KELVIN, Wen Fan, Wu Yucong, Xie Junni, Ffion Zhang, Ho Yin SUNNY CHA, Sai Bond, Man Hei KENNIF, Han PAT

Specializing Apartments
Text by Tihamér Salij

Additional research by Tihamér Salij with Martine Vledder

Drawings and images illustrated by Tihamér Salij and Claudia Mainardi with Sylwia Franczak

Apartment typologies are based on work from The Why Factory's 'Hong Kong Tower Revolution' studio at the Department of Architecture at the Hong Kong University, during Fall 2013, and of The Why Factory's 'Towers Beyond Extrusion' studio at the Department of Architecture at the Hong Kong University, during Fall 2014.

Photo collage impressions illustrated by The Why Factory: Tihamér Salij, Claudia Mainardi and the students of The Why Factory's 'Hong Kong Tower Revolution' studio at the Department of Architecture at the Hong Kong University, during Fall 2013,
and by the students of The Why Factory's 'Towers Beyond Extrusion' studio at the Department of Architecture at the Hong Kong University, during Fall 2014.

More Outdoor Space: Wrap-around Balcony by Cheng Pok Him BOB, Tang Ho Yin TIM and Chau Shek Lun ALLEN
More Outdoor Space: Seven Private Balconies by The Why Factory
Exclusive Bathrooms: Bathing in Nature by Chan Fong Tong FRED S
Exclusive Bathrooms: Swimming Around the House by Ching Ka Ho FRED and Chan Fong Tong FRED S
Dreamy Bedrooms: Sleeping Under the Stars by Kong Ho Ching ALICE, Chan Pui Yin APPLE and Qin Liting TING
Dreamy Bedrooms: Sleeping on Top of Each Other by Kong Ho Ching ALICE and Chan Pui Yin APPLE
Smart Connecting: Sky Bridges by Ho Sheung Hay TERENCE
Smart Connecting: Flexible Space by Cheng Pok Him BOB
High Class Dining: Dining with Panoramic Views by Hu Xiangdong HOCK
High Class Dining: Picnicking Sky-high by Hu Xiangdong HOCK, Ho Yin SUNNY CHA and Liu Chuen Yung VINCENT
Chef's Special: Enjoying Home-grown Food by Henao Granda Jan Esteban and Au Yeung Chun Yu JOEY
Chef's Special: Cooking with Natural Breeze by Wu Yucong and Han PAT
Extraordinary Living: The Observatory by Tang Tak Shing KELVIN
Extraordinary Living: Separated Living Activities by Chan Chung Man CM, Yeung Ho Man ARTHUR and Ma Yue
Space for Domestic Help: The Maid's own Paradise by Kwok Ka Ching JUDY, Ma Ching Yi JENNA and Sze Ying Ying FANNY
Space for Domestic Help: Meet the Maid Everywhere by Kwok Ka Ching JUDY, Ma Ching Yi JENNA and Sze Ying Ying FANNY
More Storage Space: The Central Super Store by Kwok Ka Ching JUDY, Ma Ching Yi JENNA and Sze Ying Ying FANNY
More Storage Space: Hide All your Belongings in the Walls by Kwok Ka Ching JUDY, Ma Ching Yi JENNA and Sze Ying Ying FANNY
Top Study Conditions: Books Everywhere by Wen Fan
Top Study Conditions: Secluded and Quiet Studying by Chan Chung Man KELMAN and Chak Tsz Kin KENNETH

Hong Kong Tower Revolution, Architecture and Urban Design III (ARCH 5001), Hong Kong University.
Studio Tutors: Prof. Winy Maas and Tihamér Salij with Sander Mulders and Arend van Waart
Students: Au Wing Yi, Chak Tsz Kin, Chan Chung Man, Chan Ian Yin Yan, Chan Pui Yin, Chau Shek Lun, Cheng Ching, Ip Kai Hong, Liu Kemeng, Mok Wang Chee, Tang Ho Yin, Kong Ho Ching, Kwok Ka Ching, Lau Xin Yee, Lee Kin Wai, Li Mei Yu, Lung Man Ching, Ma Ching Yi, Suen Wing Yin, Sze Ivy, Sze Ying Ying, Yeung Cho Yui, Yeung Ho Man

Towers Beyond Extrusion, Architecture and Urban Design III (ARCH 5001), Hong Kong University
Studio Tutors: Prof. Winy Maas, Tihamér Salij, Martine Vledder with Donn Holohan
Students: Au Yeung Chun Yu JOEY, Chan Fong Tong FRED S, Cheng Pok Him BOB, Ching Ka Ho FRED, Henao Granda Jan Esteban, Ho Sheung Hay TERENCE, Hu Xiangdong HOCK, Ko Pak Kan ZETH, Li Zhixin ALLISON, Liu Chuen Yung VINCENT, Ma Yue, Qin Liting TING, Tang Tak Shing KELVIN, Wen Fan, Wu Yucong, Xie Junni, Ffion Zhang, Ho Yin SUNNY CHA, Sai Bond, Man Hei KENNIF, Han PAT

Tower Scoring System - Measuring Apartment Qualities
Text by Tihamér Salij

Additional research by Tihamér Salij, Arend van Waart, Sander Mulders

Drawing by The Why Factory: Cheng Pok Him BOB

Scoring system as developed during The Why Factory's 'Hong Kong Tower Revolution' studio at the Department of Architecture (Architecture and Urban Design III, ARCH 5001) at the Hong Kong University, Fall 2013

Studio Tutors: Prof. Winy Maas and Tihamér Salij with Sander Mulders and Arend van Waart
Students: Au Wing Yi, Chak Tsz Kin, Chan Chung Man, Chan Ian Yin Yan, Chan Pui Yin, Chau Shek Lun, Cheng Ching, Ip Kai Hong, Liu Kemeng, Mok Wang Chee, Tang Ho Yin, Kong Ho Ching, Kwok Ka Ching, Lau Xin Yee, Lee Kin Wai, Li Mei Yu, Lung Man Ching, Ma Ching Yi, Suen Wing Yin, Sze Ivy, Sze Ying Ying, Yeung Cho Yui, Yeung Ho Man

How Does the Uniform Residential Tower with Typical Apartments Score?
Text by Tihamér Salij

Drawings by The Why Factory: Cheng Pok Him BOB, Claudia Mainardi, Sylwia Franczak

Image illustrated by The Why Factory: Claudia Mainardi

How Do Uniform Towers with Specialized Apartments Score?
Text by Tihamér Salij

Drawings by Claudia Mainardi and Sylwia Franczak

Additional research by Tihamér Salij and Arend van Waart

Apartment typologies used for the tower configurations are based on work from The Why Factory's 'Hong Kong Tower Revolution' studio at the Department of Architecture at the Hong Kong University, during Fall 2013, and from The Why Factory's 'Towers Beyond Extrusion' studio at the Department of Architecture at the Hong Kong University, during Fall 2014.

Hong Kong Tower Revolution, Architecture and Urban Design III (ARCH 5001), Hong Kong University.
Studio Tutors: Prof. Winy Maas and Tihamér Salij with Sander Mulders and Arend van Waart
Students: Au Wing Yi, Chak Tsz Kin, Chan Chung Man, Chan Ian Yin Yan, Chan Pui Yin, Chau Shek Lun, Cheng Ching, Ip Kai Hong, Liu Kemeng, Mok Wang Chee, Tang Ho Yin, Kong Ho Ching, Kwok Ka Ching, Lau Xin Yee, Lee Kin Wai, Li Mei Yu, Lung Man Ching, Ma Ching Yi, Suen Wing Yin, Sze Ivy, Sze Ying Ying, Yeung Cho Yui, Yeung Ho Man

Towers Beyond Extrusion, Architecture and Urban Design III (ARCH 5001), Hong Kong University
Studio Tutors: Prof. Winy Maas, Tihamér Salij, Martine Vledder with Donn Holohan
Students: Au Yeung Chun Yu JOEY, Chan Fong Tong FRED S, Cheng Pok Him BOB, Ching Ka Ho FRED, Henao Granda Jan Esteban, Ho Sheung Hay TERENCE, Hu Xiangdong HOCK, Ko Pak Kan ZETH, Li Zhixin ALLISON, Liu Chuen Yung VINCENT, Ma Yue, Qin Liting TING, Tang Tak Shing KELVIN, Wen Fan, Wu Yucong, Xie Junni, Ffion Zhang, Ho Yin SUNNY CHA, Sai Bond, Man Hei KENNIF, Han PAT

How Do Towers with Mixed Specialized Apartments Score?
Text by Tihamér Salij

Drawings and diagrams illustrated by The Why Factory: Claudia Mainardi and Anna Dolcetta with Sylwia Franczak

Additional research by Tihamér Salij with Martine Vledder and Anna Dolcetta

Photo collage impressions illustrated by the students of The Why Factory's 'Hong Kong Tower Revolution' studio at the Department of Architecture at the Hong Kong University, during Fall 2013, and by the students of The Why Factory's 'Towers Beyond Extrusion' studio at the Department of Architecture at the Hong Kong University, during Fall 2014.

The Hanging Gardens Tower:
Ip Kai Hong, Mok Wang Chee
The Garden-to-Table Tower:
Li Mei Yu, Liu Kemeng, Yeung Cho Yui
The Waterfalls Tower:
Lung Man Ching, Sze Ivy
The Isolated Functions Tower:
Tang Ho Yin, Chau Shek Lun
The Collective Activity Tower:
Ip Kai Hong, Mok Wang Chee
The Natural Breeze Tower:
Chan Pui Yin, Kong Ho Ching
The Specialized Compact Tower: Yeung Ho Man ARTHUR, Chan Chung Man
The Vertical Great Outdoors:
Chan Pui Yin, Kong Ho Ching
The Maximum Diversified Tower:
Ip Kai Hong and Mok Wang Chee

Hong Kong Tower Revolution, Architecture and Urban Design III (ARCH 5001), Hong Kong University.
Studio Tutors: Prof. Winy Maas and Tihamér Salij with Sander Mulders and Arend van Waart
Students: Au Wing Yi, Chak Tsz Kin, Chan Chung Man, Chan Ian Yin Yan, Chan Pui Yin, Chau Shek Lun, Cheng Ching, Ip Kai Hong, Liu Kemeng, Mok Wang Chee, Tang Ho Yin, Kong Ho Ching, Kwok Ka Ching, Lau Xin Yee, Lee Kin Wai, Li Mei Yu, Lung Man Ching, Ma Ching Yi, Suen Wing Yin, Sze Ivy, Sze Ying Ying, Yeung Cho Yui, Yeung Ho Man

Towers Beyond Extrusion, Architecture and Urban Design III (ARCH 5001), Hong Kong University
Studio Tutors: Prof. Winy Maas, Tihamér Salij, Martine Vledder with Donn Holohan
Students: Au Yeung Chun Yu JOEY, Chan Fong Tong FRED S, Cheng Pok Him BOB, Ching Ka Ho FRED, Henao Granda Jan Esteban, Ho Sheung Hay TERENCE, Hu Xiangdong HOCK, Ko Pak Kan ZETH, Li Zhixin ALLISON, Liu Chuen Yung VINCENT, Ma Yue, Qin Liting TING, Tang Tak Shing KELVIN, Wen Fan, Wu Yucong, Xie Junni, Ffion Zhang, Ho Yin SUNNY CHA, Sai Bond, Man Hei KENNIF, Han PAT

Studio 1 Exhibition Models.
Text by Tihamér Salij

Modelled by the students of The Why Factory's 'Hong Kong Tower Revolution' studio at the Department of Architecture (Architecture and Urban Design III, ARCH 5001) at the Hong Kong University, during Fall 2013.

Studio Tutors: Prof. Winy Maas and Tihamér Salij with Sander Mulders and Arend van Waart
Students: Au Wing Yi, Chak Tsz Kin, Chan Chung Man, Chan Ian Yin Yan, Chan Pui Yin, Chau Shek Lun, Cheng Ching, Ip Kai Hong, Liu Kemeng, Mok Wang Chee, Tang Ho Yin, Kong Ho Ching, Kwok Ka Ching, Lau Xin Yee, Lee Kin Wai, Li Mei Yu, Lung Man Ching, Ma Ching Yi, Suen Wing Yin, Sze Ivy, Sze Ying Ying, Yeung Cho Yui, Yeung Ho Man

How Do Towers with Specialized Apartments and Public Programme Score?
Text by Tihamér Salij

Developed and illustrated by the students of The Why Factory's 'Towers Beyond Extrusion' studio at the Department of Architecture (Architecture and Urban Design III, ARCH 5001) at the Hong Kong University, during Fall 2014.

The Fireplace Tower by Jan Henao
The Labyrinth Tower by Tang Tak Shing
The Vertical Shopping Street by Cheng Pok Him
The Cinema Tower by Wen Fan
The Sea-Life Tower by Li Zhixin
The Playgrounds Tower by Au Yeung Chun Yu
The Climbing Tower by Xie Junni
The Family Business Tower Qin Liting

Scoring drawings and diagrams illustrated by The Why Factory: Tihamér Salij and Claudia Mainardi with Sylwia Franczak

Studio Tutors: Prof. Winy Maas, Tihamér Salij, Martine Vledder with Donn Holohan
Students: Au Yeung Chun Yu JOEY, Chan Fong Tong FRED S, Cheng Pok Him BOB, Ching Ka Ho FRED, Henao Granda Jan Esteban, Ho Sheung Hay TERENCE, Hu Xiangdong HOCK, Ko Pak Kan ZETH, Li Zhixin ALLISON, Liu Chuen Yung VINCENT, Ma Yue, Qin Liting TING, Tang Tak Shing KELVIN, Wen Fan, Wu Yucong, Xie Junni, Ffion Zhang, Ho Yin SUNNY CHA, Sai Bond, Man Hei KENNIF, Han PAT

EPILOGUE

Flexible Regulations May Lead to More Choice
Text by Martine Vledder
based on a conversation hosted by prof. Winy Maas and prof. Weijen Wang
with Karen Chang (Partner, Globe Creative), Donald Choi (Managing Director, Nan Fung), Ivan Fu (Director, LWK &Partners), Iris Hwang (Sustainability Consultant, ARUP Hong Kong), Kar-kan (KK) Ling (Director of Planning, Planning Department HK SAR), Kelvin Tang (Student, University of Hong Kong), Rocco Yim (Founder, Rocco Design)
Moderation by Alexandra Seno (Freelance writer and Managing Partner, AXS Asia Partners)
Debate Program and Organization by Tihamér Salij with Martine Vledder and Tris Kee.

The debate was held on 23 June 2015 at PMQ, Hong Kong. With special thanks to PMQ and their team for their great support in giving us such a great venue to gather for the roundtable discussion.

Image Credits

All images in this publication were produced by The Why Factory, which holds their copyright, with the exception of the following images:

Photos p. 28-33 by Tihamér Salij
Photo p. 34-35 by Benny Lam for Society for Community Organization (SoCO)
Photo p. 36-37 First published on February 7, 2013 / 6:07 AM, © 2013 The Associated Press.
Photos p. 38-41 by Tihamér Salij
Photo p. 42 Image is online available under copyrights of Creative Commons at https://en.wikipedia.org/wiki/Public_housing_in_Hong_Kong#/media/File:Kin_Ming_Estate.jpg
Photo p. 44-45 by Tihamér Salij
Photo p. 46 Image is online available under copyrights of Creative Commons at https://commons.wikimedia.org/wiki/File:HK_Shatin_%E5%A4%A7%E5%9C%8D_%E6%BA%B1%E5%B2%B88%E8%99%9F_Riverpark_decorated_showflat_balcony_Dec-2012.JPG
Photo p.47 by Tihamér Salij
Photos p. 308-317 by Tihamér Salij

References

1 Planning Data, Land Utilization in Hong Kong 2014, Hong Kong Government, available online at http://www.pland.gov.hk/pland_en/info_serv/statistic/landu.html (Accessed 12 September 2016)

2 Public Notice - Status of Compliance, Department of Health and Family Welfare, Ministry of Health and Family, Japan, available online at http://mohfw.nic.in/index3.php?lang=1&deptid=24 (Accessed 12 September 2016)

3 2016 Quality of Living Rankings, Mercer, available online at https://www.imercer.com/content/mobility/quality-of-living-city-rankings.html (Accessed 12 September 2016)

4 Worldwide Cost of Living Index 2016, a special report from the Economist Intelligence Unit, available online at http://pages.eiu.com/rs/783-XMC-194/images/EIU_WCOL2016_FreeReport_FINAL_NEW.pdf?mkt_tok=3RkMMJWWfF9wsRovuK7AZKXonjHpfsX56%2B8vXqW2lMI%2F0ER3fOvrPUfGjI4JTsthI%2BSLDwEYGJlv6SgFTbjGMbht2bgMUhU%3D (Accessed 12 September 2016)

5 Global Living 2016- A city by city review, CBRE, available online at https://www.cbreresidential.com/uk/sites/uk-residential/files/Global%20Living%202016.pdf (Accessed 12 September 2016)

6 UBS Global Real Estate Bubble Index, available online at https://www.agefi.com/uploads/media/UBS_Global_Real_Estate_Bubble_Index_Study.pdf (Accessed 12 September 2016)

7 Housing in Figures 2016, Hong Kong Housing Authority, available online at https://www.housingauthority.gov.hk/en/common/pdf/about-us/publications-and-statistics/HIF.pdf (Accessed 12 September 2016)

8 Cities with Most Skyscrapers, Emporis, available online at http://www.emporis.com/statistics/most-skyscraper-cities-worldwide (Accessed 12 September 2016)

9 Analysis and illustrations by Dr. Ryo Fujimori in his PhD research at the Department of Architecture of Hong Kong University provided the basis for this article.

10 This article was adopted and modified from an original article by Weijen Wang and Ryo Fujimori: 'Mega-Housing Urban Form in New Towns of Hong Kong', in *OCCUPY HOUSING*, *HKIA Journal*, Issue 72, 2016.

11 Sapru, R. (2012) 'Sustainable Urban Growth: Is Hong Kong a Model for China?', available online at http://www.bsr.org/en/our-insights/blog-view/sustainable-urban-growth-is-hong-kong-a-model-for-china (accessed 30 June 2015)

12 For information on this initiative, called 'reinventer. Paris' see the programme's website at http://www.reinventer.paris/en/home/

13 Hong Kong Special Administrative Region Government, available online at http://www.gov.hk/en/about/abouthk/factsheets/docs/population.pdf (accessed 30 June2015)

14 Wilson, L (2014) 'How Big Is A House? Average House Size By Country', available online at http://shrinkthatfootprint.com/how-big-is-a-house (accessed 23 October 2015).

15 Fenton, A. H. (2014)' Hong Kong's Housing Market Facing a Slump in 2015', available online http://www.scmp.com/property/hong-kong-china/article/1645542/hong-kongs-housing-market-facing-slump-2015 (accessed 30 June 2015)

16 Yun, M. (2015) 'Hong Kong Can't Build Public Homes Fast Enough as Demand Soars', available online at http://www.bloomberg.com/news/articles/2015-02-05/hong-kong-can-t-build-public-homes-fast-enough-as-demand-soars (accessed 2 July 2015).

17 Wainwright, O. (2004) 'The truth about property developers: how they are exploiting planning authorities and ruining our cities'. *The Guardian*, available online at http://www.theguardian.com/cities/2014/sep/17/truth-property-developers-builders-exploit-planning-cities (accessed 21 August 2015)

18 Moody's (2013) 'Chinese Property Developer Margins Under Pressure', available online at https://www.moodys.com/research/Moodys-Chinese-property-developer-margins-under-pressure--PR_283206

Acknowledgements

We would like to thank all the students of The Why Factory's 'Hong Kong Tower Revolution' studio and 'Towers Beyond Extrusion' studio, held at the Department of Architecture at the Hong Kong University, during Fall 2013 and Fall 2014 for their dedication and great efforts. With Special thanks to Prof. Weijen Wang from the Department of Architecture at Hong Kong University, who initiated this collaboration.

We are grateful to the Department of Architecture at Hong Kong University, Ivan Fu from LWK & Partners (HK) Ltd., Edward Law from Gaw Capital Advisors Ltd, Donald Choi, Ada Yin Suen Fung, and Caitlin Lam from the Netherland consulate-general in Hong Kong for their generous financial support that made this publication possible.

Special thanks to Freda Fung from the Department of Architecture at Hong Kong University for her continuous support.

Credits

Concept and content The Why Factory:
Winy Maas and Tihamér Salij
with Martine Vledder, Arend van Waart, Sander Mulders, Claudia Mainardi, Anna Dolcetta and Sylwia Franczak

Editors: Winy Maas and Tihamér Salij

Text editors: Kelly Chan and Rachel Julia Engler

Proof reader: Leo Reijnen

Graphic design: www.BENG.nl
Design of The Why Factory logo: Thonik in collaboration with BENG.nl
Lithography and printing: Die Keure, Bruges (B)
Paper: Arctic Volume, 120 grs
Publisher: Marcel Witvoet, nai010 publishers, Rotterdam

Nai010 publishers specializes in the publication of books about architecture, urban design, spatial planning, visual art, photography, and design. The target readership for nai010 publishers includes architects, planning professionals, artists and designers—professionally active or in training—as well as a growing number of readers among the general public. Our publications are distinctive for their relevance to the target groups and for their stimulating contribution to contemporary sociocultural debate, thanks to their innovative and interdisciplinary character.

PO Box 21927, 3001 AX Rotterdam, NL www.nai010.nl

Available in North, South and Central America through D.A.P./Distributed Art Publishers Inc, 155 Sixth Avenue 2nd Floor, New York, NY 10013-1507, tel. +1 212 627 1999, fax +1 212 627 9484, dap@dapinc.com

Available in the United Kingdom and Ireland through Art Data, 12 Bell Industrial Estate, 50 Cunnington Street, London W4 5HB, tel. +44 208 747 1061, fax +44 208 742 2319, orders@artdata.co.uk

Printed and bound in Belgium

ISBN 978-94-6208-374-5

NUR 648
BISAC ARC003000; ARC013000

t?f The Why Factory

Department of Architecture University of Hong Kong

Kingdom of the Netherlands